"*Unexpected Joy* follows the journey to finding lasting joy in the midst of a chaotic world. Kelly does a great job of bringing good theology to life in this book written for everyday people who are seeking to find purpose and meaning in their contexts with all the challenges that come with them. Kelly shows how God uses broken people to extend His grace to the next generation because they are available to be used by Him. I would love to put this book in the hands of everyone; it won't leave you the same!"

—**Isabirye Daniel,** secondary school chaplain, The Amazima School; lead pastor of Agape Community Church, Wakitaka, Jinja, Uganda

"Like Paul, who used his skills at work to not be a burden but to bless those he served, in the same manner, Kelly and Danlyn invested their organizational skills to serve and love those who longed to be loved by Jesus. They truly were a kiss of the Holy Spirit to the sweet people of Uganda. Get ready to experience unexpected joy as you see the joy of generosity being lived out through humble and surrendered lives. A truly refreshing book!"

—**Boyd Bailey,** president, Georgia NCF (National Christian Foundation)

"*Unexpected Joy* is both a challenging and inspiring read. Challenging in the sense that Kelly pushes the reader to truly explore what Jesus teaches in the New Testament and put it into practice. Inspiring with the countless stories of his time in Uganda, living in a culture that was the opposite of what he had known up to that time. God used that difference to deepen his love for everyone he encountered. This book will stretch you and deepen your walk with God."

—**Karen Stubbs,** founder, Birds on a Wire

"Kelly Miller is a great storyteller, and his stories of life in an African mission school are filled with emotion, humor, and deep spiritual insights. *Unexpected Joy* reminds us that faith is not just a collection of abstract doctrines, but a transformative way of life. Be ready to be entertained, inspired, informed, and challenged to rediscover the joy of living in the grace of Jesus Christ. Highly recommended!"

—**Terry Glaspey,** award-winning author; professor at '

T0050117

"From the pinnacle of success pursuing the American dream to serving as dean of student life at a boarding school in Uganda, Kelly Miller's story grips readers, draws them into the narrative of grace and joy, and stimulates every emotion, often several at the same time. This is a powerful story of redemption, demonstrating the privilege it is for God's people to be involved in God's work around the globe. You will be changed by reading this book."

—**Glenn R. Kreider,** editor in chief, *Bibliotheca Sacra;*
professor of theological studies, Dallas Theological Seminary

"*Unexpected Joy* is an experiential testament to the beauty and power of surrendering to the Lord. By sharing touching stories and personal experiences, Kelly invites readers on a transformative journey toward understanding how the simple act of daily submission can lead to a life of joy and purpose in the most unlikely places and through the most beautiful people. Kelly and Danlyn's story encourages us all to embrace surrender and find beauty in the unexpected, ultimately leading us to a deeper connection with the Lord and a more fulfilling life."

—**Scott Bowen,** cofounder, Champions United, Uganda

"King David carried a certain ferocity when it came to things that mattered most to him. Whether battle or dance, he went all in with abandon. Kelly Miller is just like that. His and Danlyn's story is about courage in spite of fear."

—**Justin Dillon,** author and entrepreneur

"For the past 20 years, I've had a front-row seat and witnessed the transformational power of the ideas presented in this book in the life of the author, "Uncle Kelly"—a title he and Aunt Danlyn earned in our family nearly a decade before their adventure to Uganda. The road to the promised joy of the Christian life truly is one of brokenness, grace, and the work of the Holy Spirit, and this book provides a map for the journey!"

—**Joel Thomas,** lead pastor, Buckhead Church, Atlanta, GA

Unexpected JOY

Kelly C. Miller

HARVEST HOUSE PUBLISHERS
EUGENE, OREGON

Cover design by Brock Book Design Co., Charles Brock

Cover images © vlad_k / Depositphotos; irinelle / Adobe Stock

Interior design by KUHN Design Group

For bulk, special sales, or ministry purchases, please call 1-800-547-8979.
Email: Customerservice@hhpbooks.com

Unexpected Joy
Copyright © 2023 by Kelly C. Miller
Published by Harvest House Publishers
Eugene, Oregon 97408
www.harvesthousepublishers.com

ISBN 978-0-7369-8765-3 (pbk)
ISBN 978-0-7369-8766-0 (eBook)

Library of Congress Control Number: 2022951434

Printed in the United States of America

23 24 25 26 27 28 29 30 31 / BP / 10 9 8 7 6 5 4 3 2 1

CONTENTS

SECTION FOUR: THE "REAL HOW"

AN UNEXPECTED JOURNEY

I t didn't take me long to learn why Uganda is called "The Pearl of Africa." By any measure, it's a beautiful country. Each region offers its own stunning scenery—Lake Victoria, the Nile River, majestic mountains, rolling hills, and crater lakes. The equatorial sun is always hot, but the high elevation ensures pleasant temperatures and constant breezes. Where we live, for most of the year, the average daily high temperature is about 80 degrees Fahrenheit. Agriculturally, it would be hard to find a country more fertile than Uganda. In support of this claim, I've heard people say, "You could plant a pig's ear and grow a pig." There are stark differences between city life and village life, but people are generally friendly no matter their circumstances. Oh, and if you're into coffee, I've been told Uganda has the best in the world.

People often ask me what I like most about living in Uganda. I could talk about the warm, hospitable people, or the students I have come to know and love. There is also the visual beauty of the landscape, or the enjoyable pace and rhythm of life. For me, however, it's the peace I experience in the early mornings, when I take the school dog (Muggle) for a walk. It's also when I'm most aware of the extraordinary joy God has given me here, in this season of my life. Ernest Hemingway said, "I never knew a morning in Africa when I woke up and was not happy." I couldn't agree more.

No one would accuse me of being a morning person, but here it's not uncommon for me to be up early enough to watch the first rays of the morning sun appear over the small mountains above the school. On those days, as Muggle and I walk the dusty roads around the expansive school grounds, I thank God for creating us with the senses that allow us to experience and enjoy the beauty of his creation.

In those early hours of the day, the temperature is nearly perfect. There is a coolness to the air that seems improbable for a country on the equator. The many birds, all over the campus, greet us with a symphony of sounds. The distorted speaker of a nearby mosque broadcasting the sunrise call to prayer is a reminder of how important it is for our students to see and experience the true gospel of Jesus. Outside the fence of the school people are making their way to work— some on foot and some as passengers on the many motorcycle taxis scurrying about.

The students gather with their Mentors on the porches of their houses for morning devotions. Some of them are singing worship songs, while others are intently discussing the Word. Soon after, they will go to breakfast and then spend the day with a dedicated team of teachers committed to teaching them *how to think* instead of just *what to think*. Even though I've seen these sights and heard these sounds hundreds of times, I am always overwhelmed by what God has taught me on this unexpected journey. Above all, I am grateful for how I get to see, in the most undeniable way, the transformative work of the Holy Spirit.

When I was in high school, I was very much into what were then called hair metal bands, and somehow I convinced my parents it was okay to go to the concerts. It was 1986. I was fourteen years old and apparently old enough to go see Mötley Crüe at the old Omni in Atlanta on their "Girls, Girls, Girls" tour (please don't judge me). Tommy Lee did an upside-down drum solo, and I'm sure there was a lot of raunchy visual content, but, thankfully, I don't remember much about it. What made that night memorable, however, was the opening act. A newer group with a fresh sound, Guns N' Roses, was given an opportunity. None of us had heard of them before. The Crüe was notorious for booking opening acts that had no chance of taking the spotlight from them. Well, that night, Guns N' Roses stole the show, and it wasn't even close.

Unless you lived through the late eighties and early nineties, it's hard to appreciate how Guns N' Roses conquered the music world. This was before streaming or the internet, so the metrics were album sales and the length of lines outside record stores to get concert tickets. Guns N' Roses was on top, for years. To be at that concert, on that night, to see that opening act—that would soon become the biggest band in the world—was an experience I will never forget.

Even now, I can remember feeling like *I was privileged to be at a very special moment in time.*

Now more than thirty years later, I have that same feeling, only this time it's God who is blowing my mind, not a rock band. Over the last five years, at a secondary boarding school in Jinja, Uganda, I have seen God redeeming and transforming a generation of young people who will change their communities by how they live for him. I have seen not only *what* we are called to do as followers of Jesus, but *how* we are to do it. Serving in Uganda has put all the diverse experiences of my life into the right perspective.

The pursuit of happiness has been a popular theme for as long as anyone can remember. There's an avalanche of books, seminars, and studies, from secular and religious writers alike, that claim to show the way to joyful enlightenment. Now, in our age of digital media, we have podcasts and YouTube videos repackaging the same messages. Much if not most of this content fails its audience because it suggests, in one way or another, that we are in complete control of our own joy and can get there from our own effort and strength.

If that were true, the world would look a lot differently than it does today.

There is no ten-step program or self-help strategy to lasting joy and a contented life. The better way comes from the promises of Jesus and the transforming power of the Holy Spirit. To receive these promises, and to receive the full joy of the Christian life, we first have to make a decision. Do we believe that Jesus and the life he has promised is better than what the world is offering? All throughout my life I have heard the world telling me that happiness comes from money, power, and fame—so the solutions are simple: make more money, seek more power, and do whatever it takes to be known. Unfortunately, some churches have tried to package that set of solutions together with the idea of the Christian life.

My question is, How's that working out?

I don't think I have ever seen Americans more unhappy than they are today, and this is at a time when we have more of everything the culture is naming as the solution. All of us, at times, have struggled to find joy in this world. Why? Because we don't have a good understanding of the obstacles and perspectives that hold us back, and because we fail to see how the ways of our me-first culture lead only to defeat. Here's a paradox: on the one hand, we have access to an abundance of good, biblical teaching and theology; but on the other hand, Western Christians don't look much like the Jesus we profess to follow. To put it simply: we have great difficulty with sincere obedience.

If you're serious about growing your faith and experiencing God in a deeper way than ever before, this is the most important book you've ever read! (Maybe this is a good time to admit I'm prone to exaggeration.) It's impossible to exaggerate, however, the grace of God's plan to reconcile creation to himself, and the grace of his plan for us to enjoy him and enjoy life as we fulfill our created purpose.

Do you want to experience extraordinary joy? God tells us what to do and how to do it, and offers us the strength to make it happen. Despite this reality, we still resist, and revert to doing things our way instead of his way. Maybe we don't like to surrender control. Maybe we can't let go of what the culture has taught us. Maybe our churches have given us a picture of a legalistic God who is more concerned about rules than about love, grace, and joy. Or maybe we have never fully grasped the role of the Holy Spirit in our growth and transformation. Whatever our misunderstandings are, or where they are from, most Christians miss out on the full and joyful life God has promised.

I'm a former software executive who has spent the last five years in Uganda working as the Dean of Student Life at a unique school serving teenagers from challenging backgrounds. Living in a developing country and sharing the gospel in an honor/shame culture has helped me better understand the issues the world is facing. The underlying problems in Uganda are not greatly different from the underlying problems in the Western world, but they do manifest themselves differently here. This contrast has led to an important and helpful clarity, for which I am grateful.

I haven't been less busy in Uganda than I was in the US, but I have definitely been less distracted. As a result, I've learned a lot of new things. The most important lessons have to do with seeing the gospel, the wisdom of God, and the truth of Scripture validated in every facet of life. Even though I'm embarrassed I had to move to Uganda to learn these things, I have gained a deeper *understanding* through the *experience*, and my eyes have been opened to the right *perspectives*. I have learned how God leads us to joyful *obedience*, and how, with that posture, we grow to be more like him, for our good and his glory.

This book is an overflow of God's grace in my life. I am grateful for the opportunity to write about some of my experiences and how

God used them to bring me to a deeper understanding of what he has done, what he is doing, and what he has promised for those who love him. I write with the same deep conviction that Dr. Luke had after he carefully investigated everything and *became certain* about the risen Christ.

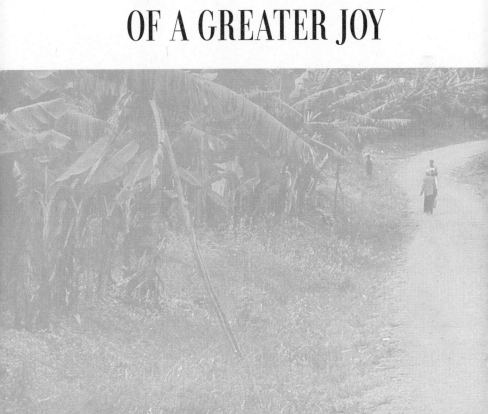

SECTION ONE

THE FOUNDATIONS OF A GREATER JOY

If our goal as Jesus followers is to grow in Christlikeness, resulting in contented lives characterized by the fruit of the Spirit—that then attract others to the gospel—then our current status is both disappointing and discouraging. We long for widespread and transformational change, but it's not happening at the rate it should or to the degree it should, especially in the light of the truth of our faith.

This is despite the great trove of resources we have, and despite our best efforts. After hundreds of years of archaeology, science, and debate, the historical fact of the resurrection of Christ stands. Atheists and antagonists are left with no good way to make their case, apart from pursuing strategies like appealing to emotional arguments about suffering and evil in the world. I don't dismiss those arguments, but, ironically, only the Christian worldview has the answer to them.

We should be seeing the greatest expansion of faith since the first century. But we're not. We must either be misunderstanding the underlying causes of the problem or looking at the world with the

wrong perspectives. I think it's both. For things to change, we need
to better know the truth, and to better avoid the obstacles that prevent us from acting obediently.

We must grow to better understand the three key topics of *brokenness*, *grace*, and *the Holy Spirit*, and how they lead us to the promised
joy of the Christian life. But before doing so, we need to appreciate
the kind of *understanding* that comes from *experience*. This is foundational. My experiences in Uganda are helpful in this regard because
they serve as a testimony to the truth and wisdom of Scripture.

CHAPTER 1

UNCLE KELLY

*Without context, words and actions
have no meaning at all.*[1]

GREGORY BATESON

Within a few days of when I arrived in Uganda, it became clear I would be known as "Uncle Kelly." All the staff and students have addressed me in this way since the very beginning. Once I appreciated the context, I understood this is a title of respect, one which I was happy to receive.

For God to use this book in your life, knowing the context of this writing is also very important since I'm writing from a unique set of circumstances and experiences. It will also be helpful to understand who I am, recognize who you are, and share the setting for this book.

Misunderstanding context, and misapplying God's Word, has led to painful errors in the history of the Christian church. The current church makes the same mistakes, but the modern manifestations are more about putting down individuals than conquering countries. In my lifetime, Christians and churches have (incorrectly) used God's word to oppress African Americans, the promiscuous, and the LGBT community, just to name a few. There are

Jesus followers who justify damaging actions by misusing Scripture, mainly by taking it out of context. We've also seen the rise of false gospels, embraced by professing Christians.

GOALS AND APPROACH

Much has been written about what needs to happen for the church to look more like Jesus, and what his followers need to do to grow in relationship with him. I will not repeat or repackage that content. I will also resist the temptation to debate theological issues.

Instead, I will present a helpful framework for living the Christian life. I will make the case for *awareness* and *understanding* as starting points for developing the right *perspectives*. I will show the importance of willful and sincere *obedience*, and the role of the Holy Spirit, in producing good fruit and good works in our lives. I will remind you that God's promises are infinitely better than anything this world can offer. Along the way, I will get in your face a little bit (okay, maybe a lot) about whether you actually believe what you say you believe.

I'm writing this book to share the experiences I've had that validate the truth and wisdom of Scripture, and to challenge you to embrace a journey of understanding the *brokenness* of the world, God's amazing *grace*, and the power of the *Holy Spirit*. I want you to fall more in love with Jesus, joyfully obey his teaching, and live in the hope of his promises. My prayer is that you will embrace the life God has created you for, for your good and for his glory. A life centered on anything other than Jesus will never satisfy in any lasting or meaningful way. Finally, I want you to become so overwhelmed by God's grace that you are actively sharing the gospel with your life.

WHO IS THIS GUY?

Like anyone else, I am the sum of the decisions I've made and the experiences I've had throughout my life. You might not expect a guy like me to be the author of a book like this. I'm not a pastor or even a pastor's kid. I didn't grow up disadvantaged or experience spectacular tragedy. I haven't struggled with alcohol, drugs, or pornography. But in my unremarkable life I've experienced a remarkable journey into a deep understanding of the Christian faith, and of how obedience unlocks the fulfillment of our God-given purpose in life.

I was born in the hippie generation and grew up in the '80s. By the time I was twenty-seven years old I reached the top of the cultural ladder of success. My life has been framed by Jesus, my marriage, international business, student ministry, travel, three-plus years in seminary (I didn't finish), and then almost five years in Uganda. I am a reformed skeptic who loves apologetics and has been wonderfully "wrecked" by the grace of God and the power of the Holy Spirit.

I know how the blind beggar must have felt when he was asked to explain his healing and replied, "One thing I do know, I was blind and now I see" (John 9:25). I'm an unashamedly emotional guy when it comes to talking about God's grace. Our students here in Uganda refer to me as "the president of the crying club" because I often shed tears when preaching on Sunday mornings. (As a side note, let it be known that about half the students are also now card-carrying members of that club.)

More than twenty-four years ago I married the most beautiful girl I've ever seen, and we have enjoyed a wonderful partnership. Danlyn also happens to be the strongest person I know. She has faced more physical pain and difficulty than any person ever should, but it has only served to grow her hope in Christ (and mine). Because of her physical limitations we don't have children, but God used that to push us toward student ministry almost twenty years ago. Nothing has influenced our lives more than the privilege of leading students to know Jesus and the gospel. Many of the students we have led are like members of our family. We call them our "kids" even though now they are in their late twenties and early thirties.

I grew up in the greatest-ever decade for just about everything, so I feel a fondness for the culture of that era, which provided so many good moments for me and my friends. As a result, you will have to endure some references you may or may not be familiar with, many of them from movies you may consider inappropriate. I will say, in advance, you're probably correct. In my defense, I grew up watching these movies on the Superstation, which did a good job in editing out the questionable content.

Paul wrote, "Whatever were gains to me I now consider loss for the sake of Christ. What is more, I consider everything a loss because of the surpassing worth of knowing Christ Jesus my Lord, for whose sake I have lost all things" (Philippians 3:7-8). I identify with Paul's story, and specifically with his perspective on his previous excesses and successes. This is the perspective God has used to grow me, and the context I am sharing with you from.

So that's who "this guy" is. Now, what about you?

WHO ARE YOU?

I have spent the last twenty years talking with a great variety of people around the world about the gospel. Most of you reading this probably share a lot in common with those I've encountered in my travels when it comes to your questions and struggles about following Jesus.

If you've ever heard the gospel, you fit into one of four categories described by Jesus in the Parable of the Sower. From that parable, Jesus explained how people were responding in different ways to his kingdom message. He described a farmer who went out to sow his seed and the four places where the seed landed. After Jesus told the parable, the disciples came to him a bit confused. Graciously, Jesus explained the parable to them:

Listen then to what the parable of the sower means: When anyone hears the message about the kingdom and does not understand it, the evil one comes and snatches away what was sown in their heart. This is the seed sown along the path. The seed falling on rocky ground refers to someone who hears the word and at once receives it with joy. But since they have no root, they last only a short time. When trouble or persecution comes because of the word, they quickly fall away. The seed falling among the thorns refers to someone who hears the word, but the worries of this life and the deceitfulness of wealth choke the word, making it unfruitful. But the seed falling on good soil refers to someone who hears the word and understands it. This is the one who produces a crop, yielding a hundred, sixty or thirty times what was sown (Matthew 13:18-23).

How have you responded to the message of Jesus? Are you one of those who has heard the message but has not spent much time trying to understand (seed along the path)? Maybe you're one of those who rejoice because the gospel makes so much sense, but then the demands of life take higher priority and push God to the bottom of the list (seed on rocky ground). Or maybe you fall into the third category, where you allow worry, along with the pursuit of wealth and comfort, to distract you from following Jesus (seed among thorns).

Likely you have struggled with life's biggest questions, about how the world began, life's meaning, morality, and where we spend eternity. As a result, maybe you have developed a worldview in which you are confident. Even so, you have a deep need to be fully known and fully loved. Perhaps, you seek personal benefit, sometimes at a great cost, more than you fear consequences. Likely you are sometimes willing to make unwise decisions, and face obvious dangers, if you think the results will make you happy. Maybe your goals are misaligned because of a misunderstanding of your true needs.

Am I getting close?

In regard to your Christian faith, maybe you avoid the hard teachings in Scripture, or resist applying them to your life, even when you agree with them. Because of this, there's a constant tension between your disobedience and your desire for faithfulness. Maybe you've been disappointed, or angry with God. There has likely been a church, a professing Christian, or someone you love, who has deeply hurt you, and in doing so has significantly affected how you relate to the gospel. I could go on, but I think you get the point.

I'm writing to Christians who have long wanted to experience the fullness of the life Jesus has promised, but are exhausted from trying, or are disappointed with the results of their efforts. I hope you are willing to be honest about what you believe and why you believe what you believe. I am writing to those who have not yet arrived at a mature, fruit-bearing faith and to anyone who desires a deeply personal, transformational relationship with God.

IN THE FRONT ROW

In 2019, I had the opportunity to speak at a donor event in Santa Barbara, California. After my presentation, a number of attendees waited to speak with me, to hear more about what I'd shared and to ask questions. Given the battle we are in for the hearts and minds of the next generation in Uganda, the first question was simply, "What's it like being on the front lines?" Without hesitation, my instinctive response was, "I honestly don't feel like I'm on the front lines. It feels more like being in the front row."

I'd never thought about it in those terms prior to that moment, but it got me thinking about the similarities between the first-century setting in which Jesus and his followers did ministry, and the village setting we are working in here in Uganda. What would it have been like to watch the first disciples proclaim the gospel in a materially disadvantaged, honor/shame culture? What did Jesus direct his closest followers to do? Well, God and his people are doing similar things, in a similar setting, here in Uganda. I've had the best seat in the house to watch the story unfold.

It's a bit frustrating that I had to move to a developing country, and face the challenges of sharing Christ here, to understand how the first-century Christians did ministry and grew in their faith. They walked away from everything they had known. They faced intense persecution. They embraced the radical, countercultural teaching of a certain Jewish rabbi. And then they were willing to die for the gospel. Why?

Because they saw a man tortured and killed, and then rise from the dead.

Even today there are people willing to die for what they believe, but that's very different from what motivated the first disciples. They were willing to die for what they *saw, understood, and experienced.* With that confidence they changed the world. They preached about the risen Christ and, more importantly, validated his teaching by how they lived. Their approach then should inform our approach today, no matter the culture.

The parallels between the culture in the villages of Uganda and the culture of the first century offer an opportunity to build an approach based on the ways of Paul, Peter, James, and all the foundational heroes of the Christian faith. If our goal is to have an unshakable faith, full of a joy that challenges and inspires others, we should already be learning from the first Christians, the group with the strongest faith ever recorded.

CHRISTIANS, CULTURE, AND CONTEXT

In his letter to the church in Galatia, Paul was frustrated with the followers there who had retreated back to legalism. Subsequently, they were losing the joy of God in their lives. Many of the problems

Paul was addressing are the same issues we face now. If Paul were alive today he could probably repurpose many of his pastoral letters and send them directly to us. Sadly, there is nothing groundbreaking about saying the Western church today is becoming less joyful, more apathetic, and less like the Jesus who gave his life for it.

In most cultures, Christians are nearly indistinguishable from nonbelievers. This is shocking! How can it be? How can people be saved by grace, have an eternal hope, and then fail to live with infectious joy and contentment? Much like the first-century church in Corinth, the modern church is lacking maturity, is going backwards, and is known for jealousy, quarreling, and worldly pursuits.[2] All of this makes it difficult for nonbelievers to come to Christ.

It's not hard to see what's happening. Leave it to Jesus followers to take the most attractive person in the history of the world and make him unattractive! As a result, the number of people identifying as religiously unaffiliated continues to grow.[3] For many years, there has been a broad sense that things are going in the wrong direction, and there needs to be some real change with the way Christians interact with the broken world around them.

In his book *Something Needs to Change*, David Platt made his case for how Christians should address the urgent needs of humanity. In his book *Letters to the Church*, Francis Chan wrote about how Jesus' followers should be the church in the way Scripture commands. In his book *Love Does,* Bob Goff talked about how believers should follow the teachings of Jesus by actively and intentionally loving one another. Despite these wonderful books and the dozens of other similar ones, the changes many say are needed are elusive.

How is this possible? It's not because the books aren't well written or the authors aren't credible. It's not because we don't know what to do or don't understand why it's important. It's not even for a lack of genuine effort! Whatever the reasons, the calls to action have not produced meaningful change.

At first glance, the COVID-19 pandemic and the events surrounding the death of George Floyd seemed to be the catalysts for the division, anger, and unrest we've seen in America over the last few years. But long before these major events of 2020, people all over the world were becoming less and less open-minded, and less and less able to consider opposing viewpoints. Useful discussion and healthy debate have become relics of the past. All of us, to varying degrees, have gravitated toward confirmation bias.

Confirmation bias has to do with only giving attention to information that reinforces what you already believe. These days it's hard to find people who watch both Fox News and CNN, or who read both *The New York Times* and *The Wall Street Journal*. Because of the groundbreaking documentary *The Social Dilemma*, we now know that social media and tech companies are programming us to become more radical about what we already believe. The reason? Money. More radical content leads to more emotional reactions, which leads to more online attention, which leads to more advertising dollars. If that doesn't scare you, it should.

Unfortunately, this is not limited to social issues and politics. Confirmation bias is also alive and well throughout the global community of professing Christians. The ancient Israelites constantly tried to make God into a god they could be more comfortable with. In the same way, we tend to read Scripture with an interpretation of convenience. Like the ancient Jews, we often abandon the one true God for false gods that fit with what we want to be true. Christians, in many cases, have adopted attitudes of platitudes like "follow your heart" or "you just do you."

All of this is further complicated by a postmodern culture that views absolute truth as an offensive concept, and worse, preaches that truth is relative. Any truth that would challenge one's worldview or beliefs is exchanged for a more convenient version of the "truth."

Instead of looking to Scripture, people seek advice from those who will validate the choices they've already made. We listen to those who support their ideas, no matter how ignorant, foolish, or dangerous they might be. Social media only makes this worse. The great news is that truth is not, in any way, relative. It is not subjective. It can be objectively tested.

I mentioned earlier that I'm a reformed skeptic. It was hard for me to maintain that skepticism, however, when I evaluated the claims of Jesus through objective lenses. My experiences in Uganda have confirmed for me that the propositions of Scripture are true, and that only the cross of Christ brings meaning to who we are. Only the truths of Scripture explain the suffering and brokenness in the world, and provide the opportunity to know true joy, justice, and peace. There is nothing else in the world that comes close!

So this is the context in which I am writing: a post-modern, post-truth, culture of criticism and self-righteousness; a world reluctant to objectively evaluate truth, out of fear of hurting feelings or offending someone.

As for me, I'm not afraid of offending anyone with this effort. Nor am I worried about the criticism that will inevitably come with writing a book like this, in our current culture. You may find this book too philosophical, or maybe you'll disagree with my theology. That's okay. Maybe you'll have strong opinions about the work I've done with students or the work I've done in Uganda. That's your prerogative. But if you are willing to set aside your personal biases for a short time, and willing to be open to the truth of God as told through some of my experiences, you might just find yourself on a path toward a greater joy, a joy that only comes from God.

> **Something to Remember:** Context is important, always. For God to use this book as an instrument of change in your life, it's important to start our journey with you understanding me, understanding yourself, and understanding what to expect on the pages ahead.

Now that you've been introduced to who I am, why I took the time to write this book, and the setting in which I'm sharing my journey to unexpected joy, let's consider the roles that *awareness, understanding,* and *perspective* have in the development of unshakable faith and, eventually, extraordinary joy.

CHAPTER 2

A NEW SET OF LENSES

*We see the world, not as it is, but as we are—or as we're
conditioned to see it…we must look at the lens through
which we see the world, as well as the world we see and
that the lens itself shapes how we interpret the world.*[1]

STEPHEN R. COVEY

For about ten years, Danlyn and I were involved with Passion Conferences, founded by Louie and Shelley Giglio, both as volunteers and as leaders. We brought high school seniors and college students to the annual event. One of the many things I always appreciated about Passion was the intentional effort to create awareness and understanding for worthy causes around the world. Reflecting back, it was where I first learned about the power of *awareness* and the importance of *understanding* as fundamental building blocks to an unshakable faith.

Passion would raise millions of dollars from the college students in attendance, to help fund organizations involved in meaningful projects that helped people all over the globe. In 2012, it shifted its focus to a single campaign, the END IT Movement, that works to create awareness about the huge problem of human trafficking and slavery.

The conference that year was at the old Georgia Dome, and we were grateful to be there with about 60,000 university students, including seventy soon-to-be graduates from the high-school ministry we were serving with at that time. Throughout the conference, leaders made us aware of the severity of the human trafficking and slavery activity that exists today. There are more than 40 million people, right now, trapped in slavery or forced labor. If you want to learn more, I encourage you to go to enditmovement.com.

The sex-trafficking side of the problem tends to draw the most attention, and understandably so. For me, however, I was more burdened about slavery in the business world, knit into the global supply chain. Maybe it was because the company I was then working for had the largest global commerce network in the world, serving millions of buyers and suppliers. Its network had more than two trillion dollars' worth of commerce flowing through it every year. Given my experience in working with supply chain technology, I was completely astounded by the statistics and stories presented about modern-day slavery.

During one of the lunch sessions, Louie Giglio moderated a panel of heavy hitters in the fight to end slavery and human trafficking. One member of the panel was a freedom fighter named Justin Dillon. He had created a very successful app and website for individual users to become aware of how many slaves were "working for them" based on the products they bought and their general lifestyle. Building on that success, he was then actively seeking the attention of large corporations, to educate them on where, in their supply chains, there might be slavery or forced labor.

I was in a unique position to understand what Justin was sharing that day. Talk of global supply chains was not exactly capturing the interest of the college students, but this was a world I knew well. I remember thinking that while it was admirable work Justin was doing, he was going to struggle to get the attention of most companies. Even if he did, the ability to scale for significant impact just wasn't there.

During Justin's presentation, Danlyn saw a Twitter post from a good friend who was proud of his brother (Justin) for speaking at Passion. When the conference ended, I called my friend to get Justin's number. I had a crazy idea for how we could get Justin's global data, on forced labor in supply chains, onto my company's commerce network. That would increase the reach of his efforts a thousand-fold. The first conversation between Justin and me lasted three hours.

Over the next few years we held summits in San Francisco and New York with some of the world's biggest brands, to talk about ending slavery in their supply chains. Justin was invited to speak on the main stage at our annual User's Conference. In a joint effort with my company, we developed a supply chain transparency tool for companies to become *aware* of their hotspots for forced labor. Justin's organization would then come alongside any company that was ready to take action, with consulting and education about best practices. Through these efforts and others, awareness and understanding of the problem of slavery has never been higher. As a result, there are now dozens of organizations working hard to fight the battle. Justin was also directly involved in new legislation passed in the US, because of the collective effort.

The END IT Movement is fond of saying, "Action starts with awareness." For me, *awareness* led to *burden*, which eventually, after seeking *understanding*, led to *action*. At the Passion Conference in 2016, the END IT Movement was still bringing awareness to the problem of slavery in the world. After four years of the campaign, they were highlighting some of the stories that resulted from people taking action. When my story was featured on the giant screens in the arena, it was hard to fathom everything God had done through my simply saying *yes* to a new burden.

AWARENESS AS A STARTING POINT

The campus in Uganda, where I live and work, sits on eighty-six acres of gorgeous property—some of the most beautiful I've ever seen. Think of a less-spoiled Napa Valley, only with higher hills and more vegetation. Because of the picturesque setting and the incredible things God is doing here, we host tours every Tuesday. I'm fortunate to serve as the main guide. Many days my phone rings around the time the tour should start, because the school is not easy to find, and I have to help visitors reach the campus. My first question, before I can give any directions, is, "Where are you right now?"

It's similar for any of us who are eager to change, grow, get closer to Jesus, or meaningfully engage in a cause. We can't set a course to go anywhere until we have a real awareness of where we are at the start.

Some people work from the idea that "knowledge is power." They diligently seek knowledge about themselves, the people around them, and the world in which they live. This is an active form of awareness. These people tend to be open-minded, and are more likely to think logically, think critically, and be problem solvers. They are generally not afraid to take action once they become aware of an opportunity to help a person or a project. They might have a problem, though, with accumulating knowledge without also seeking understanding.

Other people work from the idea that "ignorance is bliss." They aren't interested in gaining more knowledge unless it reinforces what they already believe. They don't care to learn about the problems of the world. What little information they get comes from their phones, in two-inch segments, with a lot of "swiping away," to easily move on from anything troubling. Scripture would call them "fools" because they "find no pleasure in understanding" (Proverbs 18:2). They are largely disengaged from any helpful action.

Unfortunately, most of us gravitate toward lives of ignorance, even to the point of being unaware of what we actually believe. We are prone to working from untested assumptions and can dispassionately draw conclusions about people and the world around us instead of being open to new ideas. We lack real awareness. We reject the idea of pursuing understanding because, after all, in Western culture now, truth is considered relative. As I mentioned earlier, this is made worse by our own confirmation bias and the intentional manipulation of information by social media.

Any chance of receiving the promise of God for a life of great joy starts with a posture of active awareness. We should begin by honestly asking the question, "Why do I believe what I believe?"

We must also be willing to deal with the answers and their implications. If we are willing to actively pursue an *awareness* of what we believe and why, we are then in the right place to genuinely seek a deeper *understanding* of the elements of the Christian faith that will inevitably lead to those experiences that validate the truth of Scripture.

EPIGNOSIS

The apostle Peter wrote, "Always be prepared to give an answer to everyone who asks you to give the reason for the hope that you have. But do this with gentleness and respect" (1 Peter 3:15). When I worked with high schoolers in the States, I would always tell the freshman guys, at the very beginning, that one of the goals I had for them was this: before they graduated, they would have an answer to the question, "Why do you believe what you believe?" My hope was they would experience the gospel and the work of the Spirit in a tangible and undeniable way. My goal was for them to go from "truth believed" to "truth experienced."

A faith rooted in experience, consistent with God's Word, provides an answer that can't be challenged. That, in turn, challenges others to learn more about the gospel. And when it comes to Christian witness, that "gentleness and respect" thing doesn't happen if your reasoning is purely academic and not rooted in living experience. Jesus and the writers of the New Testament agree with me on this. They consistently point to an experiential understanding of key doctrine as the catalyst for growth in Christ.

Paul described this as "the full riches of complete understanding" (Colossians 2:2). A brief look into how levels of understanding are addressed in the Greek language is helpful here. The Greek root word *eido* is most simply defined as "knowing, to know," or "to see and know." Based on its usage and context in Scripture, it's meant to describe the basic knowledge a person has after seeing something. Someone might show you something, and in response you say, "I see what you mean"—but then you take no additional steps to further understand. We might think of this as passive awareness or basic understanding. *Eido* and its various forms are used hundreds of times throughout the New Testament.

There is a deeper level of understanding, however, that only comes through experience. The root word in Greek for this kind of understanding is *ginosko*. It means to "experientially know," to understand through personal, intimate experience. This is related to the words *gnosis* and *epignosis*, that build on the definition to include prudence, discernment, and precise and correct knowledge. *Epignosis* is a deep and correct understanding derived from personal experiences.

Paul intentionally used these special Greek words whenever he wanted to stress the importance of an accurate understanding of key ideas and doctrine in the Christian faith, understanding that leads to action. Here is my favorite example:

> We continually ask God to fill you with the *epignosis* of his will through all the wisdom and understanding that the Spirit gives, so that you may live a life worthy of the Lord and please him in every way: bearing fruit in every good work, growing in the *epignosis* of God, being strengthened with all power according to his glorious might so that you may have great endurance and patience, and giving joyful

thanks to the Father, who has qualified you to share in
the inheritance of his holy people in the kingdom of light
(Colossians 1:9-12).

Paul specifically used *epignosis* when he taught about God, sin,
righteousness, God's will, assurance, salvation, and repentance.[2] Those
are important concepts! According to Paul, even Jesus wants us to
have experiential understanding: "This is good, and pleases God our
Savior, who wants all people to be saved and to come to an *epignosis*
of the truth" (1 Timothy 2:3-4).

For the early Christians, a passive awareness and a basic understanding wasn't enough to lead to transformation. Paul desired their
understanding be based on firsthand, personal, intimate experiences
with the Holy Spirit and the wisdom of God. He also cited a cau-
tionary example from Israelite history, when he wrote, "They are zeal-
ous for God, but their zeal is not based on *epignosis*" (Romans 10:2).

Two thousand years later the same principles apply to us, but we
have the advantage of having the Bible to guide us in our choices,
actions, and the interpretation of our experiences. Without that, we
might elevate our experiences above what Scripture says is true. That
error can give rise to false teaching, and worse, lead to wrong *perspectives*.

PERSPECTIVES

Once we reach high school, we think we know everything about
everything. Maybe you didn't, but I definitely did. For most people,
this posture never really changes. No matter the age or season of life,
we are confident we know what it takes to be happy and are even more
confident of the opinions we hold about the way the world should be.

Our basic beliefs and understandings naturally grow into *perspectives* through which we view all we see and experience. Think of
walking around with a pair of sunglasses on all the time. The colors around you would be filtered by the sunglasses. Eventually, after

wearing them for an extended period of time, you'd have a hard time understanding what someone else might see, through a different pair of glasses. For you, everything would be viewed through a specific lens.

Sunglasses also have frames that hold the lenses in place. Lenses can be changed but only if they fit the frames to which they are fastened. Said another way, the lenses are *dependent* on the frames. Similarly, our general perspectives are framed by our most fundamental beliefs, or what is often described as our *worldview*. The choices we make, the actions we take, and the responses we have are mostly based on our worldview. Since our worldview, or perspectives, greatly influence the choices we make—which then shape the experiences we have—we need a change in worldview and perspective if we desire different outcomes in any area of life. This is especially true when it comes to faith-related outcomes.

Mature perspectives and a growing kingdom worldview will allow us to embrace what God has created us to do. They will allow us to respond with joy to his call to obedience. Without the right perspectives we'll always struggle with obedience, or we'll obey God for the wrong reasons. In both cases, we miss the great benefits of obedience and will likely miss out on the fullness of life that God wants for us and has promised to us. As we become more actively aware of what we believe, as we seek to understand those beliefs, and as we take action on the burdens God gives us, we will have intimate experiences with him that will validate the truth of Scripture.

Unfortunately, we can sometimes be inflexible about the perspectives we hold. We can get frustrated when others don't see things the way we do. In the early nineties, there were these crazy optical-illusion pictures called Magic Eye. They had intricate patterns, shapes, and colors that contained a hidden 3-D picture that could only be seen if you relaxed your eyes in a certain way. Any time I went to the mall, there would be a crowd gathered around one of the Magic Eye posters in a shop window, with everyone trying their best to see the hidden image. Once you figured out how to see it, it became easy to do so again, but not everyone learned the trick. Perspectives are like that. What seems clear to one person is completely hidden from another. No matter the effort, the two people will never see it the same way.

Change is always hard. Changing our perspectives is crazy hard. One of the biggest challenges with it is that we aren't in full control. We can't simply "decide" to view things differently. It's a process that starts with being open, and then actively seeking the right perspectives.

There are immeasurable benefits that come from having the right perspectives. There can also be devastating outcomes from having the wrong perspectives, and from making decisions based on them. This is especially true when it comes to our faith. If we misunderstand God's plan for all of creation, our attempts to help people or to change the world will be ineffective. They might even end up devaluing people and causing great harm.

So how do we get the kinds of *experiences* that lead to greater *understanding* and, eventually, to mature *perspectives*? Unfortunately, we can't force this process. Our role is to choose a posture of active awareness and pursue a deeper understanding of Scripture. God will burden us, call us to obedient actions, and graciously allow us to experience him in the process.

Something to Remember: Embracing an active pursuit of awareness and understanding creates the environment to have the faith-building experiences with God, which confirm the truth of what God says, through Scripture, about who he is and everything in the world he created.

For me, the most meaningful experiential understanding and the most significant growth in perspective has occurred since I've been in Uganda—but this process began about twenty years ago, at a time when I thought I had everything figured out.

CHAPTER 3

A JOURNEY BEGINS

He calls us to trust Him so completely that we are
unafraid to put ourselves in situations where we
will be in trouble if He doesn't come through.[1]

FRANCIS CHAN

My journey to Uganda, to a deeper understanding of the truth, and to a change in perspective, started one Sunday in 2001, at North Point Community Church in Alpharetta, Georgia. Danlyn and I had only recently started attending, and I was still very much in the misery of my skeptical mindset. The Senior Pastor, Andy Stanley, was teaching through a series called "The Ultimate Adventure." On one particular Sunday I was introduced to the important idea that God asks us to take small steps of obedience that lead toward trusting him more fully. This process doesn't just happen overnight.

The next Sunday, Andy taught about the tension between the agenda God sets for our lives and the agenda we set for ourselves. "Who do you think is going to win?" he asked. We have a choice, he said, to embrace God's agenda and do what he says to do, or to continue to set our own course and deal with the inevitable consequences.

At that time, I had given myself permission to pursue my own agenda. After all, I was doing all the right things, like reading the Bible every day, tithing, praying, and rarely missing church. God used that sermon to turn my life upside down. As we walked out the door, I decided that God's agenda was what I wanted, and from that point onward, it would be what I would pursue.

Baby steps. The first thing I did was call my bookie. I was a sports gambler, and Sundays in the fall meant NFL football. The call went like this:

"Hello, this is N43."

"N43, you have a positive balance of $638. What are your plays today?"

"No plays today. I'm out."

"What do you mean you're out?"

"I mean I'm done. Keep my balance. Thanks for your service for the last five years."

"Okay. May I ask why?"

"Sure. It's not part of the new agenda for my life."

"Whatever you say, N43. Have a nice life."

And that was it. I never again placed a sports bet. I made other critical changes as well. By far, the most important decision I made was to begin to organize my life around Jesus, to live my life in pursuit of deeper understanding and joyful obedience to him.

BECCA

Despite that, I didn't grow as quickly as I'd expected. Andy said it wouldn't happen overnight, but I didn't think he was considering my awesomeness when he said what he did. Apparently, knowing what to do and actually doing it are two very different things. I had the knowledge, but I didn't yet have the experiences so important to the building of one's faith. A few years down the road, in 2004, I went on my first student mission trip. On that trip, I had the chance to experience God's grace in a different culture. It was also the first time I can remember thinking that some of my perspectives might be wrong.

I was still a neophyte to student ministry, and very skeptical about teenagers and their ability to be people of strong faith. We had a large team, about fifty students and leaders, that traveled to Jamaica to engage with younger kids in a Vacation-Bible-School-type program and to do some construction work for a partner church. Knowing what I know now, it's probably fair to say it was a little on the "Christian-tourism" side of things, but regardless, it was an important trip for me.

There were only four or five students on the trip I had any kind of relationship with beforehand. Again, I was skeptical, so this lack of friendship with the students didn't lend itself to a positive attitude. After a few hours on an airplane, and an even longer ride in a van, we eventually arrived in a rural place in Jamaica and settled into a hotel on the northwest coast.

As I stepped off the van, a female student was standing in front of me, wanting to talk to me. I'm ashamed to admit I hadn't noticed her before, among the other students. Her name was Becca, and she would soon become one of the most important people in my story. "Mr. Kelly, would you have time this week to talk to me?" she asked. Taken off guard and without time to process what she was asking, I said, "Sure, of course." The next day, Becca reminded me of my commitment, so we planned to get together after the day's work. We picked a spot outside on a concrete, knee-high wall, near the swimming pool that was full of our teammates. She opened up to me about what had happened to her in the prior year, and the faith roller-coaster ride she had been on as a result.

Becca and her mom had been estranged for a long time, and there was a lot of anger and animosity between them. Becca had a strong faith but struggled with forgiveness, especially as it related to her mother. God led her to finally forgive her mom, however, and eventually they reconciled and began to rebuild their relationship with one another. Tragically, Becca's mom died in a car accident soon after they started connecting again. Not surprisingly, Becca was mad at God, was questioning her faith, and was emotionally unavailable leading up to the trip.

I never found out why she wanted to share her story with me or how she even knew who I was. Regardless, God gave me some encouraging words to share with her and soon after, she was open to what God wanted to teach her on that trip. That one conversation completely changed my posture on the faith capacity of a teenager and how God uses our experiences to bring us closer to him and to validate the truth of his Word. Becca's vulnerability, love, and kindness impacted just about every person on the trip. It's truly amazing how tangible the work of the Spirit is when we simply do what we are created to do.

When we got back to the States, I assumed there would be the inevitable "backsliding" with the students from the spiritual high of the mission trip, but it never happened—partly because Becca wouldn't let us lose our focus on Christ. The next few months were filled with joyful fellowship, and we soon began planning for a return trip. Unfortunately, our bubble was popped in a sudden and devastating way.

Even now, fifteen years later, I am typing through tears as I recall the story. I was in Las Vegas for a conference, stealing a few extra minutes of sleep before getting up to prepare for my speech. I flipped open my phone (yes, flipped) and there were thirteen missed calls, all from people who were on that first trip to Jamaica. One of the seniors, John Putnam, had left a voice mail asking for a return call. I remember standing in the grand hall, where the vendors had set up their booths for the conference, listening to John tell me that Becca had died that morning in a head-on collision.

For me, that painful experience launched a search for real understanding about who God is, what he has promised, and everything he has to say about who we are and the life we live on this side of eternity. In addition, Danlyn and I started pouring ourselves into student ministry.

SEMINARY, BRAZIL, AND INSIDEOUT

After Becca died, I felt a great desire for a deeper understanding of Christian doctrine and theology. I was accepted into the master's program for biblical studies at Dallas Theological Seminary (DTS). Of all the crazy things I had done, starting seminary in that season of my life might have been the craziest. By business and cultural standards, I was an important person with an important job and a lot of responsibility. That came with lots of air miles (two million on Delta alone) and way too many nights spent in hotel rooms. In addition, I was volunteering with the little kids on Sunday morning, and then the high school students every Sunday afternoon at a ministry called InsideOut.

I approached graduate school very differently from how I navigated my way through my undergraduate degree at Auburn University. Instead of avoiding campus most days to play golf or Sega Genesis, I actually loved the classes at DTS and all the work that went into seminary. Unfortunately, the trajectory of my business career and the demands of student ministry had to take priority over finishing the degree. After about three wonderful years at DTS, I had to step away.

During that time, I was asked to lead student mission trips to Mexico and then, for seven consecutive years, to Brazil. It was on those trips where Danlyn and I really developed our burden for high school students. Many of them have become "family," and forever friends. There was one group of students, however, who God used more than any other to prepare us to eventually say *yes* to Uganda.

Over time, as we saw spiritual transformation in the students who had been participating, the number of applicants for the trips increased significantly. To address the growing demand, the decision was made to de-prioritize students who had previously participated in multiple trips. This was a logical decision, but it had a large, unintended consequence for me personally. The decision directly impacted a group of high-school seniors who had faithfully served with me in Brazil and whose energy and faith were the catalyst for the explosive growth of InsideOut.

Their passion for Jesus and for serving others was infectious. Over the course of three years, attendance at InsideOut grew from about 150 students to more than 600 every Sunday, mainly because of the efforts of these students. Somehow I was now supposed to tell them they couldn't go on a mission trip after they graduated and before they stepped into the fierce spiritual battle ahead of them at university. Fortunately, God had other plans.

WHERE THE STREETS HAVE NO NAME

Back to the discussion about objective truth, let's just agree that U2 is the greatest rock band of all time. Even though the song "Where the Streets Have No Name" is supposed to be about unity, it will always make me think about the nameless, dusty roads of Uganda, and it will always remind me of God's grace throughout my entire journey.

In 2011, I was having lunch at a California Pizza Kitchen with my good friend Scott Bowen. We had been friends since working together with students at InsideOut and had a lot in common; we were both Auburn grads, so our friendship was easy and mutually encouraging. A couple of years earlier, Scott and his ministry partner, Tom Carson, had started an organization in Uganda called Champions United. This ministry had a vision for discipling young men through football (or soccer, as we call it in the States). The idea was to hire coaches who would develop relationships with boys in order to introduce them to the gospel, and then to challenge them to live life differently than what is typical in their culture. Before we finished our pizzas, Scott asked if I might be willing, at some point in the future, to lead the first student mission trip to Champions United.

Back to the dilemma of what to do with the amazing seniors who were set to graduate in the summer of 2013 and had just been told they would not be allowed on a mission trip. What about Champions United? Were Scott and Tom ready for a mission trip to come to Uganda? I called Scott immediately and told him if there was ever an opportunity to start, it was with this group. He agreed and we started the planning process. Practically, however, there were a ton of challenges.

First, there was an Ebola outbreak in Western Africa, so that led to fear about traveling to Uganda. Africa is a massive continent and the Ebola cases were 4,000 miles away, but even so, convincing parents to let me take their children at that time was no easy task. Also, since this wasn't an official InsideOut trip, I didn't have the resources of our church to help with the logistics, fundraising, insurance, and other needs. In order for everyone to feel comfortable, I decided it would be wise to visit Uganda for a few days before moving much further ahead in the process. Scott already had a trip planned for December with a key board member and friend named Judd, so I asked if they would accommodate me for a short visit while they were in-country.

KISSES FROM KATIE

My seminary experience led to a much-needed change of perspective, as I was overwhelmed from learning more about the grace of God and the work of the Holy Spirit. I get emotional when I see, experience, or read about God doing amazing things in the lives of undeserving people, which, by the way, is all of us. Despite that, I wasn't expecting for God to use the story of a fearless and faithful young girl to encourage me for the journey ahead.

Anna and Megan, as high school students, were on that first trip to Jamaica. Eventually, they became some of the most important young people in our lives. In 2011, Danlyn was co-leading a group of high schoolers with these two. At some point during that year, the book *Kisses from Katie* was making the rounds in the Christian community; it had been on the *New York Times* bestseller list for over a year. With my schedule, I'm usually the last to know about anything viral, and this was no exception. Anna had given the book to Danlyn, and I happened to notice it on her bedside table. "What's that book?" I asked. Danlyn had grown accustomed to my unawareness of just about everything, and graciously replied, "It's a very popular book right now, and Anna said I have to read it." I was between books at that time, and wasn't traveling, so I asked, "Do you mind if I read it first?"

At that point in my life there were just a handful of books I had read in a 24-hour period—including *Seabiscuit, Redeeming Love*, the Bourne trilogy, and *A Prayer for Owen Meany. Kisses from Katie* jumped onto that list. It was challenging and inspiring to read Katie's story of moving to Uganda, and how she continually said *yes* to God, even when everyone around her thought she was crazy. The other thing that touched me was her complete surrender to the power of the Holy Spirit to accomplish anything. I recall thinking that I had never known a person with a more fruitful, trusting relationship with God.

I also recall thinking, "Good for her, but definitely not for me."

Let me be perfectly honest. I had no thoughts of moving to Uganda, and at that point, zero desire. After all, God had given us a lot of money so we could fund people like Katie and not have to think about leaving our comfortable lives.

After Danlyn read the book, we started supporting Katie's organization, Amazima Ministries. I wish I could say we started following along with the work they were doing, but (I'm embarrassed to admit) Amazima just became one more in a long list of organizations we supported. But when the time got closer to go to Uganda for the scout trip, I started to think about visiting Amazima.

I reached out and, apparently, I wasn't the only one asking, because the word I received back was an emphatic *no*. Because Katie had developed quite a following, there were a lot of people who wanted to meet her. In order to protect the children she worked with, she had to deny these requests. But three days before departure I received another email from Amazima, this time inviting me to attend their weekly discipleship program that took place on Saturdays. To this day, I still don't know how or why they changed their policy, but it would become a life-altering moment for Danlyn and me.

Scott and Judd greeted me at the Entebbe International Airport, and we made the short drive to the hotel. I still remember everything about that first night, including how unusually comfortable I felt for being in Africa for the first time. I had traveled all over the world, including to developing countries, but the feeling was different this time. For the next couple of days we visited with the coaches at the Champions United property, reserved hotel rooms and transportation for the upcoming summer mission trip, and in general, got a feel for the rhythm of Uganda.

Saturday rolled around and we set off for Jinja, about three hours away. I had an invitation from Amazima to attend the Saturday program, but I didn't have much for directions to get there. The email I had printed out said to go to something called the Nile Stage and then ask someone to point us in the direction of a village called Buziika. After about five kilometers, we were to ask a *boda-boda* guy (a motorcycle taxi driver) where to find Mama Katie. After a few misses and some interesting conversations, we finally made it to the property.

We ended up parking next to a white, fourteen-passenger van which had become somewhat famous because of Katie's book. For a successful guy, who seemed to have the world by the tail, it's surprising how anxious I was at the thought of meeting Katie, even though that wasn't the point of the visit. We were soon greeted by Bradley Lang, head of operations for the ministry. He generously showed us around and told us everything we'd ever want to know about Amazima.

We also met Doug and Amy from Nashville. Doug was considering taking the role of Executive Director for Amazima, and they were in town to get a sense of what was happening on the ground.

Near the end of our time there I stood by myself, in the middle of a worn path, taking in the view as far as my eyes could see. Uganda is breathtakingly beautiful, and I found myself thanking God for the splendor of his creation and for giving me eyes to enjoy it. Off to the side, I noticed someone walking toward me, veering off the narrow path to give me space. When I noticed it was Katie, I stopped her in her tracks. I'm not sure why, though, because I certainly didn't have anything planned to say to her. Much like other stops in this journey, however, the moment wasn't planned, nor was the conversation that followed. We shared some personal stories and talked about some items of pressing importance, uninterrupted, for almost fifteen minutes.

I don't remember what we were talking about when our dialogue ended, but at some point, a little girl walked over with tears in her eyes and stared up at Katie. At that moment I became invisible, as Katie knelt down to tend to the girl's immediate need. It was the first time (of many) I had the privilege of seeing the gospel in action in Uganda.

Looking back, I will say that a fifteen-minute conversation between Katie and a stranger, at the Amazima property, with 500 kids running around, was without question, a miracle. Like a lot of this story, however, much of what God was doing to move Danlyn and me in the direction of serving in Uganda was completely improbable, if not miraculous, given the context. Although I didn't know it at the time, a burden was building for a generation of young people in a culture which was not my own.

THE DEAN OF WHAT?

A few months later, Doug called. He had accepted the leadership role at Amazima and was putting together a small trip for donors and board members to spend a week in Jinja. He invited Danlyn and me to join the group. Since Danlyn was tired of hearing me talk about Uganda, she very much wanted to go and see everything for herself.

I was nervous about the trip because of Danlyn's health. Travel is always difficult for her, and this would involve thirty hours of flying and riding, less-than-luxurious accommodations, and long days. But she was determined, so we agreed to go with the group. Although the travel was physically difficult, I noticed an obvious, curious peace about her throughout the trip. I didn't give it much thought at the time, and instead just thanked God for bringing her through.

Maybe that's why I didn't see it coming. If I was an unlikely candidate to leave our comfortable life for the dust and dirt of Uganda, she was the *most* unlikely candidate. Why would we even consider such a move? Our life together was genuinely good, we were centered on Christ, and we sacrificially gave of our time, money, and resources for kingdom purposes. In addition, I was killing it at work and looking at retiring early if things continued to go well. So when Danlyn said, "You know, I think I could live in Uganda," I didn't receive it seriously. By no fault of her own, Danlyn was not exactly a good fit for Uganda.

Somehow, she was dead serious and there began a process of conversations and prayer that led to me calling Doug and, in a general way, letting him know we would be open to potentially serving in Uganda. Doug wasn't exactly excited about my offer. I'm not sure I was either. I mean, why would a software guy living a fruitful life want to leave the comfort of the States and put his wife in a worse situation, health-wise? But Doug and I were friends, so the line of communication remained open.

After a few months, Doug messaged me and said he wanted me to talk with a career educator named Mark. Apparently, Amazima was going to start a secondary school and had hired Mark to lead the effort. He had great experience, having been a Head Teacher (Principal) at schools both in the US and internationally. On the surface, it sounded promising.

Still, I found myself asking, *Why am I talking to this guy?*

That first conversation between Mark and me lasted about two hours and forty-five minutes. I remember, because I dialed him as we were getting on the highway, leaving Auburn after a football game, and I didn't hang up until we reached our house in Dawsonville, Georgia. Given my love for cutting straight to a solution, my first question was, "What problem are you trying to solve?" As I would eventually learn at a deeply personal level, the problems facing young people in Uganda, and in much of Africa, have not changed greatly over the last forty years. That's despite more than a trillion dollars of aid sent in to "help."[2]

Danlyn and I, like many people who've sponsored kids or given to orphanages, assumed that education is the answer to alleviating poverty. If that were the case, Africa would just need more money for more schools. Trust me when I tell you the current model does not address the real problems, nor do the present efforts result in much success or change.

Mark explained that the new school would be very different in educational philosophy. Its primary goal would be discipleship. It would seek to equip Ugandan students with the tools of learning, to enable them to live fully for the glory of God. A big part of the strategy was what would eventually be called Student Life (SL)—everything outside of the academic day, including the boarding of the students. The more I learned about the proposed solution, the more I found it brilliant, and the more I was intrigued.

What Mark needed, however, was someone to build SL from the ground up, and then lead it, without much hand-holding. Listening to Mark talk about his vision for SL and the kind of person he was looking for had me terrified, because the sum of my experience and gifts were exactly what he was describing.

We continued to talk with Amazima about the opportunity through the middle of May 2015, but for reasons I won't get into here, they went silent on us for well over three months. If I'm honest, I started feeling angry and hurt. I finally reached a point of frustration that burst out in an email to Mark, expressing our disappointment in how things were handled and letting him know we had moved on. But the next morning I received an email reply with an apology and a question. It said, "Would you consider finishing the process?"

I don't know if I'd ever experienced a simultaneous gut punch and Spirit check before, but there was no doubting that moment. Danlyn and I sat together in silence, not knowing how to respond. Ultimately, we decided to see the process through, and on October 12, 2015, I was offered the opportunity to become the Dean of Student Life at TAS. We accepted twenty-four hours later.

The following fall we moved to Uganda and almost immediately, Scripture began to come alive on a daily basis. It didn't take us long to learn that the Bible really does make sense—of all the things that otherwise make no sense at all. What happened in the years that followed has changed our lives forever.

Something to Remember: When God gives an opportunity to understand more about him, life, and the world around us, through lived experience, say, "Yes."

Fortunately for Danlyn and me, we were somewhat aware of how little we understood about the culture of Uganda, and how much would be required to become effective in building a ministry. What we didn't know, however, was how the process of seeking *understanding* would lead to more than mere knowledge. God would soon change our *perspectives*, through *experiences*, and confirm the truth of his Word in the process. It was to be my first encounter with *epignosis*.

CHAPTER 4

UNDERSTANDING UGANDA

There is freedom of speech, but I can't
guarantee freedom after speech.[1]
IDI AMIN, PRESIDENT/DICTATOR OF UGANDA 1971–1979

The first opportunity I had to get to know some of the students who would be attending the new school was during the long break before the first term of the year began. In Uganda, the school calendar runs from the beginning of February through early December. Over the break, organizations who sponsor children provide what are called "holiday programs" that bring the students together for fun, food, and fellowship. Amazima was no exception. At that time, the majority of Amazima's sponsored children were in primary school, with seven grade levels (P1 to P7). We would open as a secondary school, and we were starting with just one grade level. The students who had just finished P7 were set to be the first-ever class at the new school. If all went well, they would soon arrive at the brand-new campus to start their secondary careers.

Fortunately for me, most of the soon-to-be "first years" were at the holiday program. There was something special about this group. Even on the first day I met them, I remember thinking that God had specifically chosen them for something unique and important (I was right).

Their clothes were a bit ragged, but nothing like what I had seen in the emotionally manipulative pictures in charity commercials and the many direct-mail pieces that had come to us in the States. My white skin was one thing, but more than that, I was a curiosity to them. Who was this *mzungu* (white person) and why was he hanging around? Word quickly spread that I was to be a "boss" at the new school, so it didn't take long before I was the center of attention.

I found the students jovial, sincere, and friendly. Of course, they had many questions about America and what their new school would be like. I would learn later there was a lot of apprehension because of our very different approach and the fact that foreign nationals would be involved. After reassuring them about what to expect, they were more than willing to answer some of my questions about their lives. This was before I understood much of anything. In retrospect, I should not yet have been asking questions of the students. It was, unfortunately, an example of what happens when we aren't actively aware, when we make decisions without understanding, or when we have the wrong perspective. It was an important moment. I wouldn't make that same mistake again.

Culturally, twins are a big deal in Uganda. If you are a twin, that fact becomes part of your name, and it differs depending on whether you are the first- or second-born twin. For example, if I was a first-born twin, my name would be *Kelly Wasswa*. Translation: "Kelly First-Born Twin." It's such a big deal that many twins use their "twin" designation as their main name, and spouses may take it as their married name. Of course, I had no idea of this when the twin sisters Babirye (first-born female) and Nakato (second-born female) confidently introduced themselves to me.

Babirye would be joining our inaugural class while Nakato was a grade behind. Why were twin sisters in different grades? Well, children in humble communities generally don't start school until there is money to pay the school fees, so it's not uncommon to see twins separated. It's also not uncommon to see much-older kids in younger grades who started late because it took longer for them to get sponsored. The twins were among the first students to talk to me and if you ever met them, you wouldn't be surprised. Let's just say they were above-average confident. Anyway, it didn't take long before they were telling me their story.

Their mom was only thirteen years old when they were born and the father wasn't much older, at fifteen. Soon after their birth, the father was nowhere to be found and the mother had decided she couldn't take care of the girls. Their mother's sister decided to take them to the Nile River, and her plan was to drown them in the river. Unable to follow through with the plan, she somehow thought it would be easier to end their lives by gouging out their eyes. She preceded in attempting to remove the right eye of one of the babies and was successful in doing so. Before she could fully finish the effort, however, she stopped, unexpectedly. The twins aren't sure why they were spared that day, but nonetheless, they eventually became part of our school. The girls have been raised by their step-grandmother, who took them in shortly after the trauma.

I quickly learned that almost all our students come from very hard places and have dramatic and sometimes shocking stories in their past (or even their present). Any perspective I had about the challenges these students have faced blew up that day. As I came to know the twins' story and more importantly, the desperation which would lead their mother to make such a decision, I was shocked into the realization that my level of understanding was woefully inadequate. I also became aware of my lack of awareness and compassion. If I was going to be effective in leading these kids to know Jesus, I needed to be patient and intentional in seeking understanding.

On a lighter note, I never thought I'd be involved in a thirty-six-hour search for a missing glass eye, but it definitely happened. I was eating dinner when I got the call that we had a serious situation. After an exhaustive search that came up empty, the eye later mysteriously appeared on the mattress of the owner's bunk, with an emphasis on the word "mysteriously."

"I'VE GOT THIS!" (NOT)

Based on this experience (and many others), it became clear that if I wanted our students in Uganda to authentically know Christ and desire to make him known, I would need to better understand the spiritual setting in which I now lived and worked.

As our understanding grows, our relationship with God also grows. We can experience him in undeniable ways when we say *yes* to engaging with the burdens he gives to us. There are few things that grow your faith more than authentic experiences. Without experiential understanding and a personal relationship with God, however, what we perceive to be a burden or a calling might actually come from what we ate for breakfast, instead of coming from the wisdom of Scripture. I'm in Uganda because of a decades-long burden for teenagers and a series of *yes* responses when asked to engage with that burden.

Saying *yes* to the opportunity to build the Student Life department was the hardest *yes* of my life. There was no real precedent for what I was being asked to do, and the challenges would be unpredictable. At my core, I'm a sales guy who is used to successful outcomes that are largely in my control, so part of me was worried I would fail. There were so many unknowns. How could an American businessman build a program from scratch to disciple Ugandan teenagers, and lead a multicultural, multigenerational team in a developing country? Oh, and the Ugandans didn't really want me here, didn't believe the plan for Student Life would work, and thought the vision was a pipe dream. What a great place to start!

On paper, I was a good fit: fourteen years of student ministry,

thirteen overseas mission trips, three-plus years of seminary, a successful business career, foster-care experience, ruggedly handsome, and,
for good measure, I had read every book on poverty, missions, and
the developing world. Okay, maybe I'm exaggerating; I haven't read
every relevant book. Whether I was actually qualified or not, it was
my responsibility to create a safe, nurturing environment, centered
on Christ, where our students could authentically know him, desire
to make him known, and be prepared to go out and live fruitful lives.

Good process is good process regardless of the context, so *being
actively aware* and *seeking to understand* were number one and number
two on my list. Okay, there wasn't actually a list yet, but that was the
approach I started with. Learning as much as possible about Uganda
was crucially important. I needed to learn if I were to develop the
right perspective, to make the best decisions from.

I first had to consider my frame of mind if we were going to be
successful. Instead of problems to be solved, there were people to
be loved. My mind was racing with a lot of "what-to-do" items, but
much more critical were the "how-to-do" items for serving in this
unique context. To love these students in the right way, I needed to
better *understand* the culture in which they had grown up. I needed
to learn about family dynamics, education, identity, faith, and how
women are viewed and treated. I put together a plan to gain as much
understanding as possible in the weeks leading up to the first day
of school. Fortunately for me, some important colleagues were willing to spend a lot of time with me and answer my endless barrage
of questions.

The Scholarship Mentors at Amazima are a team of Ugandans
responsible for the school's relationship with the community, and,
more specifically, with the families of our students. They are social
workers (and much more) who come alongside people and play a
critical role in empowering them to live self-sustaining lives in Christ.
For me, however, they knew our students and their families better

than anyone and provided the best possible chance for me to better understand the culture. They were generous with their time and never showed frustration with what must have been a very exhausting couple of weeks with me. You might not have guessed it, but I'm capable of being a little *too* passionate. Throw in the language barrier and the preconceived notions about white people, and you can begin to understand the level of awesomeness required to coach me through my learning process. To this day, if God has used me to accomplish anything meaningful in this country, I look back to that period of discovery as a crucially important season.

HONOR AND SHAME

Fundamentally, Uganda's culture is based on the concepts of honor and shame. This framework greatly influences every area of life, including identity, family, social conventions, relationships, money, education, and especially, matters of faith. It's been said that *guilt* is being sorry for what you've done but *shame* is being sorry for who you are. If at our core we are ashamed of who we are, it can be a significant barrier against accepting the gracious love of God. How do we communicate to students that are not valued by their culture, that they are valued by God? How do we help them see they are created in the image of God, and therefore of incredible value, when that truth is so distant from what their culture has been telling them?

This is the great challenge we face in sharing the gospel in Uganda. The starting point for almost every student I've led is one of shame and rejection. Because of this, the concept of an honor/shame culture was the most important thing for me to understand if I were to be effective in executing the plans for our ministry programs in Student Life.

Historically, honor/shame cultures have been characterized by class systems where a small but powerful and wealthy ruling class sits high above the rest of the population. Important decisions are made for the benefit of the few and at the expense of the many. One's identity and opportunities are largely related to family heritage and the tribe or kingdom the family comes from. Some leaders in the faith community also take advantage of the honor/shame dynamic to create their own class system, to their own benefit.

To make this even worse, the teachings and grace of Jesus are often set aside in favor of legalism. So, our students face difficulties that stem from the hard places they've come from, and then they face difficulties that stem from the culture in which they've grown up. This dynamic shows up in simple ways almost every day.

For many years, my response when I've missed a phone call was to send a text saying, "Sorry I missed your call. How can I help?" It had always served me well, so I continued this practice after moving to Uganda. I don't know how many times I sent that same text before I received a reply that surprised me, from a good friend who worked with me at the school. He texted, "Why do you keep offering me help?" I immediately went to his office to find out why he had reacted this way. He explained that asking for help can be a source of shame, and an offer of help can be demeaning, because it assumes help is needed.

If you ask our students what they would like to have as a profession after completing their education, at least half the responses would be, "I'd like to be an accountant." With all due respect to my CPA friends, why would a teenager aspire, above all other options, to be an accountant? Well, village culture considers accounting to be an honorable profession, and that sometimes matters more than anything else. Even though there are probably fifty credentialed accountants for every open opportunity, Ugandans still pursue that degree because of the honor associated with it. Sometimes, being unemployed with an honorable degree is preferred over being employed in a field seen as less important.

Fortunately, the approach for leading people to a living faith in the risen Christ, in an honor/shame culture, was modeled for us 2,000 years ago. At the time of Jesus, first-century Palestine had been under Roman rule for about eighty years. By any measure, most of the people were oppressed by the elites standing above them, and disadvantaged. Whether Jewish or Roman, leaders consistently wielded their power to enrich their own lives, no matter the consequences to those under them. Power and position were fiercely protected. It's why they had to kill a Jewish carpenter with no visible resources or political influence. His teaching was a threat to their entitled way of life and that was not okay. Of course, killing Jesus failed to stop the movement because of that whole rising-from-the-dead thing.

Emboldened by the resurrection, the earliest leaders of the Jesus movement organized their lives completely around his upside-down teachings. In kingdom culture, love (not power) would be the ethic, the last would be first, the poor would be blessed, leaders would serve their followers, women would have equal value, and most importantly, a right standing with God would no longer be based on individual works but rather on the finished work of the cross (grace over law).[2]

Since the experience of our students, in their communities, so closely paralleled the cultural experiences of the first-century Christians, we would approach Student Life in a similar way, with Christ and his teachings at the center of everything. Kingdom culture above any other culture.

That doesn't mean there isn't tension in making program decisions when you have a mix of cultures, ideas, faith experiences, and pride thrown together. It also doesn't absolve us of the responsibility of building a kingdom culture that respects and understands the culture our students have known their whole lives. A kingdom-culture mindset doesn't mean we don't set goals, or don't work hard to be efficient, unified, and successful. Just because our students and their families are people to be loved and not problems to be solved doesn't mean there aren't systemic problems in Uganda, problems that we hope and pray a generation of transformed students will seek to solve, applying their gifts for kingdom progress.

Ultimately, coming up with the *how* for building a kingdom culture and seeking to lead our students to know Jesus and desire to make him known, has been the biggest (and most enjoyable) challenge of my lifetime. To whatever degree we have been successful, it started with an active awareness and a desire to understand through experiences. Understanding the faith of our students, however, would prove to be the most critical of all understandings.

IT'S NOT JUST UGANDA

After spending quality time with the Scholarship Mentors and getting to know our students better, I learned that many of the fundamental problems our students and their families face here in Uganda are the very same problems people face in America. This was a surprise, though maybe it shouldn't have been. Honor and shame may not be commonly associated with Western culture, but it's a prevalent and persistent reality. The difference, though, is that in the West its influence is more subtle and in the background.

If we examine issues of gender and family in the US, marriages are falling apart at alarming rates, leading to well-documented, dire consequences, especially for wives and children. Regardless, American dads aren't around very much, men are still mostly in charge, and despite "progressive" thought, women are devalued in most aspects of society. As in Uganda, faith is more inherited and taught rather than chosen, and false gospels are frequently preached and accepted.

At the time of this writing, the United States is rapidly moving toward a traditional honor/shame culture. Again, similar to Uganda, the real and growing division in America is based on economic class. Increasingly, low-income communities have become victims of failed government policies that lack compassion, and at their worst, devalue the very people they purport to help. In my experiential understanding, living under the weight of honor and shame will kill the soul.

Like all honor/shame cultures, the primary goals in America are wealth and fame, and with them, an obsession with self-promotion. Although the cultures are very different, the same problems exist in both countries. The problems aren't necessarily worse in Uganda, but they manifest differently, in a way I was able to clearly see and experience. There were huge benefits to understanding that the fundamental problems in Uganda are not very different from the problems in the culture and subculture of America. This reality validates what Scripture says about these problems and reinforces the solution: Jesus and his teachings. It also greatly reduces the temptation to look at solutions through the lens of our Western perspective.

If we can understand that material wealth and comfort are not the solution, nor indicators of God's favor, then we can humbly look to Jesus for how to live and enrich the lives of others. People often say America is a blessed country, and that is true. The blessing, however, is the availability of the gospel and access to the Body of Christ, not our economy and the benefits that come with it.

Something to Remember: When we diligently seek to better understand the culture in which we live and do ministry, God will shape our perspectives, through intimate experiences that testify to the truth and wisdom of his Word.

While my experiences in Uganda have reframed the experiences I've had in the United States, living in both cultures has also led to a greater understanding. Even as we grow in Christian maturity and our perspectives change, however, they are still framed by the fundamental beliefs we have about where life and faith intersect and collide. Perhaps most fundamental to the Christian faith is our view of brokenness.

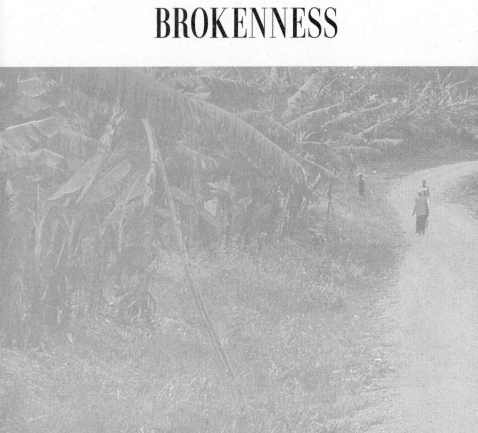

SECTION TWO

BROKENNESS

As I mentioned before, there are fundamental beliefs (worldview) that frame our general beliefs (perspectives) that largely dictate our decisions, choices, and actions. The same paradigm exists for those who follow Jesus and live in the hope of his promises. Our view of *brokenness* is perhaps most fundamental because everything and everyone around us is tragically broken.

Brokenness frames our perspectives on sin, suffering, identity, value, and how to meaningfully engage in the world. Most importantly, it frames our perspective on the gospel. Without a correct view of brokenness, we can't have the right perspective on our complete need for a Savior, and any deviation from the true gospel has devastating consequences.

If you don't like the concept of brokenness, at least acknowledge that not much of anything is as it should be. Deep down we all know it.

From seminary I was fortunate to gain the correct, academic perspective on the brokenness I encountered in my early years in student ministry. It wasn't until I moved to Uganda, however, that I experienced and understood brokenness in a deeper way, that validated what God says in his Word.

My prayer is that this section will challenge you to confront what you believe about brokenness and most importantly, your perspectives associated with it.

CHAPTER 5

FALSE GODS
AND FALSE GOSPELS

His divine power has given us everything we need
for a godly life through our [epignosis] of him
who called us by his own glory and goodness.

2 PETER 1:3

One of the core values at our school is "Servant Leadership" (the others are "Nurturing Relationships" and "Academic Excellence"), and in the Student Life Department, we work to create opportunities for our students to serve each other and their communities. Our students live in "houses" that each have three dorm rooms; every dorm room in turn has six beds. In the center of each "house" is an apartment where a married Family Mentor couple lives, who are responsible for modeling a Christ-centered marriage.

Every Saturday morning one of the houses on campus, according to a schedule, goes out to the surrounding community to serve a vulnerable family by cleaning, washing clothes, cooking, repairing damage, and most importantly, sitting and talking with them. The service projects are arranged by our Scholarship Mentors who are out in the community every day. Most of the time we have no knowledge of the situation before we arrive, so sometimes we can be confronted with difficult living conditions that are hard to process. On one particular Saturday, that was especially true.

The family we served, like most in that area, lived in a small mud house on a small piece of land. There were six young kids running around who were being raised by a *jaja* (grandmother). Our students began their work around the compound and eventually made their way into the little house. Soon one of our students went to his Family Mentor to raise concern about a young girl he found in one of the rooms. The Mentor found a smiling, somehow joyful, teenage girl sitting in the corner, unable to move. There were visible sores covering her body that, as we would later learn, were a result of sitting in the same spot for almost four months. You read that right: four months. She'd fallen out of a mango tree and broken her back. Since they were unable to afford medical care, this girl, Natasha, was resigned to a life of sitting on a dirt floor.

Uganda is well known for its friendly people and hospitality. No matter how materially poor they might be, people will welcome others into their homes without hesitation. When it comes to helping a neighbor, however, it gets a little complicated. In the paradigm of an honor/shame culture, people are hesitant to ask for help, and hesitant to offer it. That's how a situation like Natasha's is possible. My instinct has always been to jump immediately into a situation to apply a solution. But, thankfully, I learned early in my time in Uganda that *how* an intervention is done matters as much or more than *what* the intervention might be. I have good Ugandan friends with sincere hearts for people in need, who I trust to guide the *how* when intervention is needed.

After getting permission from her family, we made arrangements for Natasha to be transported to a specialty hospital in the city of Entebbe, to have her back injury evaluated. As we expected, her back was broken. It was also beyond repair. Somehow Natasha never lost her joy, however, even when the bad news came. She volunteered that her joy came from her faith in Christ and that he had sustained her every day since she fell out of the mango tree. We would have helped her regardless, but we were extra motivated because of how she received our assistance with such gratitude.

I remember being truly amazed by her faith…the kind of unshakable faith we should all have.

The first step in her recovery was to deal with the sores on her body. They were badly infected and the situation was serious. We moved her to a local hospital here in Jinja and made sure she had the best care possible. After a month in the hospital, her wounds were almost healed. What she didn't know was that people were making a custom wheelchair for her, and there were discussions about bringing her into the scholarship program so she could go to school. Everything was going great…until it wasn't.

I was getting ready to kick off our Wednesday night chapel service when my phone rang. It was my friend Rebeccah, who was managing the plan for Natasha. I assumed she was calling to tell me she had received the wheelchair we'd been waiting for, but unfortunately, it was another kind of update. With just a few days to go before Natasha could be safely released from the hospital, her biological mother, who had not been seen by anyone for a very long time, had gone there and taken Natasha away. Rebeccah and others had been searching for about two weeks but were unable to find her until that afternoon. Devastatingly, one of the unhealed wounds had gotten infected, and as a result, Natasha had passed away.

That's when the absolute absurdity of the prosperity gospel went from being academic to being personal. Everyone involved had great faith and was praying constantly throughout the whole process. Where was Natasha's healing? Where was her "prosperity"? In Uganda, the prosperity pastors would say she wasn't favored because she'd been unable to give financially and her faith was weak. This wrong thinking ignores the truth of our brokenness and that of the world around us. As heartbreaking as it is to face the reality of stories like Natasha's, events like this provide an *epignosis* (experiential understanding) that moves us to the correct perspectives. The importance of this can't be overstated.

FALSE GODS

The first time Danlyn and I made the drive from Jinja to Kampala, we had a driver take us, since we were nowhere close to being ready to drive in the chaos of the big city. It wasn't long before we were caught in a jam, which means we sat in one place for close to an hour. The reason for the traffic was that thousands of people were lined up, holding jerry cans (used to transport water), waiting to get into a very large place of tents. It seemed odd, even for Uganda, to see so many people queued up in one place, so I asked our driver, "What's going on?" He chuckled as he replied, "Oh, they are waiting to buy holy water from a prophet."

In most developing countries, people are vulnerable to false teaching because of the difficult circumstances they face in life. Survival takes precedence over almost everything, so even the most outrageous claims may be taken seriously, if there is a promise of a better life. There is a church in Kenya called Breast and Honey New International Church, which was very popular until the pastor was exposed by an undercover news person. The pastor taught that the spirit of a woman lies in her breast, and in order to be "delivered," he must personally perform the action in the same manner a baby would get nourishment from their mother. You may laugh, but this is one example in a long list of ridiculousness. Different tribes and regions in Uganda believe in different things, so it was important to fully understand what our students believed.

My desire was and is for students to know and experience the true gospel. To help make this happen, and to help me understand,

I had the best possible resource I could imagine. Our Campus Pastor, Daniel Isabirye, is one of the smartest, most humble, and most faithful Jesus followers I've ever known. He also has a master's degree from Southeastern Baptist Theological Seminary (North Carolina), and his thesis was entitled *A Biblical and Theological Analysis of the Tenets of the Wealth, Health, and Happiness Gospel, in Jinja, Uganda.* Prior to coming to work at the school, Pastor Daniel spent his time teaching at the local seminary, educating local pastors on the true gospel and how they could lead people to know the real Jesus. If any Ugandan knew the culture of faith in Jinja, it was Daniel.

The first time I interviewed Daniel for the role of campus pastor, he said something to me I have never forgotten. With noticeable passion, he said, "Ugandans are tired of *hearing* the gospel. They need to *see* and *experience* it."

That statement crushed me, but more importantly, reminded me of just how important the *how* can be. Missionaries and ministries have been preaching in the rural villages for decades, but according to Pastor Daniel, the culture of faith has remained largely unchanged. Apparently, people have been hearing the gospel but not understanding it, due to the complexity of their context.

I spent a lot of time asking questions and listening to what Daniel had to say about the local churches our students were attending. The civil war of 1986–1994 left behind a high number of widows and orphans who lived in extreme poverty. Many "pastors," with no theological training, descended on Jinja and began preaching a message of "transactional" blessings to those who would give money and have enough faith. Over time, this became the dominant theology and subsequently, has caused immeasurable damage. A common phrase used by pastors here, to pressure people into giving more, is "no coins, just paper."

As my understanding about the influence of false gospels began to change, it allowed me to think more strategically about how we would do ministry in Student Life.

When our students first arrive at school, Pastor Daniel and our Bible Department have them describe their faith background (on paper) and why they believe what they believe. This is an important first step to create a self-awareness about their individual faith, and to help create an environment where they can embrace a pursuit of *understanding*, resulting in a change in *perspective*. Usually they struggle to answer because they don't understand the question.

For most of our students, faith is more familial than individual. In other words, the faith of the family is the faith of the student. A student will often identify as a Muslim or a Christian but have no meaningful understanding of what their faith is about. Many local Christian churches preach mainly from the Hebrew scriptures and are very legalistic, controlling, money-driven, and heavily oriented to prosperity teaching. Jesus is often presented as a god among other gods, but as the best of them because he offers eternal life and a way to escape hell. Witchcraft is still very prevalent in the local villages, so there are practices and rituals that get combined with Christianity. Faith leaders are given an elevated status, and often claim that their divine inspiration and experiences trump the Bible.

There have been many a night when I've cried myself to sleep after learning of the abuses our students have experienced at the hands of pastors, local church leaders, and even immediate family members. In addition to the spiritual abuse from being taught false versions of God and/or the gospel, there are way too many stories of emotional and physical abuse at the hands of people who are supposed to love and care for them. In this context, brokenness is used as a tool to frame the wrong perspectives.

What troubles me most is that many of our students have a false sense of spiritual security and no instinct to understand more, because they've "accepted" Christ many times. For many of them, their "acceptance" came out of fear of losing a sponsorship, or simply to please a person who might provide them an advantage. Sadly, very few of our students arrive on our campus with a genuine faith of their own.

I've come to realize we face the same challenges with students (and adults) in the States.

THE GOSPEL OF PERFORMANCE

In my experience, some of those who walk away from Christian faith in America do so because of harm from a church or a professing Christian, but most who walk away do so because of disappointment with God. Disappointment is inevitable if someone prays to a version of God who doesn't exist, or if someone believes in promises God never made. Then when God doesn't act as expected, doubt creeps in and things fall apart. When you talk with people who have walked away from God, you'll almost never hear they have rejected the person of Jesus or the truth of Scripture. What they have rejected is a version of God who doesn't exist.

This is nothing new. God performed many astounding miracles in the presence of the Israelites, but they still couldn't resist worshipping false gods. Even when Moses was up on the mountain meeting with God, receiving further instructions for their benefit, they said to Aaron, "Come make us gods who will go before us. As for this fellow Moses who brought us up out of Egypt, we don't know what has happened to him" (Exodus 32:1). "This fellow Moses"?! Really? After all God had done for them, and with the critical role Moses had played, they quickly moved to making a golden calf to worship as a god. This kind of action would continue throughout Israel's history, and although our idols look different today, Western Christians keep on making the same mistakes.

Many of Paul's letters addressed the issue of wanting to add things to Jesus and to the gospel of salvation by grace through faith alone.[1] In the current Western church, adding to Jesus or shaping God into something he is not comes in many forms. Just as with the Christian

house churches in the first century, there is still a drift toward legalism and creating unnecessary (and harmful) obligations for believers.
In airport bookstores there are piles of books about how to be happy
through some form of positive thinking, and most of these books are
written from an (incorrect) Christian point of view.

Americans desperately want to believe things like, "God helps those
who help themselves," "Good people go to heaven," or other platitudes assuming a version of God that has him serving us or rewarding
our performance. Worse, and most alarming, is the increased enthusi-
asm for the prosperity gospel, which has God rewarding people with
good health and material wealth, for their faithfulness in service to
him. No matter how damaging false gospels are, there is something
appealing about a perspective that avoids the truth of our brokenness and at the same time (falsely) fulfills our desires.

Why are we so willing to trade the gospel of grace for a gospel of
performance? To start with, we like to be in control and we like guar-
antees—even if it's guaranteed trouble! We also want a justification
to pursue the comforts of this world, with the freedom to enjoy the
spoils of success. If we can have salvation and have control over the
"blessings" we receive from God, we are all for it.

I think even those of us who abhor the prosperity gospel would,
to some extent, like it to be true, at least partially. That makes it easy
for pastors to get away with teaching it and enriching themselves in
the process. Throw in a cancel culture that makes it difficult to speak
truth, and you have a recipe for disaster.

I can't move on from here until I express how deeply saddened
I am by what's happening in America in regards to faith, because
Jesus and the gospel are just as available there in the US as here in
Uganda. The allure of material wealth, however, leads people to miss
the difference between the truth and any theology that seeks to add
to the gospel. Worse, we are largely unaware of this, and instead of
seeking understanding, we readily accept theologies that justify our

behavior, or that depict God as who we would like him to be instead of as who he actually is. No matter the culture or the context, wrong beliefs, that come from false teaching, block the path to unshakable faith and real joy.

THOSE WHO WANT TO GET RICH

Prior to moving to Uganda, my awareness and understanding of false gods and false gospels was mainly academic. Because the teaching of prosperity is the complete opposite of the true gospel, I hadn't spent much time seeking a better understanding. Also, the theological problems with prosperity teaching are so obvious, I naively didn't think educated people would take it seriously. I know I'm prone to "enhancing," but in this case I'm not exaggerating when I say that every text which is used in prosperity theology must be completely removed from its context if it's to be used in support of this false teaching. God's blessings are completely at his pleasure and not connected, in any way, to our performance.[2] The prophet Isaiah said, "All our righteous acts are like filthy rags" to God (Isaiah 64:6). Ouch!

I don't mean to go off on a rant here, but any suggestion that good health and material wealth are given as a direct result of our performance or faithfulness has to ignore the current and historical reality of material poverty. It also has to ignore the fact that very many righteous people, in both the Old Testament and the New, were persecuted despite their demonstrated, unshakable faith in God. Health and wealth are not a reliable indicator of God's favor.

Even if we allow for the fact that in the old covenant there are examples of God blessing people with material wealth, any honest understanding of the new covenant must acknowledge there are no specific health-and-wealth promises related to performance. It's actually quite the opposite. The cause-and-effect language in the wisdom literature does not, in any way, support prosperity teaching. It's the book of *Proverbs*, not the book of *Promises*.

Jesus and the apostles consistently warned of the dangers concerning wealth, and more importantly, the love of money. In his letter to Timothy, Paul said, "Those who want to get rich fall into temptation and a trap and into many harmful dangers and desires that plunge people into ruin and destruction" (1 Timothy 6:9). I don't think I need to say anything more.

JUST JESUS

For at least half the school year, we teach through one book of the Bible in our Sunday morning worship service. A couple of years ago we chose to go through the book of Colossians. In this particular letter, the apostle Paul was addressing the heresy that had people believing there were additional obligations believers had to meet to be saved, and worse, that certain people were given special revelation superseding the teachings of Jesus. In theological terms, we would say the letter reinforced the supremacy and sufficiency of Christ. As cool as that sounds, try explaining that concept, with those words, to students for whom English is a second language.

The first Sunday of teaching through Colossians was devoted to the context of the book, since a lot of the challenges Paul addressed were similar to what our students had experienced in their local churches. I love preaching in Uganda because of the obvious contrast between the true gospel and the false gospels so widely taught and accepted here. Most of our students have had very little exposure to the New Testament, so when they are presented with the truth it doesn't take long before they are eagerly seeking to understand.

As I was explaining Paul's motivations and the issues he was trying to address, I found myself listing all the things *not* required to be secure in Christ. "It's not about your church, pastor, priest, or spiritual advisor. It's not about your good deeds or your bad deeds. It's not about your family. It's not about rituals or sacrifices. It's not even about your prayers or specific words. It's only about faith in Jesus and his finished work on the cross. That's it. Just Jesus."[3]

And there it was. A simple way to approach the next five months of preaching through Colossians. Just Jesus. An easy answer to all the questions from the students that start with, "Yes, but what about…?" Just Jesus.

Even before the school opened this had been our ministry strategy to combat the false teaching they had been exposed to, but it had never before occurred to me how beautifully simple the gospel of Jesus Christ is, until that spontaneous moment in a sermon. I wish I could say this concept was an Uncle Kelly original, but the apostle Paul beat me to it. "For in him all things were created: things in heaven and on earth, visible and invisible, whether thrones or powers or rulers or authorities; all things have been created through him and for him" (Colossians 1:16).

It's hard to explain what it's like to see God so dramatically call and reconcile these students to himself. As they begin to grow in their *epignosis* of their brokenness, and of the fallacy of the health-and-wealth gospel, we get to watch their faith explode and the Spirit begin to produce fruit in their lives. Our role is to constantly point our students to Christ in everything we do, but especially in the trusted relationships we build with them. We don't seek to create dramatic moments for our students to come to Christ, but rather, we facilitate relationships through which God will bring them to a saving knowledge of the truth, in his time.

Conventional wisdom would look at the difficulty of doing ministry with these students, considering the level of brokenness they have experienced, and would predict a low level of success, in terms of bringing them to an authentic, fruitful faith in Christ. At TAS, we have defied those predictions. I would sell more books if I could give a step-by-step process to follow, but offering an experiential understanding of the true gospel, presented with an understanding of the audience, does just fine by itself.

Something to Remember: At certain times and in varying degrees, we're all prone to view the gospel through a lens of performance and reward. The only correct perspective, however, is one that doesn't move beyond "just Jesus" and the finished work of the cross.

When we accept the correct perspective on the true gospel, we are then in a position to understand what is probably the most tangible expression of brokenness: suffering and hopelessness.

CHAPTER 6

SUFFERING AND HOPELESSNESS

Any discussion of how pain and suffering fit into
God's scheme ultimately leads back to the cross.[1]

PHILIP YANCEY

Ugandans experience loss much more often than Americans do. Close relatives of our students pass away on an almost-weekly basis. This happens so often that we had to write a specific policy about which burials can be attended, how many friends get to go, and so on. To suffer so much loss results in a remarkable resilience to tragedy and suffering, that can sometimes be misinterpreted as a callousness about death. So when my friend Jeff walked up to my house to share about what had just happened near campus, his unusually subdued demeanor caught me off guard.

"Hey Jeff, what's wrong?"

"Well, I've just returned from a terrible moment at the bridge [over the Nile River]."

"What happened?"

"The police have killed a taxi driver and thrown him off [more than 100 feet down to the water]."

As crazy as this sounds, I wasn't shocked. Violence from the police is not uncommon in Uganda and I'd heard many stories like this before. The full story, however, is what had left Jeff broken.

He continued, "Apparently, the driver's wife was in labor giving birth to their fourth child, and he was rushing to the hospital. The police stopped him, and when he tried to hurry them in their inspection, they pulled him out of the taxi, beat him, and threw him down to the river. The wife has now given birth but doesn't yet know why her husband never arrived."

At that moment, I felt a great compassion for the wife of the taxi driver. I immediately asked Jeff if he could find out who she was and get her phone number. Jeff is very well connected, so within the hour we had the information we needed to reach out to her. I called my friend Ruthie who was on my Student Life leadership team, and a person who I greatly trust to guide me in coming alongside people in moments of need. Ruthie called the woman, named Jackie, and set up a time for us to go see her.

Only a few days had passed since the tragic event at the bridge. Jackie lived in a small community called Chzungu, in a rented space. We entered her home and took our seats while she settled to a spot on the floor. She held the newborn baby girl in her arms and stared down, unable to make eye contact with us. Jeff handled the customary Ugandan greeting protocols that, regardless of the situation, must be observed. Ruthie then asked Jackie to share her story with us.

Jackie told of how her husband was a good man and a loving father in a culture that doesn't generally value such character traits. I felt completely devastated in hearing about her husband and would have loved to have personally thanked him for setting such a good example in the community, but instead I was sitting in a small room with his grieving widow.

In addition to the newborn, Jackie had three other daughters who were all in school, and she was proud to say her husband had never failed to pay their school fees. Because of the strength of their relationship (he had no other wives), she had been a stay-at-home mom for all her adult life and hadn't been trained in any vocation. Tears were streaming down her face, and there was a deep sadness in her tone as she talked about the life she had enjoyed, the life just taken from her. I was fighting back tears myself. Although I had seen grief like this before, there was something different this time, a greater level of despair. Without thinking, I blurted out, "Jackie, what are you going to do?"

She didn't speak English but somehow understood my question. For the first time since we had arrived, she raised her chin and looked me right in the eye. It was then I saw it, more than any other time in my life: hopelessness. She had faced a terrible loss and was experiencing an intense suffering that her culture said must be a result of someone's sin or lack of faith. Even if she somehow knew that what had happened wasn't a punishment from God, Jackie certainly had no understanding that would indicate there might be some meaning or purpose for her suffering. Without the right perspective:

Suffering has no meaning and God can't be trusted.

If God can't be trusted, there is no hope.

If there is no hope, this life is worthless.

If this life is worthless, we are worthless.

Soon after meeting with us, Jackie started attending our Sunday morning worship service at the school. The sermons were in English, but Ruthie would sit next to her and translate the messages in real time. It didn't take long for Jackie to see the truth of Scripture and place her faith in Christ. In addition to moving from death to life, Jackie was also freed from her despair and received the peace that only comes from hope in Jesus and an understanding of our suffering.

Soon after, she had the confidence to present a promising business idea she was excited about. We came alongside her with an initial investment, and some short-term support to allow her daughters to get back in school. Within one year the business was self-sustaining and remains so until this day. Jackie works hard and her life is still fraught with difficulty, but you will never find her without peace and joy. She knows, beyond the shadow of any doubt, that she is valued by God.

There are many things I love about my life in Uganda, but the greatest of all is seeing the truth and wisdom of Scripture come alive, as God leads me to engage with it in the world around me. God promises that our suffering matters. With a proper understanding, we can trust him to bring us through our trials with peace, hope, and even joy.

As our students here in Uganda come to understand that the suffering they and their families experience is not meaningless, hopelessness is replaced with hope, and sadness is replaced with an unexpected joy. In the last term of the first year, we taught through the apostle Paul's letter to the Philippians on Sunday mornings. It is also known as the joy letter. God used that season, and his words about suffering, to touch nearly every student at the school. Just as with Jesus and his first-century followers, their inexplicable peace in the worst of circumstances is changing the people around them.

As we visited families over the term break, we kept hearing stories about how our students were teaching the community that suffering isn't meaningless, and about the peace, hope, and joy that comes through true faith in Jesus. This may be hard to believe, but I can report that even three years later the joy has not left our students, even though (especially during the COVID crisis) their circumstances have not improved. I can't take credit for this transformation, however. Once they experienced the truth of God's promises, their *perspectives changed* and their faith became unshakable.

I've said this before but it's worth repeating: Uganda is not more broken than any other country, including the US. The brokenness just manifests in different and more visible ways. When you live here it's difficult to ignore it, like we do so often in the States.

TWO KINDS OF POVERTY

Whether in Uganda or in the US, how we understand brokenness and suffering will either strengthen our faith or destroy it. In this context, our trials may have a positive or a negative effect. It all depends on our perspective, our awareness and understanding (*epignosis*) about what we have experienced or what we have seen others suffer. Living in Uganda I have become much more aware of the widespread suffering that exists in this world.

No matter where we live or the culture we've experienced, our understanding and interpretation of the trials we face will have an enormous impact on how we see the world, ourselves, other people, and God. A proper understanding of suffering encourages a trusting posture toward God and prepares us to face trials in a healthy way. But with a wrong understanding, suffering or trials can lead to a crisis of faith.

Paradoxically, I don't think the world has ever been more broken, while at the same time, people have never been more unaware of the actual brokenness all around them. This is especially true in the Western church. People of all faiths (and non-faiths) would agree the world is not as it should be, but for most there is an unwillingness to seek a greater understanding, or to engage in a way to make things better. Worse, it seems like technology has made us less compassionate. There is also now a sort of "awareness avoidance" with which people can just "swipe away" the bad news and move on. Although we have an abundance of information about the plight of suffering people all over the world, there is a disappointing lack of large-scale engagement.

Some kinds of suffering are obvious—like death, poverty, hunger, and chronic pain. People also suffer from mental illness, addiction, relational abuse, and issues of worth and identity. Americans associate suffering with the homeless and the materially poor, but much of the suffering we face has been relegated to the background. The highlight-reel culture of social media puts pressure on people to present a rosy picture of their lives, so real suffering is quietly suppressed or even intentionally hidden.

After living in Uganda, where suffering is more tangible, I have developed a different perspective on suffering in America. The worst kind of suffering is not related to material wealth but is related to hopelessness, the feeling that comes when suffering seems to have no meaning or purpose. Because of this, I would say the suffering in America *is more severe* than the suffering in Uganda. A poverty of hope is worse than a poverty of money.

Every day for the last eighteen years, my first prayer to God has been for my wife Danlyn's physical suffering to end. God has consistently said *no* in spite of her unwavering faithfulness and my (sometimes) devoted service to him. Our trust in God, however, has only grown stronger, and we've never been happier. As promised, he has grown her faith (and mine) through perseverance, and she has more peace and hope than humanly possible. Her story has challenged many people to look at their trials differently and ask the question, "What is the right perspective?"

WHY GOD ALLOWS SUFFERING

Jesus made it clear we would experience suffering. With a proper understanding of what he's said and promised, we can avoid hopelessness and receive the full *benefit* of God using our trials for our good, and ultimately for his glory.

Before we get to what God has promised regarding suffering and hopelessness, let's be clear about what he has *not* said or promised.

God has *not* promised that if you pray hard enough or are good enough he will end your suffering.

God has *not* promised to protect you from suffering, regardless of your faith or actions.

God has *not* said your suffering is a result of your unfaithfulness.

God's actual promises, however, offer peace, hope, confidence, a deeper appreciation for his grace, and the opportunity to have joy no matter the suffering.

1. God has promised we will suffer, but it's not random.

This promise is a tough one and not exactly our first choice for Vacation Bible School. He is sovereignly in control and our suffering is part of his plan. Paul wrote:

- "Everyone who wants to live a godly life in Christ Jesus will be persecuted" (2 Timothy 3:12).

- "For it has been granted to you on behalf of Christ not only to believe in him, but also to suffer for him" (Philippians 1:29).

- "Now if we are children, then we are heirs—heirs of God and co-heirs with Christ, if indeed we share in his sufferings in order that we may also share in his glory" (Romans 8:17).

Ouch. My boss here in Uganda likes to say, "Clear is kind." If that's true, then God is extremely kind in being so crystal clear. If you're a Christian, you will suffer for Christ. Full stop.

2. God has promised to bring us through our trials with a supernatural peace, and then to strengthen our hope in him.

In Jeremiah 29:10 the prophet told the Israelites they would be in exile for seventy years. After sharing that bad news he said, "'For I know the plans I have for you,' declares the Lord, 'plans to prosper you and not to harm you, plans to give you hope and a future'" (Jeremiah 29:11).

As it relates to suffering, this verse is one of the most important and encouraging in all of Scripture. But of course, the prosperity hustlers still can't help but to abuse and misuse it to serve their own purposes. Through Jeremiah, God had just told the people of Israel they would be suffering for the rest of their lives (verse 10), but not to worry because he would bring them through, with prosperity and hope. About that prosperity: the Hebrew word used here is *shalom*, which in this verse means an intimate, transcendent peace in God. Incredibly, Jesus had the exact same message for his disciples, the night before he was crucified. "I have told you these things, so that in me you may have peace. For in this world you will have trouble. But take heart, I have overcome the world" (John 16:33).

This verse is part of what is known as the Upper Room Discourse, containing some of the most important words ever spoken. Like Jeremiah, Jesus promised that life would be difficult, but there is a peace in him to carry them through their trials. The world is hopeless without Christ, and "overcoming the world" is about the gift of hope that comes from faith in him.

3. God has promised that our suffering matters and that it has purpose for our good and his glory.

While we may not know the specific reasons for our suffering, we can be comforted in knowing there is great purpose and meaning in it. In his letter to the Christians in Rome, Paul wrote, "We know that in all things God works for the good of those who love him, who have been called according to his purpose" (Romans 8:28).

The good Paul is referring to is growth in Christlikeness, and not the good our finite minds might desire. This idea is also taught in the first few verses of James's letter to Jewish Christians. "Consider it pure joy, my brothers, whenever you face trials of many kinds, because you know that the testing of your faith produces perseverance. Let perseverance finish its work so that you may be mature and complete, not lacking anything" (James 1:2-4).

Perseverance is a faith muscle, and as it gets stronger through trials, God uses that faith to do good works for his glory. In his grace, he allows us to benefit from this same work. People will say, "God has a plan for your life," which is true. But his plan for us includes the experience of suffering, that allows us to grow in Christlike character, co-reign with God over creation, and glorify him in all we do. An *epignosis* (experiential understanding) of suffering also leads us to where to put our hope.

An understanding of what God says about suffering and hopelessness is critical to developing a correct view of brokenness. Only in the Christian worldview does suffering have a meaningful and intended purpose. Only in the Christian worldview can we trust that God knows our suffering. Only Jesus offers any hope to a hopeless world.

> **Something to Remember:** God has promised that the suffering believers experience is for our benefit and for his glory, and that in him we can persevere with peace and joy.

Having the wrong perspective on suffering leads to hopelessness, but the most damaging result of the wrong view is found in the way people are mistreated—especially women.

CHAPTER 7

EQUALLY CREATED, EQUALLY VALUED

In Christ Jesus you are all children of God through faith, for all of you who were baptized into Christ have clothed yourselves with Christ. There is neither Jew nor Gentile, neither slave nor free, nor is there male and female, for you are all one in Christ Jesus.

GALATIANS 3:26-28

COVID was the biggest trial our students and their families had ever faced. Ugandan schools were shut down longer than any other school system in the world. During that time, the next day's meal was never a certainty, and with every student in Uganda home for eleven straight months (and for more than twenty months overall), there were more mouths to feed, since many students receive one or two of their daily meals at school. There was also not much work available. Among teenagers, the country saw shocking and hard-to-process numbers of dropouts and pregnancies.

If there was ever going to be a time for our students to give up hope and fall back into what was culturally normative, it would have been during that crazy time. I will be honest: I expected to hear a lot of discouraging stories, and wouldn't have blamed any of our students for falling down. Incredibly however, our students continued to thrive in the face of the tallest odds, including our girls.

About halfway through the COVID shutdown I was reminded of just how critically important it is for girls to understand their worth, so they can have the confidence to make wise decisions for the present and the future. I had been asked to meet with a small number of students about whom there was specific concern. My second meeting was with a girl who, reportedly, was running around with an older man. She was sixteen years old, a first-year student, and when COVID hit, she had been at school for less than half a term. She had heard the "value" message, and her Family Mentors were doing a great job of modeling good values at their house, but generally it takes longer for our girls to "get it," and six weeks at the school hadn't been enough time for her.

I asked her about what she liked best about her "boyfriend," and she said, "He buys our supplies." That's not what I was expecting, so I asked, "What if he stopped buying supplies? Would you still be with him?" She replied, "No, of course not." I quickly pivoted to talk about the future:

"What do you want your husband to be like?"

"Uncle Kelly, what do you mean?"

"I mean, how do you want to be treated?"

"He will provide."

"Don't you want to be treated well? Have a good marriage?"

"Uncle Kelly, I don't understand what you are asking. I won't want my husband to be around."

"Do you think you deserve to have your husband treat you well?"

At this point, she lowered her chin, and while staring at the ground, simply shook her head. I turned to my Ugandan friend, who was part of our Community Engagement Team, and asked him to repeat my questions in the local language, to make sure she understood what I was saying. She understood. Same answer.

At that moment, my emotions were a cocktail of rage, compassion, and conviction. I don't know why, but when the brokenness of this world manifests in this way, with teenage girls, it affects me more deeply than anything else. Given what she had shared, there was nothing more I could say, so I simply asked if I could pray for her. When I was finished, she gave me a hug before setting off. In the US a hug wouldn't have been unusual, but here in Uganda it was not the normal protocol, especially given my role at the school.

I got the sense that something was wrong about the whole situation, so we did some investigating. Apparently, when she was only thirteen years old, an older man had offered to pay for school and home supplies in exchange for "spending time" with him. This did not seem unusual to her because some of her sisters and cousins had done the same. She had been taught that her sole purpose as a Ugandan girl was to find a man to pay for food and supplies. That was it. That was her value.

Eventually we got the authorities involved, and the man was arrested and taken to jail. You might not be surprised to learn that he had three other young girls in the same arrangement. For our student, we were able to use the situation to reinforce what she had been learning about her value as a daughter of God, made in his image for a purpose. We moved her to a safer location where she could start the process of healing and, hopefully, feel confident about joining her classmates when the school opened again.

I wish I could say this was an isolated or surprising story, but unfortunately it wasn't. Because many of our girls have gone through similar circumstances (and worse), I wasn't at all surprised about her situation. Even in the first few months of living in Uganda, I had the firsthand opportunity to observe the fundamental damage that often comes with the wrong perspectives.

BOYS AND GIRLS

Before the school opened in February 2017, there was a week-long program for the sponsored students at our land in Buziika, which is the home base for our community and family engagement initiatives. At the land there is an open-air chapel with a grass roof that covers enough space to hold 200 to 400 people, depending on the age group in attendance. On one particular afternoon during the program week, the chapel was packed with older students who were considered upper primary, including the students who would soon become part of the first graduating class of the new school.

I was still in my learning phase and doing my best to stay in the background, so I found an inconspicuous spot from which to watch the students and listen to the presentations. The Country Director for Amazima, began his passionate speech with a simple question: "By a show of hands, who thinks boys are better than girls?" I'm not exaggerating when I say almost every student, both male and female, quickly raised their hand. I had come to understand that the broader culture of Uganda viewed women as secondary to men, but I wasn't prepared to see it so overtly accepted as truth. It was one of many times my heart was broken by students not understanding their value.

I have a God-given burden for teenagers, but I am especially burdened for teenage girls, with the particular challenges they face in a world that teaches them, directly or indirectly, that they are created for the service and pleasure of men. I needed to understand what our Ugandan students believed about the value of women so I could design an effective ministry approach. So many of the problems that continue to plague our world can be traced back through history to a perspective that devalues women, so it's helpful to look at how women were viewed in ancient Israel and the Roman world. With this view, it is easier to see how it manifests in Uganda today.

There's no debate that women were devalued in first-century

societies around the Roman Empire. Women were mostly defined by the men who "kept" them, either through marriage or ownership. In the first-century honor/shame culture, this meant they had almost no individual rights.

In Israel during the time of Jesus, women could not vote, hold political office, or even testify in court. As it related to participating in temple activities, they were restricted to the Court of Women, which men were also allowed to enter. Despite the prominent place of women in Israel's history, and clear instructions from the Torah, men made rules that limited opportunities for women and elevated themselves. Mostly, men interpreted or applied the Old Testament law to favor themselves.

> At dawn [Jesus] appeared again in the temple courts, where all the people gathered around him, and he sat down to teach them. The teachers of the law and the Pharisees brought in a woman caught in adultery. They made her stand before the group and said to Jesus, "Teacher, this woman was caught in the act of adultery. In the Law Moses commanded us to stone such women. Now what do you say?" (John 8:2-5).

Actually, the law of Moses says, "Both the adulterer and the adulteress are to be put to death" (Leviticus 20:10). My question is, Where was the adulterous man in the story? The men in Israel at that time surely knew the law, but after centuries of intentionally devaluing women, nobody in attendance asked that question. Their perspective didn't require it. Fortunately for the first-century women, and ultimately for most of the world, Jesus changed everything. But in the humble villages of Uganda, even almost 2,000 years after Jesus honored women, not much has changed in how women are (not) valued.

FOLLOWERS AND COWS

I spent many hours with our Scholarship Mentors, discussing the context in which we would be doing discipleship. None of that time was more valuable than when I learned about family dynamics, and more specifically about how women are treated in the villages our students come from. First, I learned it is not uncommon for men to have multiple wives and many children. The father of one of my students has twenty-one wives and fifty-three children, for example.

In the local language, the word for "cook" and "wife" is one and the same. Women are often given to marriage at a young age in exchange for a dowry, that is usually characterized by how many cows a woman is worth, assuming she can bear children. There can also be a serious "try before you buy" mentality. I have a good friend who waited until the wedding night to consummate his marriage, and he was almost thrown out of his family as a result. If it had turned out his bride was barren, they would have considered her to be worthless as a wife.

Unfortunately, some communities also have a culture of abuse, that is generally accepted as normal. In one of the kingdoms in Uganda, women are taught to believe their frequent beatings are a sign of love. On more than one occasion, a first-year student has asked a male Family Mentor why he doesn't beat his wife. It's also worth noting that this practice is consistent across Muslim and Christian families. As I mentioned before, faith is often more about heritage than true belief, so culture and tradition often stand above any religious teaching. All of this and more creates an environment in which women can be devalued and abused.

Because of my background with student ministry in the States, I thought I was ready to help our Ugandan students understand their value. That was my assumption until I started asking questions about what our students had experienced and been taught in the communities they came from. I quickly realized I was not ready. The challenge was much bigger than I anticipated, and my previous experience was not going to be very helpful, at least not in the way I had expected. But the perspective I gained in Uganda helped bring clarity to my understanding of how women are also devalued in America.

Danlyn and I have walked alongside many young girls in the States who've experienced a devastating brokenness resulting from following the path that US culture says will empower them. From a young age, girls in America are exposed to a steady stream of content that degrades their value and erodes their confidence. At the same time, boys have easy access to pornography, significantly inhibiting their ability to value the girls around them. In my opinion, based on working with teenagers, social media is destroying a generation of girls. Because of this, it's never been easier for teenage boys to prey on their insecurities. Looking back now, it's hard to believe I missed the severity of what is going on in American culture.

In addition, despite all the laws, initiatives, and movements in the US that have claimed to empower women, we haven't yet seen a meaningful paradigm shift in how women are valued. While the #MeToo Movement has been a great start for awareness, it will likely not change how the culture values women. In 2018 in the US, there were more than 2,000 rapes reported per day, with women as 90 percent of the victims.[1] Think about that for a moment. If that doesn't make you sick to your stomach, then I don't know what will. Maybe we are so desensitized that we lack awareness and have little desire to pursue any real understanding. Based on the argument I'm making, this means that in general, we also have the wrong perspective.

I firmly believe things are getting worse. Teenagers in the US have never been more depressed, and according to the CDC, suicide rates among teens and young adults are the highest on record (even before COVID).[2] In my view, there is also an added exhaustion from seeking likes and followers on social media, and trying to maintain an online profile that projects an image consistent with what the culture values. Male celebrities and athletes are often given a free pass when they treat women poorly. Whatever the measure, America is #trending in the wrong direction.

After testifying against Larry Nassar, who abused 100-plus girls over a twenty-year period without much resistance, gold-medal gymnast Aly Raisman said, "I think we need to change the way society views women." What she called for is a collective change in perspective, #ImwithAly. Even with a proper awareness and understanding of how things are in the States, there is still a temptation to think that what's happening in Uganda (or other places) is worse. It's not. It is just a different presentation of the same brokenness. People in the West overlook how women are treated having been desensitized by years of looking at value from the wrong perspective.

I AM JESUS, HEAR ME ROAR

Feminists who don't love Jesus have always been an enigma to me. Before Jesus came, women were assigned very little value by the societies in which they lived, and one could argue that every society where women have advanced has been influenced by Christianity. The cultures of the world where women are most abused and mistreated are those where Christian influence is weakest.

Through word, deed, and association, Jesus reinforced the idea that women are created equally in the image of God and share equally in the responsibility to represent him in reigning over creation as he works out his plan for redemption.[3] Jesus came into a world where women were second-class citizens whose testimony lacked any credibility. Even so, Jesus consistently and dramatically engaged women throughout his ministry and broke sharply from Jewish tradition in doing so.

- Jesus healed a paralyzed woman on the sabbath and called her a daughter of Abraham.[4]

- Jesus healed a woman who had been subject to bleeding

for twelve years and who also touched the tassel of his
rabbinical cloak.[5]

- Jesus forgave and saved a sinful woman at a dinner in the
  house of a Pharisee.[6]

In each case (and there were many more), Jesus lovingly engaged
women who were considered untouchable, and did things that would
have gone first-century viral. If there had been social media back then,
Jesus would have been trending for sure. The problem for Jesus was
that most of what he said and did, especially as it related to assigning
equal value to women, was a direct threat to the system of privilege set
up by the male Jewish leaders. Jesus even called them out on divorce!
He was ruining everything for them, and as a result, he had to die.

What they didn't know was his death would lead to a resurrection
and a vindication of everything he taught and modeled, including
how women were to be treated and valued. Unfortunately, men are
still fighting against those things, despite how perfectly clear Jesus was.
In many places, man-made laws have been enacted to protect women,
but they are powerless to change the hearts of men. The questions
I kept asking myself were, *What can we do, with our students here in
Uganda, to achieve a different outcome?* and, *How can we lead them to
understand what God says, so they can live with the perspective of Jesus?*

NEW YEAR, SAME SERMON

The standard in the Western world is that women are to be valued, so people put a lot of effort into sharing that message. Because
of this, most girls, as they are raised, are told they have value—so
when they eventually face the many ways in which their culture does
not value them, they at least have a foundation from which to discuss
the concept of their value. Here in Uganda, girls are mostly taught
they have less value, so it's very difficult to even start the conversation.
How do we explain to them their value as precious daughters of God?

The good news is that what God says about women is almost the complete opposite of what our girls have been taught. If we could help them come to an awareness and *epignosis* (experiential understanding) of their actual value, as people created equally in the image of God, we could potentially change the culture of their communities, and eventually of their country.

The strategy was simple. We would frequently share truth, as it relates to the value of women (and men), and consistently model what it looks like to value each other (especially husbands and wives). When students arrive for their first year, we always have an assembly to introduce this important topic that will be discussed, in various ways, over the next five to seven years of their lives. I have had the privilege of delivering this message each year.

From the beginning, I leaned heavily on my Ugandan staff for the *how* in talking about such a sensitive issue to an audience who had been taught so many dangerous things, and had experiences I can't begin to understand. Even in our home cultures and in a familiar setting, we can accidently do the right thing in the wrong way. For a white person in Uganda, it happens all the time, even with the best of preparation. The one advantage I had for this particular message was that the problem of women and their value is not a Ugandan problem, it's a global problem stemming from a common brokenness. In my opinion it's *the* problem in the world. This shared problem and brokenness, however, makes it much simpler to present the truth of God's Word in an honor/shame culture.

Giving this message to our students is my favorite talk of the year because there is no ambiguity in God's view of women, even if it may not be obvious on the surface. From Genesis 1 through the end of Revelation, God is remarkably clear and consistent in saying that men and women have equal value.[7] As we discussed earlier, Jesus also went out of his way to make sure there was no doubt, and consistently challenged the men in charge. My favorite part of this annual sermon is when I go through some famous verses in chapter 5 of Ephesians:

> Submit to one another out of reverence for Christ. Wives, submit yourselves to your own husbands as you do to the Lord. For the husband is the head of the wife as Christ is the head of the church, his body, of which he is the Savior. Now as the church submits to Christ, so also wives should submit to their husbands in everything.
>
> Husbands, love your wives, just as Christ loved the church and gave himself up for her to make her holy, cleansing her by the washing with water through the word, and to present her to himself as a radiant church, without stain or wrinkle or any other blemish, but holy and blameless. In this same way, husbands ought to love their wives as their own bodies. He who loves his wife loves himself.
>
> After all, no one ever hated their own body, but they feed and care for their body, just as Christ does the church, for we are members of his body. "For this reason a man will leave his father and mother and be united to his wife, and the two will become one flesh." This is a profound mystery, but I am talking about Christ and the church. However, each one of you also must love his wife as he loves himself, and the wife must respect her husband (Ephesians 5:21-33).

As a starting point, this whole passage should be understood in the context of mutual submission. It's lazy exegesis to read this passage in a way that suggests husbands can dominate their wives, or that women should submit as if they are secondary in value. Paul is assigning leadership and followership responsibilities, and if you pay attention, who gets the better end of the deal?

- Men are called to love their wives as Christ loved the church and give themselves up for them.

- Men are called to love their wives like their own bodies.

- Men are called to love their wives as they love themselves.

- Women are called to submit to and respect their husbands.

God has given husbands an incredible burden to love and protect their wives in a manner that can only suggest the highest value for women. Paul, like Jesus, was speaking into a culture where women had little value and men had all the advantages, so to direct husbands in this way was radical and countercultural. It would have been met with serious resistance. Women, of course, would have embraced and celebrated such teaching.

How do our students receive it? Well, you might be surprised to learn that after some initial pushback, our boys accept the truth much easier and faster than the girls do. Ugandan boys come to school with a lot of pride and swagger about their cultural norms, but when confronted with the truth of God's Word, combined with seeing their Family Mentors model it every day, it doesn't take long to see significant change in the way they treat the girls.

For the girls, however, it's much more difficult to accept. Most of our girls have been sexually active, but not because they wanted to be, nor because they enjoyed the experiences. It's not uncommon for girls in vulnerable communities to trade sex for a few dollars, and in some cases the transaction is facilitated by a parent or guardian.

When I explain that God created sex to be enjoyed in a loving marriage, I get nothing but blank stares looking back at me because the idea of *enjoying* sex doesn't make much sense to our girls. But after they hear the message of their value consistently repeated and modeled by their Family Mentors, there is a point in time, for almost every one of our female students, when they understand how much God loves them and who he created them to be. Of all the miracles God performs on our campus, this transformation shows the most dramatic, tangible, and practical results.

In the last four years I have seen Ugandan boys become men who respect women, and who genuinely desire to have the kind of marriages that have been modeled for them. At the same time, our girls have become young women who are very confident and who have little problem keeping the village boys at bay. It's these outcomes that remind me of just how important it is for us to never tire of leading people to understand their value, apart from what any culture or worldview says. With that, we guide them to experience the love and grace of God, that confirms this truth in their hearts.

I believe there will be a time, in the not-so-distant future, when the students of TAS will have healthy, Christ-centered marriages and be the kind of fathers and mothers God has designed them to be. God will use their lives to change their communities! I am certain of it.

> **Something to Remember:** Men and women are equally loved by God, are equally created in his image, and have been given equal responsibility to co-reign with him over creation.

When a person has an understanding of their inherent value, everything God says about their relationships makes sense. For our perspectives on ourselves to fully align with what God says, however, we have to face who we are in our sinful nature.

CHAPTER 8

WHO WE ARE
(ON OUR OWN)

*Therefore no one will be declared righteous
in God's sight by the works of the law; rather,
through the law we gain* [epignosis] *of our sin.*

ROMANS 3:20

Coming alongside families is the heartbeat of Amazima Ministries, so we are very careful not to disempower them by providing everything for them. In support of this important philosophy, all the students of TAS must meet a set of requirements when they arrive for each term, including bringing a small monetary contribution.

The day they arrive for a given term ("reporting day") used to be tough. Mainly because students were often sent home for not meeting all the requirements, and they couldn't return until everything was fulfilled. It was emotional and stressful as we waited for them to return. By the time we reached the second year, however, reporting days were going much more smoothly. The students and their families now understood the program and worked hard to have their supplies ready for each term. To that point, no student had ever failed to return after being sent home. One student's pride, however, changed that record in a devastating way.

Brian was one of those older students who didn't start school until later in life. He was at least eighteen years old when he started his second year (the equivalent of seventh grade). We have many students in this situation, and they have an additional layer of difficulty, as adults in a boarding school with years of life experience already behind them. Brian and his younger brother Thomas, who was coming to school for his first year, showed up on reporting day with a mix of joy and swagger. Brian was one of the more popular students and he was excited to have Thomas now joining him.

The brothers had no parents or guardians and had lived on their own, with assistance from Amazima, for almost ten years. As part of a child-headed home, the set of supplies they were required to bring was substantially smaller, and their uniform fee was reduced. In addition, they had to get a medical form signed by one of the Scholarship Mentors. Disappointingly, they failed on all three requirements on reporting day.

We were a little frustrated with Brian because a kind person had provided work for him during the break, so if he was out of money (as he claimed), then he had squandered what he had earned and was expecting TAS to pick up the tab. Brian and Thomas were sent back to the community with instructions to get their medical forms signed and to sort out their missing supplies and money. Brian didn't like being sent home and took great offense at the question of how he had spent his money. I remember feeling a sense of foreboding because it was obvious his *perspective was all wrong.*

When he got back to the village he started spinning stories of how we didn't care about him, together with a bunch of related lies, all stemming from his bruised pride. When his Family Mentors tried to reason with him, he wouldn't budge. He was getting a lot of street cred for standing up to authority, and unwittingly got himself past the point of no return, both figuratively and literally. If he were to go back to school at that point, he would have looked weak and foolish to his friends, so unfortunately Brian said *no* to the many pleas for him to return. Thomas did come back for a short time, but being at the school without his big brother was too difficult for him to bear. He ran away in the middle of the night a couple of weeks after returning.

Although devastated by what had happened, we eventually moved on and finished the year incredibly well at the school. The Mentors would check in on Brian and Thomas occasionally, but neither of them was open to assistance nor relationship. Not anymore. Brian's pride was still dictating his choices, and because of this he was making poor decisions for himself and his brother. Unfortunately, Thomas would be the one to bear the most serious consequences.

I had only known Thomas for one term (before he ran away), but even in that short time, we could see a transformation. Growing up without parents or guardians had led to many difficult emotional and behavioral issues that set him in a poor position for a fruitful life. His noticeable progress was an encouragement to almost everyone, but leaving the nurturing environment of the school prevented him from continuing to grow. In addition, Thomas had a condition requiring constant medication, which in Uganda is available free of charge through organizations like Amazima. Despite our best efforts, though, there had been no consistent management of Thomas's health once he left school, and we lost track of him.

The students had returned to start the next school year for just a few weeks when I got the news. I was walking Muggle just after sunup and enjoying a few moments of quiet before the chaos of the day was to begin. My phone vibrated in my pocket, so I pulled it out to check to see who was calling at such an early hour. Seeing it was Pastor Daniel, I nervously answered. I could barely understand him because of the combination of his Ugandan accent and his emotional state. After taking a deep breath, Daniel told me that Thomas had died earlier that morning. Apparently, because he hadn't been taking his medication, he contracted a preventable infection that was discovered too late.

It was another moment of crushing loss, which, like so many others I've experienced here, could have been easily avoided. Although our kids deal with death on a frequent basis, this one was different. There was a tension that came from the fact that Thomas's passing was so unnecessary. Predictably, Brian blamed himself, and I expected our students would do the same. That's just where my head was.

Miraculously, our students expressed only genuine love and grace for Brian. We were able to use that tragic story to show our students the danger of pride, and how important it is to be aware that it's in all of us. Much like in the Bible story of Jacob and Esau, where the latter traded his birthright and future for a bowl of stew,[1] Brian traded his future, and likely his brother's life, in favor of holding on to his pride.

When I was in high school the football players wore a T-shirt that said, "Pain Is Temporary, Pride Is Forever." I always thought it was an annoying and foolish slogan, but I never realized how absurd it was until I gained a proper understanding of our sin nature. The slogan shows just how unaware we are about who we really are. Whoever coined that phrase certainly got one thing right: the "forever" part. Pride and its accompanying destruction can certainly last forever if we remain unaware or don't understand the danger.

Pride is present in almost every sin and even present in our efforts to do good in our own strength. When we are selfish, or disobedient, or choose to treat others poorly, pride is there. World wars have started over pride. It's also pride that prevents us from acknowledging our pride. By any measure, pride is the sin most likely to keep us from a mature relationship with Jesus, characterized by the life-giving fruit of love and joy. Just in case your pride has you thinking that I'm judging you, let's look at how God feels:

- "The Lord detests all the proud of heart. Be sure of this: They will not go unpunished" (Proverbs 16:5).

- "God opposes the proud but shows favor to the humble" (James 4:6).

So, God "detests" and "opposes" prideful people. Yikes! Pride is extremely dangerous, and unfortunately, it's a part of all of us. For our growth in the Spirit and living the Christian life, nothing holds us back more than pride.

THE SIN NATURE

Pride also serves as a marker of our brokenness and a reminder of our sin nature, that persists even as we grow in faith. It's an important moment when we become aware and acknowledge that even as Christians, we are still broken. The perspective we have about our sin nature either increases our ability to live the fullness of the Christian life, or limits it. Living and working in Uganda has only reinforced this important truth for me.

I realize that by bringing up the topic of our sin nature, I've introduced a point of potential tension or confusion. This is both critically important, and at the same time, very difficult to accept. Maybe you're asking, "What about being created in the image of God?" or "I thought we were a new creation in Christ?" Both are true, but even as image-bearers who are now in Christ, our sin nature still looms large. One of my favorite professors at seminary used to say that God's image in us has been "defaced but not erased."[2]

This reality manifests in the difference between the way we as Christians are supposed to live and how we actually live. Gandhi summed up this idea perfectly when he reportedly said, "All you Christians... must live more like Jesus Christ." I agree. In Uganda, false teachers take the fact that believers continue in sin and leverage it to create a legalistic culture over which they can yield power and control. A misunderstanding of who we are as sinners, even as we are also new creations in Christ, creates a vulnerability to be exploited, especially in an honor/shame culture.

A general lack of understanding about this also explains the continuing brokenness in the world, and why there is so much apathy in the Christian community. Without a proper understanding of our sin nature, we operate from a baseline of false assumptions and make choices out of our flesh that lead to unintended outcomes. In other words, *we are the problem*, in whatever culture or circumstance we find ourselves in. We are brokenness personified. We either over-legalize behavior or fail to respect our capacity to do harm. Both extremes flow from the wrong perspective.

It is said that G.K. Chesterton, a British writer who lived in the early twentieth century, replied to the question, "What is wrong with the world?" by writing, simply, "I am." If we are the problem, then logically we can't also be the solution. Or can we? As image-bearers, chosen to co-reign over creation, we are appointed to be part of the solution, as God works his plan of redemption through us. Accepting who we are in our brokenness changes our posture toward God and encourages us to embrace our true identity in Christ.

In order to believe in and accept the finished work of the cross for salvation, we have to know we are incapable of coming to God on our own merit. The same principle applies to knowing our real needs and growing in Christlikeness. In and of ourselves, we don't have the power to do it. Unfortunately, despite the known consequences and obvious benefits, we resist pursuing self-awareness and understanding as it relates to matters of faith.

TO KNOW WE ARE SICK

People in the United States aren't at all resistant to the concept of "awareness" when it comes to the various causes that people consider important. There are awareness days/weeks/months for just about everything:

Domestic Violence
Awareness Day

National Sleep
Awareness Week

Mathematics and Statistics
Awareness Month

Self-Injury
Awareness Day

Bowel Cancer
Awareness Month

Allergy Awareness Week

STD Awareness Month

Endometriosis
Awareness Month

National Cyber Security
Awareness Month

Tinnitus Awareness Week

Down Syndrome
Awareness Week

National Salt
Awareness Week

There are hundreds of other examples, but I think you get the point. We aren't against self-awareness when it's fun, anecdotal, helpful, or amusing. As such, there are all kinds of temperament and personality tests that sort us into colors, shapes, letters, numbers, or animals. But when it comes to self-awareness about matters of personal faith, or if there is the potential for negative feedback about who we are, we can be resistant or even unwilling to seek understanding. Why is it so hard?

The biggest reason, in my view, is self-righteousness. Most people believe that they themselves are good. Even many Christians believe that good people go to heaven—so Christians have "double" credit. The culture of the world leads people to believe their wealth, fame, or power marks them as good. Does that make sense? Not to Jesus.

To some who were confident of their own righteousness and looked down on everyone else, Jesus told this parable: "Two men went up to the temple to pray, one a Pharisee and the other a tax collector. The Pharisee stood by himself and prayed: 'God, I thank you that I am not like other people—robbers, evildoers, adulterers—or even like this tax collector. I fast twice a week and give a tenth of all I get'" (Luke 18:9-12).

I'm not saying this is you, but I will say that it's me (at least sometimes), and it's ugly. Based on our man-made, Christian "good" scale, I can think of myself as better than most. Right? Wrong! Let's see how Jesus finished the parable.

> The tax collector stood at a distance. He would not even look up to heaven, but beat his breast and said, "God, have mercy on me, a sinner." I tell you that this man, rather than the other, went home justified before God. For all those who exalt themselves will be humbled, and those who humble themselves will be exalted (Luke 18:13-14).

The difference between the two men was their awareness and understanding of their sin nature. The tax collector didn't feel unworthy because of any specific sins, but rather, because he knew he was a sinner. He went home justified before God, while the Pharisee, well, he just went home.

Another thing that keeps us from being aware of our sin nature is material comfort, that deceives us into thinking we don't need God, especially if we view ourselves as good, or at least better than most. When Jesus said, "It is not the healthy who need a doctor, but the sick" (Matthew 9:12), maybe he could have added, "it is not the healthy who need a doctor, but the sick who also know they are sick." The problem is that we are all very sick (broken), but only those who know it will seek healing.

The journey to self-awareness and understanding about our sin nature is not a fun process, but it is better to learn it through self-discovery rather than to learn it through pain.

MY GUT-PUNCH MOMENT

When I was twenty-nine years old, I was the poster boy for the American Dream. In comparison to my friends, I had the best job, made the most money, had the nicest house, drove the most expensive car, and married the hottest wife. At the time, those things were supremely important to me because they proved I was better than all the guys who peaked in high school (I'm not bitter, I swear!). In addition, I was doing all the "right" things in playing the part of a good Christian, including reading the Bible most days and going to a Southern Baptist church. My life was great, or so it seemed.

In fact, things were not at all great, but there was no way I was going to acknowledge my misery. That would mean the American Dream was a lie, which for me at that time was incomprehensible. No matter how many signs and indicators were in front of me—including a struggling marriage, shallow friendships, poor choices, judgment of others, and more—I couldn't see them. Nor was I interested in any kind of self-examination or self-discovery. Why should I be? I was awesome.

Fortunately, God used my best friend from high school to "slap me upside the head." Chris and his wife, Katrina, came over for dinner, and as the late afternoon sun descended behind the horizon, he and I were on the back porch enjoying our cold beers and reflecting on how much our lives had changed in the seventeen years we'd known each other. The conversation shifted to talking about a mutual friend of ours who was prone to sharing about how much money he made, his accomplishments, and in general, how much better his life was than everyone else's. Because this other friend about whom we were talking also happened to be a rival of mine for the top spot on the ladder of success, I did not hold back my criticism of his haughtiness. It was at that exact moment that God opened my eyes to who I was in my flesh. I'm convinced it was the power of the Holy Spirit, but either way, Chris summoned the courage to say, "Dude, I don't know how to tell you this, but that's what most people think about you."

Tears started to well up in my eyes as I began to process the gravity of what I'd just been told. I've had my share of gut-punch moments in my life, but none has been equal to that one. Somehow, in a life-long effort to prove to everyone, including God, that I was good enough, my identity was found in all the wrong things. I had resisted self-awareness and embraced comparison in order to convince myself of my high status in the hierarchy of the American Dream, and in so doing had severely limited my ability to experience the love and grace of God. An experience that only comes from an understanding of just how "not good" we really are.

ALL OF US?

About twenty years ago, the phrase "Mean people suck" took its place in American culture. You would see it on T-shirts, coffee mugs, and bumper stickers everywhere. More appropriately, however, the slogan should simply be "People suck," because all of us, in fact, suck. This assessment of our condition isn't merely philosophical or theoretical if you accept the authority of Scripture.

From Genesis to Revelation, Scripture is consistent in its perspective on the condition of mankind. Apart from God's saving grace and the transforming work of the Holy Spirit:

- Every part of every person is corrupted; there is nothing good about us.[3]
- There are no exceptions.[4]
- We are all slaves to sin and incapable of choosing good.[5]
- Even our good deeds are, well, not good.[6]

I would certainly understand if you're pushing back hard right now. Even though Scripture is clear, this reality about ourselves is not easy to accept. Maybe Jesus can convince you. In asking a question, a "certain ruler" addressed Jesus as "Good teacher" (Luke 18:18), which, I think you would agree, was a very reasonable and respectful approach. Here is how Jesus replied: "Why do you call me good?... No one is good—except God alone" (Luke 18:19).

Got it. We all suck.

Wait a minute. What about following your heart? If we are Christians, shouldn't we follow our hearts? No. Again, not if you believe God's Word to be true:

- "It is from within, out of a person's heart, that evil thoughts come—sexual immorality, theft, murder, adultery, greed, malice, deceit, lewdness, envy, slander, arrogance and folly" (Mark 7:21-22).

- "The heart is deceitful above all things and beyond cure" (Jeremiah 17:9).

Are we having fun yet? I'm not. Maybe you're feeling justified in your pushing back because you don't think Scripture can be trusted as God's Word. Okay. Even so, if we are brutally honest, everything about our experience in the world around us suggests we are not inherently good. You don't need seminary training, Calvin's *Institutes*, or Luther's *Bondage of the Will* to know it's true. Did you have to teach your children not to sin? How often do you hear yourself instructing your children to be kind or play nice? We are not naturally loving and kind to others or obedient to God. We are, however, naturally self-centered and disobedient.

It's too easy to point to the Holocaust, slavery, genocide, human trafficking, or the caste system in India as evidence for the depravity of others or as a way to minimize the severity of our own actions. Ask yourself: are you truly content, or are you still chasing some version of the American Dream? Do you value everyone equally or is there a scale of good against which you judge the actions of others? Perhaps the most telling sign is our level of pride and how it shows up in all areas of our lives.

If at this point you're not motivated to better understand your sin, I don't know what to tell you. Either way, let me go down swinging by reminding you of the apostle Paul, whose self-awareness and understanding of his own sinfulness is well documented.[7] He was so aware of the dangers of pride that he viewed any glory for himself as completely unacceptable. Here are my two favorite translations of how he described it:

- "May I never boast except in the cross of our Lord Jesus Christ, through which the world has been crucified to me, and I to the world" (Galatians 6:14).

- "God forbid that I should glory, save in the cross of our Lord Jesus Christ, by whom the world is crucified unto me, and I unto the world" (Galatians 6:14 KJV).

Maybe we could say Paul was a "good" Christian…?

Something to Remember: Even as new creations in Christ, our sin nature persists and can't be managed or lessened by human strength. Only in Jesus and with his strength can we overcome sin.

A growing respect for our sin nature is required if we are to mature to a right understanding of our brokenness. Without it, we will fail to receive the *epignosis* (experiential understanding) we need and will struggle to actually help others. Before broken people can help broken people, we need to better understand when helping doesn't help.

CHAPTER 9

WHEN HELPING DOESN'T HELP

*To those who through the righteousness of our God and
Savior Jesus Christ have received a faith as precious
as ours: Grace and peace be yours in abundance
through the [epignosis] of God and of Jesus our Lord.*

2 PETER 1:1-2

I've had the privilege of hosting groups on our Tuesday tours since
TAS opened in 2017. Before COVID the typical tour consisted of
twenty to thirty people from a variety of NGOs and mission teams.
Often, there was a group of foreign nationals who were in the country to check on some ministry, school, or orphanage they had started
or supported. They were always very proud to share about how well
things were going with their organization.

One Tuesday a group was in Jinja to visit a primary school their
church in the States had started and funded. It had been established
about ten years prior and had grown to have hundreds of kids in
attendance. The group of Americans had spent a few days touring
the school, meeting the kids, and visiting with the teachers. Apparently, their time at the school went very well and they could not have
been more exuberant about their experience.

They talked about how happy the children were and the number of students who had accepted Christ during the week. The school grounds were clean and the uniforms were perfect. By every measure, this was a great school and the students were grateful to be part of such a fine institution. I was skeptical, but had no real reason to doubt as they regaled us with their tales of success.

Also joining the tour that day was a married Family Mentor couple on my staff who had attended the church in the States that this group was from. They were familiar with the school and knew about the church's support of it. It was exciting for them to hear the positive report, because even though they had only lived in Uganda a few months, they had seen the unfortunate reality of other schools in the area. After the tour was over they spent some time with the group from their church, and then headed down to their house to meet their boys who were then returning from a full day of classes.

Coincidently, there were four boys in their house who had attended that primary school before coming to TAS. As the couple began to share the positive report from the American group about their former school, those boys started laughing and eventually interrupted the story.

"Auntie, you're talking about '*mzungu* (white person) week.'"

"What's *mzungu* week?"

"A few times a year the *mzungus* who pay for the school come and we put on a show for them."

"Put on a show?"

"Yes. They put clean uniforms on us and make us pretend everything is great."

"What? How is that possible?"

"If the *mzungus* knew what it was really like they would take their money away."

"What's it like when the *mzungus* aren't there?"

Many of the Ugandans I know have a curious way of talking about trauma and abuse. I don't know if it's a defense mechanism or something else, but most of the time, they are smiling and jovial as they share difficult experiences from their lives. The Family Mentors listened as their boys talked about their former school. When the visitors from the States were not in town, they wore tattered uniforms and the environment was dirty and unsafe. Their "education" consisted of memorizing information and recopying, over and over, the notes in their books. Discipline was mainly administered through caning, which is a beating with a sugarcane rod.

There are many reasons why I would say that education, in developing countries, is often not the final answer to poverty. In my experience, most of the schools where sponsored children attend use rote memorization for learning. In secondary school, the students can be in a classroom thirteen or fourteen hours a day. The outcome, after sixteen years of being in school, is a mostly worthless certificate that affords little to no opportunity. More than a million students finish secondary school in Uganda every year, and only a small percentage go on to further education.

In my opinion, the education system in Uganda actually contributes to poverty because the environment in most of the schools further erodes the child's dignity and significantly limits their ability to see themselves as valuable. It's not uncommon for a dormitory to have 300 beds in a single room, with only one adult supervising. Classrooms are overcrowded and have very limited resources, and the methods of discipline are shaming and caning. I could go on, but the point is, at most other schools, the welfare of the student is not a priority. And just to be clear, money is not the issue.

IDENTITY AND DIGNITY

The best solutions to global poverty have been well researched and identified. There are proven ways to come alongside people in need that lead to self-sufficiency. There are also decades worth of examples, from all over the world, of *when helping didn't help*. The mistakes to avoid and the right steps to take are known and available to anyone who would seek to understand. So what's the problem?

With a proper awareness and understanding, you can actively become a part of the change you want to see in the world. Two helpful books are *When Helping Hurts*, by Brian Fikkert and Steve Corbett, and *Toxic Charity*, by Robert D. Lupton. These books teach that we should not look at poverty primarily in material terms, but instead, we should look primarily at the issue of human identity and dignity, as all people are made in the image of God. If you want to actually help people, focus on the identity and dignity of the person; don't just give them the material things or resources you think they need. Of course, this is easier said than done.

It takes work to learn how to help people grow to a dignified identity, which is needed for climbing out of material poverty. The easier path is to just sit back and judge the work of others, send a check, and move on, or at worst, leave it for government programs.

If you've made it this far you know I'm an outcomes-driven person. Because of this, I use the measure of *effectiveness* to evaluate any effort that intends to help people. In my experience, most of the "help" offered to people in material need has failed to guide them out of poverty. This doesn't mean the money and hours spent addressing material needs are not important. They are. I'm also not advocating for less effort or passing judgment on motivations. What I'm saying is we can do better, and we can see more effective, transformational outcomes.

I'm not a political person, but when it comes to public policy relating to the materially poor in the US, too many government initiatives have created dependency, and thus eroded peoples' sense of value. The problem has to do with addressing only material needs instead of the universal need to be fully known and fully loved. America has long been a lifestyle culture, driven by spending and debt, so the solution to poverty has been seen in terms of providing money, to buy stuff, and to improve lifestyle. It's impossible to overstate how misguided and unproductive this perspective is. Its outcome is a perpetual welfare state that continues to grow despite the hundreds of billions of dollars invested and the frequent "benefits" given to the materially poor. The US government's approach to this disadvantaged segment of the population ignores the problem of identity, and thus makes it more difficult for people to break the brutal cycle of poverty.

A couple of years ago I was invited to speak at my alma mater, Auburn University, on "Passion and Vision" to a few thousand students as part of a leadership development program. I remember telling the students their generation had great passion and vision for the way they thought the world should be, but lacked reasonable and practical plans to get to their desired outcomes. I spoke with students afterward and found many who had good ideas for how to engage in their burdens. Unfortunately, for most of them I could see that just wanting and demanding justice for people had replaced actually helping them.

The broader activist crowd is all about doing what feels right or using the catchphrase of the day instead of seeking understanding about how to really help people. The irony is that very often they are screaming about identity. It's just that they have the wrong concept of it.

JUST TEACH A MAN TO FISH?

The famous adage says, "Give a man a fish and he eats for a day. Teach a man to fish and he eats for a lifetime." It sounds nice and might be true for some parts of the world, but for Uganda and other developing countries, it's incomplete because it doesn't deal with the poverty of identity. Here is a more appropriate version:

> Give a man a fish and he eats for a day. Teach a man to
> fish; teach him his value as an image-bearer of God; teach

> him he is worthy of love; walk alongside him in friendship,
> and then, maybe, he eats for a lifetime.

My version doesn't exactly roll off the tongue, but you get the point. So many efforts to help people ultimately fail because they focus purely on the physical or economic needs of a person. Of course, there are times when direct, material relief is necessary to help people in crisis. In those times it's logical to set priority on those needs. But aside from those times of crisis, addressing the poverty of identity is required to ultimately help someone become self-sufficient.

As I've mentioned before, a group of students from TAS go out into the community on Saturday mornings to serve a vulnerable family. Sometimes we encounter situations that are difficult for our non-Ugandan staff to process. Our Ugandan staff, however, are more familiar with the challenges people face here; only rarely are they (outwardly) emotionally moved by what they see. On one Saturday, however, the situation was so dire that I found one of my Ugandan Family Mentors completely distraught after arriving back on campus.

His name is Simon and he's an incredible Jesus follower, husband, father, and mentor to the twenty-three students in the Peter House. One Saturday, shortly after returning from a nearby village, I found him by the chapel. He was visibly upset, so I asked him what was wrong. Simon, through tears, told of the conditions of the family they had just spent a few hours with.

A mother and nine children were living in squalor and the overall environment was unsafe. They all slept together in a single room, on a bug-infested mattress that couldn't lay flat because of how small the room was. Nothing was clean, and there was animal feces everywhere. She had a job in a factory where they paid her about fifty cents a day. The children were not in school, and were left to fend for themselves while she was at work. I will stop there.

Simon is Ugandan and grew up in a humble community, so as

bad as this situation was, it wasn't unique and couldn't have been a shock for him to see. What had him so upset? Well, Simon was broken by the woman's self-acknowledged, complete feeling of worthlessness. We cleaned the compound, got a new mattress, sprayed for bugs, and provided a small gift of rice, but my outcomes-driven brain was wanting to do more.

"Simon, does she have any skills? What if we helped her start a business? We could do a loan or a grant and dedicate some time to coming alongside her. What do you think we should do?"

"Uncle Kelly, this lady doesn't believe she is worthy of any help. There is nothing we can do to help her until she comes to understand that she has value in this world."

Since living in Uganda I've had many moments I won't forget, but that one is near the top of the list. I'm always most bothered by situations that seem to have no viable, practical solution. It's one thing to be aware of principles, and even to seek understanding, but when you see things play out in real time and with real people, well, that's *epignosis*, an experiential understanding that validates truth and changes the way you engage in the world. Fortunately for me, I've seen far more success stories than disappointments.

A STICK AND A SMILE

In the town of Jinja there is one end of Main Street that is, shall we say, a little more *mzungu*-friendly. On the corner sits a lovely restaurant and grocery store called The Deli that is a favorite spot for many of the foreigners who call Jinja their home. There is also an abundance of street kids and adults there who are looking for a handout or trying to sell something to make a few shillings.[1] Generally we see the same faces whenever we go to town, and especially at The Deli.

A couple of years ago an older-looking man started hanging around who I'd not seen before. He was easily distinguished from the others because he used a five-foot stick to walk around. After a few months of exchanging pleasantries, he finally decided to approach me. At my car window, and with his customary smile, he asked for a moment of my time. A letter appeared from his breast pocket and he handed it to me with a simple request: would I take it home and read it?

His name was David and he'd been the sole proprietor of a secondhand clothing business that recently had been lost to a fire. His entire inventory was gone and he had no capital to move forward. The letter was eloquent and sincere. Clearly, David was an intelligent man, and apparently had been successful until the fire. He was married and had five children who, at least until that point, were all in school with no outside assistance. The letter was requesting a loan to start a new business, and included a very detailed business plan and accounting for every shilling he was requesting.

About a week later, I was back in town and David was at his usual spot in front of The Deli. He hobbled over with the same big smile, eager to know my response to his letter. I thanked him for his thorough effort and asked him a simple question, "Why not get a loan from a bank?" With a confused look on his face, he simply answered, "Because I'm disabled."

There is a great stigma with disability in Uganda, and even though David had an advanced degree (MA in accounting), no bank would give him a business loan. I was excited about investing in David because there was a high likelihood of a positive outcome. More importantly, David had a strong faith, and his identity was in Christ, not in his disability or his poverty. He knew his value as an adopted son of God, and at this point just needed a boost and someone to come alongside in friendship.

The next couple of months were fun. Not only did I invest in David, he allowed me to help him with inventory strategies, sales, marketing, and more. I should note that I leaned heavily on my Ugandan friends for the *how*, but regardless, I am happy to report that David's business continues to thrive and his family is strong.

David hung around The Deli for almost four months, always with a smile on his face, before we had that first conversation. Regardless of his circumstance, and despite a culture that said he was worthless, he knew his real value. Because he understood his worth as an image-bearer, the help provided to him became a path out of poverty.

THE MODEL OF JESUS

A world of brokenness makes for a world of people who need help. As Jesus followers we are created and called to help. Anyone with a working knowledge of the gospels knows that Jesus prioritized the poor and outcast members of society. In a powerful moment at the start of his ministry, Jesus quoted the prophet Isaiah:

> The Spirit of the Lord is on me,
>> because he has anointed me
>> to proclaim good news to the poor.
> He has sent me to proclaim freedom for the prisoners
>> and recovery of sight for the blind,
> to set the oppressed free,
>> to proclaim the year of the Lord's favor (Luke 4:16-19).

And then, in a drop-the-mic moment, Jesus said, "Today this scripture is fulfilled in your hearing" (Luke 4:21). With that, he was saying he was the Messiah who would finally bring good news to the poor, and at the same time he established who would be his priority. Hint: it wouldn't be the rich or advantaged.

The earliest sermons of his ministry were also focused on the undervalued, with a message of inclusion and acceptance. He went out of his way to engage with them, to teach them about the kingdom of God and how to live. Rather than directly address their material needs, Jesus focused more on their inherent worth in his crazy, upside-down value system. He often addressed their spiritual needs and their value before healing them physically.

Even though Jesus provided the model for engaging and helping the poor and disadvantaged, Western society continues to resist the kingdom culture he taught, and instead assesses value in material terms. With this fallacy it's no wonder so many well-intended efforts fail to lead to transformational outcomes.

Setting and pursuing goals focused on material gain, without addressing the poverty of identity, doesn't lead to good consequences, no matter the culture. But in developing countries, where the investment for such efforts mainly comes from Western sources, there is an even greater likelihood for ineffective ministry. Because the Western mindset for charity is typically set in monetary terms, donors can assume good things are being achieved wherever money is flowing. Success may be measured by metrics like the size of the investment, the number of kids sponsored, or the number of meals distributed. What about reporting on progress toward people understanding their value? It may sound like I'm criticizing, but I'm not. I've served on the boards of ministries and NGOs that couldn't exist without funding. Impressive-sounding statistics are required to get people to invest. I get it. But that doesn't mean we can't strive for better outcomes.

If organizations would follow the model of Jesus by addressing the value and dignity of the people they serve as the highest priority, the resulting transformation would be broad and deep. I'm not suggesting anyone abandon a specific mission or activity, but rather that they integrate the matter of the value of individual people into how they go about their work. Since I work at a school and for an organization that provides scholarships for vulnerable children, let me give a practical example.

The vast majority of child-sponsorship programs in developing countries provide everything a child needs to go to school, including all the fees, uniforms, and school supplies. This makes sense, right?

At the beginning, the receiving family is happy, the child is happy, and the sponsorship organization feels good about the assistance they are providing. Unfortunately, in most cases, there is no ongoing way for the family to participate in the education or welfare of their child. The result? Over time, resentment grows in all directions.

- The students may resent their parents because they aren't providing for them.

- The parents may resent their students because of their attitude of entitlement.

- The parents then resent the sponsor organization, that they blame for the broken relationships with their children.

These are unintended consequences of good people, giving good money, doing good things, so vulnerable children can attend school. The biggest consequence, though, is that the child moves through the education system while the underlying problem of their impoverished identity is not addressed, for them or their parents. When the child eventually finishes school, they are not, as a result, in an advantaged position. I would argue they are even more likely to live a life of poverty, because of broken relationships and their perceived lack of value.

In my experience, intentionally adding a policy allowing the family to play a role in their child's education leads to a much more positive outcome from the generosity. More importantly, it helps develop relationships that build dignity and develop an understanding of participants' value. This is what we have seen at our school. Asking families to contribute financially, regardless of their means, has had a huge, positive impact on the relationships our parents and guardians have with their students. Our kids see their parents making big sacrifices to ensure they get to school, and in return there is appreciation and respect instead of resentment. Honestly, it's extremely difficult (emotionally) to send a kid home on reporting day for lack of a few pencils or a can of shoe polish, but over the last four years, this has thankfully become a rare occurrence.

In addition, our Family Mentors develop close friendships with our students' families, through which they come to understand their value to us, to their children, and most importantly, to God. Those friendships never include material assistance but instead are completely focused on mutual respect and trust.

There is a real temptation to look at the material poverty in the developing world and think that people in America have it so much better. Jesus doesn't think so and neither do I. I'm seeing our students and their families, who live in a very humble community, embracing their value and created purpose like nowhere else, resulting in a faith that is far more valuable than anything money can buy.

> **Something to Remember:** We'll fail to meaningfully help people unless we provide them with an understanding of their value as persons, instead of just providing them with material aid.

Embracing this idea of guiding impoverished and disadvantaged people to understand their inherent value, as a foundation for truly helping them out of poverty, starts with coming to the right view of *brokenness*. But on the journey to living the fullness of the Christian life, there's another "frame" that also leads to important perspectives: *God's grace*.

GRACE CHANGES EVERYTHING

A correct understanding of *brokenness* is perhaps the most essential of the perspectives we need to have, because of how other concepts are built on it. Now that I've unpacked the reality and truth of our brokenness, we are in a great position to explore how God's *grace* frames our understanding of God himself, of who we are in Christ, our circumstances, and how we respond to his rules for living.

If brokenness is the most *essential* frame, then God's grace is the most *influential*, because everything related to our faith is affected by our view of it. This is a bold statement, but I would say that most, if not all, of our spiritual problems are related to a wrong view of God's grace. I don't say this to be critical. Grace is hard. Grace makes no sense. The grace that pervades God's kingdom is the complete opposite of the ways of the cultures of the world. As the writer of Hebrews bluntly wrote, "It is impossible for the blood of bulls and goats to take away sins" (Hebrews 10:4).

I took a class in seminary, Spiritual Life, that brought this tension into focus. Ninety percent of our grade was based on a single, semester-long project culminating in a paper to be turned in at the end. When we arrived for the last day of class, the professor offered a curious choice to the students. We could turn in our work to be graded on its merit, or take out a blank sheet of paper, write our name on it, and then simply add the grade we would like to receive for the course!

The students who had worked hard on the project still wanted to have their work evaluated and graded. Believe it or not, many of them submitted their work rather than take the automatic *A*. For everyone else (including me), the choice was simple: take the *A* and celebrate! Not surprisingly, there was some resentment toward the students who accepted the automatic grade. By any measure, it wasn't fair for the students who worked hard to receive the same grade as others who did not take the project as seriously. But that was the point.

How you react to this story should tell you something about your current view of God's grace and how open you may or may not be to changing your perspective. Regardless, that's where we're heading in this section. Before we look at the perspectives most framed by our view of God's grace, let's start by looking at what we believe about it, and seek a better understanding.

My prayer is that God will use this section to bring you into a right understanding of his grace and reframe your perspectives about him, yourself, and his call to obedience.

CHAPTER 10

GOD'S GRACE

*In the same way, the gospel is bearing fruit and
growing throughout the whole world—just as
it has been doing among you since the day you
heard it and truly* [epignosis] *God's grace.*

Colossians 1:6

Because of the shame aspect of Ugandan culture it's a big challenge for our students to understand God's grace, but when they truly get it, the response is overwhelming. They come to school keenly aware of their own performance as it relates to sin and good works, because they've been taught it's the way to salvation, health, and wealth. When they understand God's grace, it dramatically and beautifully shatters the shame they feel and leads to an unshakable, fruit-producing faith.

A student who (coincidentally) was named Grace came to us from a home situation that was extremely difficult, even in the context of the material poverty of Uganda. Her dad wasn't around, so it was just her mom, her brother, and herself in a rented "house." The mom struggled with alcohol and was often abusive to Grace and her younger brother. To support her drinking and to make some additional money, the mom decided to use most of the house as a makeshift bar. Not surprisingly, the clients were not exactly respectable people. Grace's family lived on the banks of the Nile River at a spot known for violence and feuding. It was a dangerous place.

A critical part of the Student Life ministry strategy is to develop trusted relationships with the families of our students. This is accomplished through what are called "home visits." Twice a term, Family Mentors visit the families of each of their students. The goal of each visit is to grow dignity through friendship. Our families are not "projects" for us, nor do we force spiritual conversations during the visits. Most of the people in these families do not believe they have inherent value, so the friendships serve to break down that attitude and hopefully support a dignity and confidence that can lead to self-sufficiency.

Grace has been a part of the Hannah House since she arrived on campus several years ago. For her first three years, her Family Mentor team consisted of Uncle Zach and Auntie Mac (a married couple) along with Auntie Jackie. The three of them diligently pursued a relationship with Grace's mom, even though she'd usually been drinking and could be somewhat combative during their home visits. If the Hannah House Mentors had come to me and said they couldn't handle visiting Grace's mom anymore, I would have been okay with it. The situation was so dire that at times it wasn't safe for Grace to stay with her mom over the breaks between school terms.

In spite of the danger and potential abuse, Grace refused to give up on her mom. Even when she wasn't sleeping at the house over a break, Grace would visit to help her mom and talk to her about Jesus. No matter what the mom did, and sometimes her actions were unconscionable, Grace would not withhold grace. Her Family Mentors, after observing Grace love her mom unconditionally, decided they also could not give up, no matter what difficulty they encountered.

Two years after Grace began at TAS, the Hannah House Mentors came for a visit to the mom's house, but this time she was sober. She expressed a desire to place her faith in Christ, shut down the bar, and stop drinking. The consistent, undeserved grace she received from her daughter and the Mentors finally broke her. There was no explanation for such grace apart from this Jesus she'd been hearing about. She wanted to know him.

Admittedly, I was a bit cynical about her conversion and her expressed desire to clean up her life. I've had a dozen or so friends who said the same sort of thing, but the eventual results were discouraging. In addition, the price tag in Uganda for alcoholic detoxification is outrageous. Even though the odds were definitely not in her favor, I'm thrilled to report she proved me wrong. She managed to get the resources needed to join an in-patient detoxification program and long-term counseling. Grace's mom began to authentically change. She joined a local church that was ready to come alongside her in fellowship.

Unfortunately, we were soon reminded of the inescapable brokenness all around us. The years of drinking had ravaged her body, and not too long after her conversion God called her home. Grace's mom died during a school term, so it was her Family Mentors who told Grace the news of her mother's passing. She received the news with sadness, but also with the joy of knowing they will be together with Jesus for eternity. I'd previously had the privilege in the States of walking through the loss of a parent with teenagers, but never before had I seen such a response. Since Grace had the right understanding of God's grace, she was able to accept the loss. Her actions stemmed from having the right perspective.

RESISTING GRACE

You would think people would be eager to accept the free gift of God's grace, but if you look at the lives of most Christians, you'll see that's not the case. Instead, we more often choose the exhausting path of *performance* and live with the disappointment of not getting what we think we deserve, in a culture of comparison and criticism. Why is that?

During our time doing ministry in the States, it wasn't difficult to see the obstacles that made it difficult for our students to understand and receive God's grace. They grew up in an American culture where rewards are based on performance; the idea of grace makes no sense. Grace, after all, is completely unnatural. If something were to be accepted through grace alone, it would mean the credit goes elsewhere and there would be no recognition for efforts.

In addition, social media became a showplace for performance (and failure) that further moved the idea of grace to the background. There was also that pesky sense of entitlement that came with the millennial generation. The problem with entitlement is that the moment we think we deserve something from God, we lose sight of his grace. I used to think of premillennialism in theological terms, but now the word reminds me of a time when students were more relationally available—but that's a discussion for another day.

For students to accept God's grace, they'd have to accept the idea that they weren't good enough on their own, and that they weren't better than those around them. American culture doesn't allow for such ideas.

What our Ugandan students have heard about grace before they come to campus has usually been negative. Their pastors have sometimes talked about grace as a dangerous enabler for sin. They say people will use grace as an excuse to sin more, since they will be forgiven anyway. God's grace stands in opposition to the prosperity gospel, so it has to be downplayed at every opportunity for the false teaching to persist.

When our students are finally confronted with the truth of the gospel of grace, they react much like the first-century Jewish Christians did—with resistance and confusion. God's grace is rarely taught in the churches they come from. Much like the first-century Pharisees (and legalistic pastors in the US), many Ugandan faith leaders are offended by the idea of God's grace because it threatens their power and position. They work very hard to maintain a legalistic framework of control, so grace can't be allowed to sneak in.

Our Ugandan students have the added difficulty of growing up in an honor/shame culture. Their typical pattern is to resist grace—not because it threatens their sense of deserved rewards, but because their personal shame won't allow them to accept it. This is a different dynamic than what had been my experience with American teenagers, but I'd prefer to have to deal with the Ugandan pattern, because the starting point is closer to what's required to truly understand God's grace.

AN UNDESERVED GIFT

In 2007 I was working for a large software company led by a President who liked to do grand things to fire up everybody for the work ahead. His favorite gesture, always done in dramatic fashion at the annual sales conference, was to award a new Porsche to the number one global sales executive. I was fortunate to earn this award after my first full year with the company.

Before you judge me (probably too late for that), know that I went to the President and asked if he could use the money to buy a couple of minivans for single moms in need, instead of using it for the Porsche. The lease payment was so large that we could have bought two ordinary cars instead. He laughed out loud at my suggestion. For him, the point was to have a very big, very public award, that the entire sales force would see, so they would be incentivized to work harder, knowing the potential for a brand new Porsche was real. With no other options, I begrudgingly accepted...okay, at that point maybe it wasn't so begrudgingly.

So, I went to the local Porsche dealer and picked out a Carrera 4S convertible.

I won't spend too much time talking about the car but good grief what a machine. It's important you know that at this point in my life, I had received more than twenty speeding tickets (all of them were unfair, by the way). Cops were always singling me out for some reason. But one day there might have been a good reason to pull me over…

Danlyn worked at North Point Community Church in the children's ministry, so that meant we had to get there very early on Sunday mornings. I'd never before driven the Porsche to church, but that Sunday morning it was the vehicle to use, so there we were, enjoying the smooth ride down Highway 400. We came to a stretch where it's dead straight for as far as you can see, and we were the only ones on the road, so naturally I had to step on the gas a little.

I didn't know exactly how fast I was going because my eyes were glued to the road. By the time I slowed down, my hands were stuck to the steering wheel and my heart was racing a bit. And then—blue lights.

"Babe, I don't know how fast I was going but I'm pretty sure I'm going to jail."

"Well, you can call your parents to bail you out. I need to get to work."

It was a Georgia State Patrolman, and he was furious, as in the screaming-and-cussing kind of furious. Since I'm a sales guy, I was concentrating on an excuse and not really paying attention to what he was saying. After quickly processing, I started to say something in my defense. Before I could get two words out, he said, "Don't you say a word. Do you have any idea how fast you were going?"

"I…"

"Don't answer that," he snapped. "I was going one hundred fifty-five miles per hour, and you were pulling away."

I'm going to be honest. For a brief moment there was a smidge of pride. Then he started yelling again, while questioning my character and my capabilities as a husband. Fun stuff. Unexpectedly, and without any explanation, he then casually walked back to his car and proceeded to sit in the driver's seat with the door open and his legs stretched outside the car. After about sixty seconds, his left arm went up in the air, above the roofline, and it looked like a "get outta here" kind of wave.

"Babe, I think he's letting me go."

"There is no way he is letting you go."

"You're right; I must have misunderstood."

But after another sixty seconds, he did it again. This time, there was no misunderstanding. I was free. I put the car in first gear and drove, at a snail's pace, all the way to church.

I was completely in the wrong and there was nothing I could say in my defense. For his reasons, completely of his own choosing, the patrolman decided to give me the gift of freedom. There is no record of my offense. He didn't even take down my name.

I wasn't free, however, until I accepted the gift.

IT'S NOT UNCLEAR

In my opinion, based on almost twenty years in student ministry, there is nothing more critical to walking closely with Jesus than an *epignosis* (experiential understanding) of the grace of God. God's grace may be both the most important and the most misunderstood aspect of the gospel, but I doubt you'd find many believers who would admit to not understanding God's grace.

Scripture is not ambiguous or confusing about grace. If you ask most Christians to define grace you will hear correct things like "unmerited favor" or "undeserved gifts." You'll also likely receive a nice assortment of Bible verses like these:

- "All have sinned and fall short of the glory of God, and all are justified freely by his grace through the redemption that came by Christ Jesus" (Romans 3:23-24).

- "So too, at the present time there is a remnant chosen by grace. And if by grace, then it cannot be based on works; if it were, grace would no longer be grace" (Romans 11:5-6).

- "By the grace of God I am what I am, and his grace to me was not without effect. No, I worked harder than all of them—yet not I, but the grace of God that was with me" (1 Corinthians 15:10).

- "He chose us in him before the creation of the world to be holy and blameless in his sight. In love he predestined us for adoption to sonship through Jesus Christ, in accordance with his pleasure and will—to the praise of his glorious grace, which he has freely given us in the One he loves" (Ephesians 1:4-6).

- "For it is by grace you have been saved, through faith— and this is not from yourselves, it is the gift of God—not by works, so that no one can boast" (Ephesians 2:8-9).

The Old Testament law and sacrificial system set the stage for the dramatic and culturally disruptive grace of Jesus. After the Jews failed to follow the law, Jesus fulfilled the righteous requirements of the law, satisfied the wrath and justice of God, paid the penalty we rightly deserved, and invited all the world to be saved through belief in him.[1] The cross of Christ represents the greatest act of grace in the history of mankind. All of Scripture points to Jesus, who is the embodiment of God's grace.

It is, has been, and always will be about God's grace—in everything. When Jesus told stories about the kingdom of God, he was often explaining God's grace. It seems straightforward and awesome, so why do most Christians live as if they don't get it? There are a myriad of reasons, but the main one is that grace makes no sense in a world of performance, measurement, and comparison.

UNDERSTAND SIN TO UNDERSTAND GRACE

The key to experientially understanding God's grace is to pursue an active awareness of our sin. I have often said that a mature and growing Christian is *not* necessarily someone who sins *less*, but someone who is keenly aware of their sin and feels great sorrow over it. Instead of trying to be good enough, it's more about knowing we are not good enough and never will be. Said more simply, how we view our sin determines our perspective on God's grace.

For those of us who think we are pretty good, God's grace isn't that big of a deal. Anyone who is not overwhelmed by God's grace is likely underwhelmed by their own sin. On the other hand, if we have a proper awareness of the severity of our sin and our inability to offer anything meaningful to God, his grace becomes immeasurable and completely transformative.

In the Porsche story, I was given complete, undeserved freedom even though I was driving more than 100 miles per hour over the speed limit. Do you think I would be telling this story if I was going only fifteen miles per hour over the limit? Of course not. My view of the grace I experienced was dependent on my view of the offense. Because the offense was so egregious, the grace given was equally enormous and made no sense whatsoever. To be sure, I will never forget that experience of grace.

In addition to pursuing a better awareness and understanding of your sin, it's helpful and practical to pay attention to how you react to the common grace in your life. Are you truly grateful in those moments? Do you celebrate when grace is given to others? What about people you don't know personally? When people teach about the famous parable of the prodigal son(s),[2] the focus is often on the grace given to the younger brother who squandered his inheritance only to be accepted back, without condition, by his father. Equally as important, however, is the reaction of the older brother, whose sense of justice can't handle the grace given to his undeserving brother.

Be honest: how do you feel about the grace given to me in the Porsche story? Is there part of you that doesn't think it's fair that I was given a free pass for such a dangerous offense? Do you have a posture of "grace for me but not for thee"?

We've all had common-grace moments in the course of our lives. Whether or not those moments were meaningful depends on your view of the grace given and how deserving or entitled you think you are (sorry, that sounds harsh). If you want to know your level of understanding as it relates to God's grace, look no further than your typical response.

If you truly understand God's grace, it will show in how you extend grace to those around you—even to those who have hurt you deeply, and don't deserve it. That's the point, actually. If you are hesitant to extend grace to others, you may not have a proper understanding of the grace you've received. If you don't think much of God's grace, odds are you think you're a pretty good person, at least in comparison to the people around you. To say God's grace is just undeserved favor is limiting. Everything we have is by God's grace, including the awareness of his grace. As Paul said in his letter to the Christians in Rome, "If by grace, then it cannot be based on works; if it were, grace would no longer be grace" (Romans 11:6).

There is nothing more encouraging and strengthening than to personally experience the truth and wisdom of Scripture. For me, understanding and experiencing God's grace has shaped my life more than anything else. God has taught me, through students like Grace, what a real Jesus follower should look like, and that there is grace for us in every situation.

> **Something to Remember:** Everything God has done for us, and everything he has promised to us, is completely out of his grace; it has nothing to do with us, our actions, or our good works.

Now that we're (hopefully) willing to let go of performance-driven faith, let's dig into some perspectives that, when viewed correctly, have the potential to dramatically transform your faith.

CHAPTER 11

GOD, US, AND IDENTITY

*He chose us in him before the creation of the world
to be holy and blameless in his sight. In love he
predestined us for adoption to sonship through Jesus
Christ, in accordance with his pleasure and will.*

EPHESIANS 1:4-5

When our first students in Uganda arrived at school, there was an emptiness and sadness among them that is hard to describe. I must admit, it took me by surprise. In my naivety, I assumed they would be overjoyed and grateful to be here. Instead, it was the opposite. They didn't want to be a part of this new school. They could not process, through their perspectives, that this school would change anything for them.

As I mentioned earlier, the churches they grew up in had mostly presented a false gospel, resulting in a devastatingly incorrect perspective on God. God was presented as a cosmic judge who rewards and punishes based on performance. Jesus is only different in that he is better than other gods. Predictably, this wrong view initially prevented our students from accepting what God says about those who are in Christ. When our students walked through the gates of campus, the shame they felt about themselves and their families, and the shame they felt about their failure to live up to unrealistic standards, was on full display.

In the first few months of school, I came to understand how some of the local pastors and leaders use wrong perspectives to foster beliefs that allow for a level of "control" over people. One example comes from a great kid named Moses, who was also the first-ever Head Boy at TAS, which is like a Student Body President at a US high school. Moses came from a sponsorship organization that had sent only two other students to TAS that first year, so unfortunately he did not arrive with any friends.

Being somewhat shy and short in stature, Moses did not stand out on campus and struggled to get noticed. Despite the fact he was kind to others and therefore not unpopular, he was an unlikely candidate to win the highest office at the school. Still, he won—by executing a clever campaign and by delivering a strong speech to his fellow students during the election process.

Part of my role at the school is to teach our young leaders how to lead like Jesus (as servants). As time went on, and as I mentored him, Moses and I developed a good rhythm together. I learned that his perspectives on God and himself were mainly shaped by the leader of the children's home where he had been living for the previous seven years. From that, it was difficult for him to process a different theology.

Because Moses trusted that leader, there was a lot of tension when I tried to discuss the many issues that came from his wrong perspective. Any time he was faced with teachings different than what he'd heard before, he would feel additional shame for going against his prior Mentor at the children's home. His biggest hang-up was that he lived in almost constant fear of blaspheming the Spirit. He had been taught that he could instantly lose his salvation if he were to do that, even unintentionally.

It's always tempting (at least for me) to blow up someone's

wrongly held beliefs when the truth of the matter is so evident in Scripture. That approach rarely works, however, because it doesn't consider the deeply rooted experiences of a person, or why they believe what they believe. It's better to start with a perspective of God, and then on who we are in Christ, that can lead to bringing down the theology of shame and fear that makes it so difficult to embrace the true gospel.

Rather than debate with Moses (or any of our students) about their various positions on specific issues where there might be tension, our strategy was to model, through trusted relationships, what a life looks like lived through the correct perspectives. Often after a long period of time, discussions about questions stemming from false teaching would be based on a foundation of common understanding and trust. At some point, after patiently holding to this strategy, Moses came to view both God and himself correctly. The transformation was nothing short of remarkable.

I ran into Moses one day and spent a few minutes catching up with him. The students had returned for a couple of months before being sent home again because of COVID. We talked about the difficulty of the pandemic and how things were going for him. With a smile on his face, he said he was doing very well, in spite of being kicked out of his home by his father! Feeling awkward, I asked Moses why he had to leave his home and he said, "My father said I had to reject Christ or leave the family, so I left. How could I not?"

I have learned not to be surprised by the unshakable faith of our students nor by their courage in facing a culture which, generally, rejects the true gospel. But in this case I was a bit stunned, because he was willing to leave in the middle of the COVID crisis, and during a time when food was scarce and available work even more so. This young man who came to TAS with the wrong perspective of God and himself was now so assured in the truth that he joyfully proclaimed Christ even when it meant difficulty and uncertainty. Oh, and that leader who had (unintentionally) misled Moses? He has also come into a right understanding of grace, and in doing so, is now pastoring a church that preaches the true gospel. #graceisawesome

Scripture says that following Jesus comes with great cost. If we have the right perspectives about God and how he views us, we can also have the confidence to follow Jesus even when it costs us greatly.

A correct view of God and who we are in Christ requires an understanding of the grace of God. Apart from grace, it is impossible to accept God's unconditional love for us and his invitation to become adopted sons and daughters. The right perspective on God is critically important because all other perspectives are directly influenced by that. If we don't view God in the right way, we will always struggle to develop any other healthy or mature perspectives. A.W. Tozer wrote, "What comes into our minds when we think about God is the most important thing about us."[1]

The correct perspective on God is also required to develop the critically important perspective on who we are in Christ or, as C.S. Lewis described it, how God thinks of us: "How God thinks of us is not only more important, but infinitely more important. Indeed, how we think of Him is of no importance except in so far as it is related to how He thinks of us."[2]

I don't think Tozer and Lewis are in conflict here. Rather, the two statements support each other, because we can't really know how God thinks of us unless we first have the correct perspective on God. Both perspectives are very important to our growth in Christian maturity. If we desire to move toward real joy, we must recognize that it's impossible to do so without the right view of God and an understanding of how he views us.

Unfortunately, based on how the church (largely) looks today, I would say most Christians have an incorrect view of God, who they are in Christ, or both. The evidence supporting this assertion is, in my opinion, overwhelming.

WHY DON'T THEY LIKE US?

In the book *UnChristian: What a New Generation Really Thinks About Christianity…and Why It Matters,* Kinnaman and Lyons reported on data from the Barna Research Group about how the church is currently viewed by outsiders.[3] The top three descriptors for Christians were: (1) anti-gay, (2) judgmental, and (3) hypocritical.

I've known this information for a long time, but even now as I type, I feel sick to my stomach. How is it possible that twenty-first-century Jesus followers, who are supposed to be known by their love for others,[4] can be characterized this way? In my experience, the reason people view Christians this way is…wait for it…because many Christians *are* this way. Christians who misrepresent Jesus and the gospel with their hatred, judgmentalism, and legalism likely carry a grave misunderstanding of who God is and who they are in Christ.

There are many other troubling signs and trends that indicate wrong perspectives about who God is and who we are. These include unintended false teaching, devaluing those with disabilities, movement toward "religion," disappointment with God, prioritizing performance over people, and in general, walking away from faith. With the correct perspectives, there is no way these things would be happening with such frequency and on such a grand scale.

Reverence for God has almost been eliminated from Western culture. It wasn't always this way. Harvard University[5] and Yale University were both founded by Christians. Along with other Ivy League schools, they were originally established to educate clergy and further the Christian faith. In addition, a large number of colleges in the US were founded by Christians for the purpose of spreading the gospel through academic work. Clergymen were respected, and the Bible was considered a sacred document by just about everyone. The movement in American culture away from a favorable view of Christians has only happened because professing Christians have acted out of false perspectives on themselves and God.

Perhaps most disturbing is how wrong perspectives on God or ourselves are manifest in our view of others and in our actions toward them. In Christian history the church has, at times, ignored the teaching of Jesus and the model of the early disciples, set aside the frame of grace, and singled out groups of people for judgment. At those times, the church has been an impediment to people coming to faith in Jesus. The apostle Paul consistently warned Christians about this dangerous practice:

- "Let us stop passing judgment on one another. Instead, make up your mind not to put any stumbling block or obstacle in the way of a brother or sister" (Romans 14:13).

- "It is my judgment that we should not make it difficult for the Gentiles who are turning to God" (Acts 15:19).

In Paul's ministry, he always adjusted his approach for the people to whom he was speaking. Although he was not afraid of speaking truth, it was always done with grace and compassion for the context and experience of his audience. Like Jesus, Paul knew how to draw the marginalized and disadvantaged people of society to the gospel. Unfortunately, this effective practice slowly eroded and gave way to legalistic denominations and generations of Pharisee-like judgmentalism, often with disastrous consequences.

Alternatively, if we had had correct views of God and how he views us, our actions would attract others to the message of Christ and our churches would be overflowing with broken people seeking Jesus. Is it that easy? Clearly not. Western culture has gotten to a point where having a perspective that is not approved by popular opinion can get you fired (or worse).

Another big problem we face, in helping others develop the right perspectives, is that any wrong perspectives people carry have come from their personal experience, or from someone who they trusted. If we suggest to someone they may have a wrong perspective, we are indirectly questioning their background and experience, or implying that whoever they trusted was wrong. This is the biggest challenge we face with our Ugandan students. We are up against deeply ingrained culture and traditions, which are often elevated above Scripture.

ABOUT GOD

Debating topics like evolution and the age of the earth can be fun, but in my opinion, not very helpful. Whether or not the earth is 7,000 years old or four and one-half billion years old doesn't change that Jesus was crucified and rose from the dead. In fact, the death and resurrection of Jesus is the best-documented event in ancient history. Our faith is in the person of Jesus Christ and not in anyone or anything else. The most important thing about the creation story is not *how* or *when* God created, but *why* and *who* he created. It's about God and who he created us to be.

All throughout Scripture we see a consistent picture of God. He is the same now as he was with Adam and Eve in the garden. He is the same in the Old Testament as he is in the New. His purpose for creation and his plan to redeem it (and us) has not changed. I'm not saying it's a simple thing to study all of God's words and deeds, across thousands of years, and pull together a single portrait of God. But Scripture tells us so much about his character and attributes that we can engage in thoughtful discussion, regardless of our experience or background.

With our students in Uganda, we start with an understanding of their current perspectives and then present what the Bible says about who God is. A good place to start is in Exodus, when God described himself.

> The Lord, the Lord, the compassionate and gracious
> God, slow to anger, abounding in love and faithfulness,

> maintaining love to thousands, and forgiving wickedness, rebellion and sin. Yet he does not leave the guilty unpunished; he punishes the children and their children for the sin of the parents to the third and fourth generation (Exodus 34:6-7).

Now, this is God speaking about himself directly to Moses, so as a starting point, we can take seriously that God's character includes compassion, grace, patience, love, forgiveness, and justice.

The other reason Exodus 34:6-7 is a great passage to start with is because of the last part of verse 7: "He does not leave the guilty unpunished; he punishes the children and their children for the sin of the parents to the third and fourth generation." This is one of those widely misunderstood verses that leaders in honor/shame cultures use to gain power. We draw on other scriptures and the context to help our students understand what is actually meant by the words of this verse. From that, they are more open to understanding God, in harmony with his attributes taught in the earlier part of the passage. It's amazing how the verses that are often used in false teaching, when understood correctly, can be used to disprove the same false teaching.

For the record, God does not hold a generation accountable for the sins of its ancestors. Instead, history shows that each generation repeats the same mistakes as the prior one. This is especially clear with the example of ancient Israel at the time of the Exodus. In that context, God punished people for the same sins as their parents, *not because* of the sins of their parents. Jesus was clear about this when his disciples asked him about a man who had been blind from birth.

"Rabbi, who sinned, this man or his parents, that he was born blind?"

"Neither this man nor his parents sinned," said Jesus, "but this happened so that the works of God might be displayed in him" (John 9:2-3).

As we move through the Hebrew scriptures, the Gospels, and the letters of the earliest disciples, we find a consistent reinforcement of those descriptions in Exodus 34 and additional attributes of God like sovereign, trustworthy, mighty, and merciful. Directly and indirectly, through examining stories throughout the Bible, we can also learn the following about God:

- God cares about people, not performance.
- God offers unconditional love to us.
- God has promised us hope and peace in difficult times.
- God pursues us even when we are disobedient and lost.
- God wants the best for us, and (more importantly) knows what's best for us.

All this stands in stark contrast to the God presented to our Ugandan kids by many of their pastors, their culture, and the traditions around them. If we have modeled patience and love through relationships, the truth of Scripture will lead the students to the one true God who is infinitely more appealing than what they've known. There is no comparison!

Even though we teach our students systematically—and there is great value in studying God throughout the Scriptures—there is an easier and more direct path to the correct perspective. God has not made it difficult to know who he is, because, as Scripture teaches, Jesus is God.[6] As he said to Philip on the night before he was to go to the cross, "Anyone who has seen me has seen the Father" (John 14:9).

In other words, if you want to have the correct perspective on God, just look at Jesus. Again, it's "just Jesus." It may seem overly simplistic but it's not. As the writer of Hebrews said, "Jesus Christ is the same yesterday and today and forever" (Hebrews 13:8). If your view of God doesn't match up with Jesus, you have the wrong perspective.

However long it takes for our students to develop a mature and correct perspective on God, it takes less than half that time for them to accept who God says they are as new creations in Christ. The right view of God clears the obstacles to gaining a right perspective on us and sets the course toward an unshakable faith in Jesus.

MERMAIDS AND DIAMONDS

We all struggle, to some extent, with the tension of how we view ourselves, how we believe we are viewed by God, and how we are viewed by others. Because of this, many of our decisions and actions come from "identity management." Now we also face the need for *online* identity management. For most people, their online identity is all about the person they think they want to be, or the person they want others to see. All of it is exhausting.

For some, identity is found in things that are outwardly visible like talents, family, job, success, heritage, race, or physical appearance. Others find identity in sexuality, politics, advocating for causes, or being victims. There is also a growing trend to identify oneself with many attributes at the same time. At the 2020 Democratic Convention there was a speaker who identified themself as a "Black-Vietnamese, transgender, nonbinary/gender-transcendent, mermaid Queen-King."[7] My point isn't to judge this person, but to say that most of us will go to great lengths to define our identity. The question is, Why?

I'm not against acknowledging or even celebrating those things that are distinctive about a person, nor do I have a problem with the concept of individuality. The problem arises when we take things that may be true about ourselves and decide that those things are, in fact, who we are. If our identity is wrapped up in the things of this world, we'll fall prey to performance orientation. Whether we realize it or not, our choices about how we understand our identity inevitably determine how we value ourselves and others. This makes it difficult to accept who we are, limits our desire to seek understanding, and leads to almost constant discontent.

For eighteen years I was at the highest level for frequent fliers on Delta Air Lines (Diamond Medallion) and enjoyed the elevated status that came with it. The "Diamonds" are particularly proud of their status and make every effort to let everyone in the airport and on the plane know about it. They are typically demanding and entitled, and look down on lower-level frequent fliers and especially on those who don't fly often.

I wasn't consciously aware of how important that status was to me. After living in Uganda for a couple of years and losing that status, however, I realized just how much of my identity was connected to being a Diamond flier on Delta Air Lines. I now had to wait on hold to speak to an agent, and when I flew, there was no first-class seat for me, nor any special treatment or acknowledgment. Losing my status bothered me so much that I felt tempted, various times, to explain to people that I used to be a top-level flier! I know this is beyond pathetic, but it taught me a lot about the consequences of finding identity in the wrong things.

The perspectives we have of ourselves create the framework from which we compare and judge ourselves and the people around us. There is no escaping this principle. The consequences can be more severe, however, when we operate with an incorrect perspective about how God views us. If we believe God is without grace and views us through our performance against a set of rules, we will naturally compare ourselves to others in the same way, and judge those who are performing poorly. In Uganda this creates a devastating system of honor/shame in which the material circumstances of a person's life (health and wealth) are seen as evidence of how God views that person.

Fortunately, a proper understanding of how God views us, which is our identity in Christ, elevates us above the principle of comparison and spares us the personal and relational consequences of self-judgment and the judgment of others.

I AM WHO I AM SAYS I AM

One of the reasons we all struggle with managing our identities is because we so badly desire to be accepted—by ourselves, by God, and by others. I don't need to make a case for this statement because we all know it's true. When our primary identity is in things of this world, our identity management will always include the pursuit of acceptance, and we'll always be dealing with rejection. It is an exhausting, endless cycle that never leads to contentment and joy. But if we understand who God says we are as new creations in Christ, we find absolute and unconditional acceptance. With that we can begin to let go of the toxic practices of comparison and judgment.

Everything changes when we accept that we are accepted and loved by God.

The cross and resurrection not only confirm God's unconditional love for us, but allow us to fully and confidently accept that we are who God says we are as believers: new creations in Christ[8] who have received the Holy Spirit,[9] free from the bondage and eternal penalty of sin,[10] chosen for a purpose,[11] forgiven and loved by his grace,[12] and fully adopted into the family of God.[13] In addition, God says we are all equal in our God-given identity in Christ.[14]

I once heard Louie Giglio say, "Our identity in Christ is received, not achieved." What could be more gracious than that? When *God's* view of us becomes *our* view of us, there is no longer a need for comparison and judgment as it relates to who we are.

As I have remarked previously, my life experiences, especially here in Uganda, bear witness to the validity and wisdom of Scripture. For me, the most dramatic example is how our students come to view other people. After students place their faith in Christ, understand who he is, and accept what that means for their own identity, it's amazing how that changes not only how they see, but how they treat others. God's Word says that if we understand who we are in Christ, we should more naturally seek to love others unconditionally.[15] That's not always easy, but if we don't see value in others, we won't love and serve them as God has commanded us to.

There is an enormous stigma set on people with disabilities in Uganda, especially with children. It is not uncommon for children with physical and mental challenges to be abandoned by their families, or worse. Children with disabilities are often viewed as cursed, or worthless to their community. Many of our students come to school with similar beliefs about disability because they've been taught to believe such things. This dynamic creates a difficult challenge. How do you create value for people who are given no value in the culture in which they live? The short answer is, you don't. Only God can change the heart of a person.

In Jinja there is a phenomenal ministry serving children with disabilities, called Ekisa ("grace" in the local language). Their goal is to provide love and rehabilitation for the children in their care, work with their families to break the stigma of disability, and ultimately resettle the children back into their communities. Along the way, with our students at TAS, we decided to trust the faith and transformation we were seeing, and partner with Ekisa in what would be called the Buddy Program.

The idea was simple: to pair up our students with Ekisa kids and offer an opportunity for them to spend some time together. To get things going, Ekisa came to our campus and did a presentation on the truth about disability. As part of it, they presented the option for our students to voluntarily join the pilot program. The response was huge. Over half the students in our school expressed interest, which meant we would have multiple teams going on different days. Admittedly, I was surprised, and if I'm honest, I was skeptical of their motivation to participate.

While we have gotten more efficient over the years, the basic program has remained unchanged. Most Saturday mornings, a buddy team from TAS takes a bus over to Ekisa and spends a couple of hours playing, singing, dancing, and sharing with their buddies. As our student population has grown, the percentage of those wanting to participate has grown at an even higher rate. As it turns out, my skepticism was unfounded.

I'm not exaggerating when I say the most tangible evidence of the Holy Spirit I've ever seen has come from watching our students love their buddies at Ekisa. It just doesn't make any sense. How can Ugandan teenagers, in a culture that sets no value on kids with disabilities, find so much joy in loving and serving these children? Well, when we embrace God's grace and develop the correct perspective on God and how he views us, we begin to view others differently, and are motivated to serve. The response of our students is simply the gospel in action.

> **Something to Remember:** The cross of Christ confirms that God loved us, redeemed us, and saved us, completely by his grace, and that he desires a relationship with us. Accepting his invitation to be adopted into the family of God forges a new identity.

With a better understanding of God and how he views us, let's take a look at how the perspective on our circumstances impacts our faith and what it reveals about what we really believe.

CHAPTER 12

GRACE AND CIRCUMSTANCES

I know what it is to be in need, and I know what it is to have plenty. I have learned the secret of being content in any and every situation, whether well fed or hungry, whether living in plenty or in want.

Philippians 4:12

I knew our circumstances were going to dramatically change when we moved to Uganda, but if you had asked me before we left, "Are you ready for this?" I would have said *yes* with confidence. Even though we'd lived in material comfort for most of our marriage, I thought the trials we'd experienced, and how God used them to grow our faith, had prepared us to be content in all circumstances. Here's the thing: you never really know how you will do with living "in want" until you're no longer living "in plenty."

For our first three months in Uganda, we lived in a tiny cottage that we (not so) affectionately called "the brick oven." I've mentioned the weather in Uganda is close to perfect but that doesn't mean the direct sun isn't extremely intense. We're on the equator after all. The cottage sat on a compound with a ten-foot wall around it, that effectively shut out the wonderful breeze that is almost constant here. The roof's overhang was only twelve inches wide and there were no trees to shade the house from the sun. Throughout the day the sun would bake the brick walls with no relief until twilight. The bricks would retain the heat they'd received throughout the day so there wasn't a single moment when the inside of the house was not HOT. Multiple fans were pointed toward us from a couple feet away but it still felt like a hair dryer was blowing in our faces, even as we tried to sleep.

I'm a person who likes to be cold when I sleep. Regardless of the time of year or the temperature outside, the first thing I do when I get to a hotel room is turn on the AC and set it to the coldest-allowable temperature. I was once at the Grand Hyatt in Manhattan during winter, which at that time, still had a central heating and cooling system. You could control the temperature of your room, but only within the boundaries of hot or cold set by the hotel. To me, this was unacceptable. People who get cold can use blankets, but people who get hot have no options. So I convinced the hotel manager to switch the entire hotel to AC. All this to say, I was not at all content in our Ugandan home. Brick ovens should only be for pizza.

Soon after arrival we were struggling to find our footing. Within ten days of being in the country, Danlyn had somehow picked up a nasty bacterial infection. She went to the recommended clinic, which didn't do much to build our confidence in local medical care. Graciously, the nursing director at Amazima brought IVs to Danlyn at the cottage so she could avoid spending more time at the clinic. I was asked to go to the pharmacy to get some additional medicine.

I had been driving in Uganda for only about a week, so I wasn't exactly sure of myself behind the wheel. Worse, the streets in Jinja do not have stop signs, and right-of-way is more of a suggestion than a rule. After retrieving the medicine, I was carefully going through an intersection when out of nowhere, a *boda-boda* (motorcycle taxi) drove right in front of me and I T-boned it, hard. The driver and passenger were both thrown from the vehicle and were laying in the road. I pulled over and got out of the car to check on them. Immediately a small, angry group of men had formed and was coming right at me. I jumped back into the car and started rolling up the window but before it could reach the top, two sets of arms were grabbing for me and the keys in the ignition. There was also a mob around my car banging on the hood and preventing me from moving. In the moment, it was as terrifying as it sounds.

With adrenaline taking over, I managed to push the arms out of the window and started moving the car without much thought for the guys in the way. I yelled to them that I would go to the police station, that happened to be about a block away. I made it to the station but was probably more scared there than at the accident site. Fortunately, the guys on the motorcycle had no broken bones and were able to make it to the police station so we could sort everything out.

If you've seen the movie *Zootopia* and remember the sloth at the DMV, you now have an understanding of the inefficiency of Ugandan government processes. I am not exaggerating when I say it took almost two hours for the officer to handwrite my statement. After sitting in a small, windowless room for over three hours, I learned that the driver of the *boda-boda* was not licensed and certainly not approved to take payment for transport. In addition, there was no doubt the accident was completely his fault.

In Uganda, however, fault doesn't necessarily matter if there is a white-skinned person involved. My car was impounded, and I was ordered to pay for the smashed *boda-boda*, the medical bills, and an "appreciation" payment to the police. If I wasn't scared out of my wits I might have been frustrated by the unfairness of the whole thing, but in reality, I was extremely fortunate to be able to walk away from a situation that could've been much worse.

I made it back to the "oven" to find Danlyn sitting on ice (to cool off) with an IV in her arm hanging from a light fixture. We were both in tears over what we had experienced that day, and even more over the sum of the circumstances that were now our new normal.

Only an understanding of grace would allow us to view these circumstances with the right perspective.

Eventually we moved from the "oven" into a little house on campus that was an upgrade in every way. In addition to being a comfortable space, it also happens to be at the best spot to catch the breeze. With the move our circumstances had changed for the better and so, not surprisingly, life overall seemed better. Over the years we've often had to deal with snakes, rats, giant roaches, and all kinds of bugs. Our house is also home to many geckos who, for some reason, like to poop on Danlyn's belongings (even her toothbrush). We have had a 100 days without power, dozens of days without water, and those special moments without either.

Of course, circumstances are not just external. The hardest times for Danlyn and me come when our lives get connected with the difficulties facing our Ugandan students in their communities. In other words, their circumstances affect our circumstances. Regardless, we learned early on that, like many people, we didn't have a mature view of our circumstances. Somehow, we had moved away from grace as the foundation.

LIFE IS TOUGH

In the eighties, "Life Sucks Then You Die" was a saying that found its way into the culture after appearing on a T-shirt in the classic (and surprisingly excellent) film *Teen Wolf*. As with many trends in the eighties, the saying was exaggerated but not too far off the mark. The reality for most of us, most of the time, is that life is difficult. As much as we want to believe improving our circumstances is the answer to improving our lives, that has never been the case. Obviously, better circumstances help, but they are much less significant than we want to believe or are willing to accept.

My life has had many moments (and seasons) of what would be considered wonderful circumstances, both personally and professionally. But without exception the worldly good I've experienced had very little value when life and relationships got difficult. Even the sum total of my positive circumstances have had no lasting or mitigating effect. None. I believe this is equally true whether I'm talking about my time in Uganda or life in the States.

Even though history and personal experience tell us that improving our circumstances will never ensure a happy life, most of us are willing to bet we are the exception to the rule. We tend to put a lot of faith in the ability of our circumstances to give us happiness. For those of us who grew up in America, this idea is almost unavoidable. From birth we are bombarded with the idea, from every direction and through every medium, that a lifetime of happiness is found through pursuing the best possible environmental, relational, and material circumstances. This idea is so ingrained that we lack any awareness of the danger it brings, and of how opposed it is to the gospel of grace.

Somewhere along the way, subconsciously, we've come to feel entitled to a certain lifestyle. At the time of this writing, our political class wholeheartedly agrees. Trillions of dollars have been spent trying to improve the circumstances of disadvantaged people, but has this solved the problem? Of course, better circumstances can cover a lot of problems for a time, and deliver seasons of happiness, but make no mistake: ultimate joy can't be found in the things of this world.

Far more important than the circumstances themselves, whether they are positive or negative, is our perspective on those circumstances, especially as it relates to our faith.

THE BEST OF TIMES?

There is that moment in *The Matrix* when Neo, for the first time, saw the world around him for what it actually was. From that point forward everything changed...well, actually, nothing had changed.

What changed was his perspective on everything. I had a similar experience related to my perspective on the "best" of circumstances.

In the late nineties the founder of Oracle, Larry Ellison, decided he would take the idea of a reward trip to an entirely new level. The highest achievers at Oracle would be treated to an all-expenses-paid trip to an exotic location where they would be showered with fancy gifts, entertained by popular music artists, and have access to activities most people would only dream of. My former company was Oracle's biggest rival at that time, and desired to beat them in every feasible way, so our CEO decided that our reward trip had to be the best in the corporate world.

I don't know if it succeeded in being the actual best, but if there is a more expensive reward trip out there, I would be surprised. Prior to 2016, if you had asked me about what that trip was like, I would have given you glowing stories of the most wonderful place on earth (at least for that week). My perspective completely changed, however, when I went on a reward trip shortly after returning from a visit to Uganda.

Maybe it was because we had recently made the decision to serve in Uganda, but regardless, nothing felt right. We were in Maui with 1,000 other winners and their guests. As usual, there were no expenses spared and everything was outrageously over-the-top. They flew in Katy Perry for a private concert on the beach, Gary Player for a golf clinic, Lindsay Davenport for a tennis clinic, and six members of the German national team (that had recently won the World Cup) to play soccer with us. They also brought in people from Ray-Ban and Tiffany to set up "stores" at the resort. Every attendee was allowed to pick out whatever they wanted, for free. Upon returning from dinner each night we would find a "pillow gift" usually worth more than $300. Obviously, everyone in attendance was super grateful...NOT!

Almost every conversation we had with other attendees centered on a complaint or disappointment:

- "Katy Perry didn't play long enough," or "Katy Perry was a terrible choice."

- "I can't believe we are required to attend the CEO's speech."

- "I didn't get the massage appointment I wanted."

- "The Oakleys from last year were way better than the Ray-Bans."

- "Why is it Tiffany every year? Can't they pick a different jeweler?"

And on, and on, and on. Many people were stressed out, and the brokenness of relationships was obvious. Moreover, many of the winners had planned to leave the company shortly after the trip. It was a sobering moment for me because it was obvious that this was likely how it was every year, but this was the first time I'd noticed. My perspective had changed, so the ungrateful and entitled responses were painful to hear. I shouldn't have been surprised, because after all, we'd all earned the right to be there. There was no place for grace.

The best that material culture has to offer failed to produce widespread joy and contentment, even for just one week. It was actually quite the opposite. If we pay attention to the world around us we will notice very little correlation between lifestyle and authentic happiness. What does this say about circumstances? Circumstances, on their own, aren't the answer to a better life. For the record, we can only be fully satisfied in Jesus.

Unfortunately, at any given moment, the perspective on our current circumstances also directly impacts the strength of our faith. When life is good, so is God—or so we think. Why is it that when people are in a season of better circumstances they also tend to talk about how good God is? Maybe it's because the prosperity hustlers say that wealth is a sign of God's favor, and a reward for strong faith and good deeds. Maybe it's because blessings have come to be defined in material terms. More likely, it's because peoples' perspective on their circumstances is framed by performance and not by God's grace.

The other consequences of the wrong perspective are that when circumstances are difficult (which they often are), it's hard to avoid feeling like a failure, or feeling that God is withholding blessings because of our actions. When things aren't going as we'd hoped, our faith begins to wane and we find ourselves fighting fear and doubt, unnecessarily. Our responses to difficulty are not surprising because they frequently come from immature perspectives rooted in a system and culture of performance, comparison, and deservedness. In Uganda, the churches will sometimes intentionally teach the wrong perspective to maintain a level of control, which, because of the honor/shame paradigm, is an effective strategy. What a mess!

When things get difficult, our first instinct is usually to try to change our circumstances. Instead, we would be better served by paying attention to our *response* to circumstances, that will tell whether we have the right perspective or not.

FIRST-CENTURY CIRCUMSTANCES

I'm not suggesting we pretend everything is rosy when life is hard, or that we should avoid celebrating when God graciously allows us to enjoy what he has given us. To deny the reality of difficulty wouldn't be a helpful change in perspective, but would only be a way to try to cope. If you genuinely want to face reality in a better and healthier way, trying to control our feelings about our circumstances is futile. The goal is not to just learn how to respond correctly, but instead to develop a perspective from which the correct response *naturally* comes.

Fortunately, that right response to our circumstances, from the right perspective, is not a mystery. The first-century Christians, and especially the leaders of the early church, modeled for us how to view and respond to the circumstances of our lives in the most helpful way, the way that leads to the best possible outcomes: unshakable faith and abundant life in Christ. So what were their circumstances like?

While some of the first converts to Christ were wealthy (like Nicodemus, and Joseph of Arimathea), the vast majority were materially poor. After the resurrection they were both poor and persecuted. By the world's standards, their circumstances were dismal to begin with and got worse when they became Jesus followers. That was certainly the case for the apostle Paul. In his second letter to the Corinthian church, he listed some of the challenges he faced in comparison to other believers.[1] Paul

- worked much harder,
- had been in prison more frequently,
- was flogged more severely,
- was exposed to death repeatedly,
- received from the Jews the forty lashes minus one (five times),
- had been beaten with rods (three times),
- was pelted with stones,
- was shipwrecked (three times),
- was constantly on the move,
- was in danger from rivers, from bandits, from his fellow Jews, and from Gentiles,
- in danger in the city, in the country, and at sea,
- in danger from false believers,
- had labored, and toiled, and often gone without sleep,
- knew hunger, and thirst, and been cold and naked.

On top of everything, Paul also faced "daily the pressure of [his] concern for all the churches" (2 Corinthians 11:28). Other believers may

have not been able to match Paul's resume of suffering, but we know
that the early church suffered greatly and was persecuted constantly.

HOW DID THE FIRST-CENTURY
CHRISTIANS RESPOND?

There is an old poem that was used by a comedy artist in the
1940s which says,

> It's easy to grin
> When your ship comes in,
> And your life is a happy lot.
> But a man worthwhile
> Is the man who can smile,
> When his shorts creep up in a knot.

A bit trite for sure, but not entirely wrong. Our response when
circumstances don't go our way says everything about our perspective on them, and on God.

The apostle Paul's response, even in the midst of the direst of circumstances, was *complete gratitude*. No matter the circumstances in
which he was writing (four of his New Testament letters were written while in prison), he expressed his gratitude to believers for their
faith, their love for one another, their faithfulness and obedience, and
for how their actions encouraged him. Paul also frequently shared
how grateful he was to God, for just about everything, including his
suffering for Christ.

Throughout his writings he taught the critical importance of being
grateful. He boldly told the Ephesians they should be "always giving
thanks to God the Father for everything" (Ephesians 5:20). He had a similar message to the church in Thessalonica. After telling them to rejoice
always and pray continually, he said, "Give thanks in all circumstances;
for this is God's will for you in Christ Jesus" (1 Thessalonians 5:18).

Wow, that's a serious call to gratitude! It's one thing for an apostle like Paul to do it, but does he really think the rest of us can give thanks in all circumstances? In his defense, he's obviously never been the fan of a lowly sports team or had to stress about followers on Instagram. We can't brush off this imperative, however, because of what follows. He said it's God's will for us to respond to our circumstances, good or bad, with gratitude. God wants us to be grateful even when life sucks.

Despite his suffering and his frustration with the young churches under his leadership, we have to recognize that Paul was joyful. James, the brother of Jesus, considered it "pure joy" when he was called upon to suffer.[2] The apostle Peter said we should rejoice and praise God when we, as Christians, suffer.[3] This outcome comes from a grateful response to our circumstances, which is only possible with the correct perspective. As I said earlier, we can't just force ourselves to respond differently to our circumstances; our response is determined by our perspective.

Okay, so what is the correct perspective we should seek? What perspective induces a grateful response to all circumstances and contributes to joyful living? Before we go there, let's see what the apostle John says it is NOT. "Do not love the world or anything in the world. If anyone loves the world, love for the Father is not in them" (1 John 2:15).

Youch! John doesn't seem to put much stock in the things of this world, so any perspective that relies on worldly circumstances for happiness, or as a measure of divine reward, is pointless. He also suggests you probably aren't a true Jesus follower if you're all about the "the world." Now, if we take John seriously, we might be in big trouble, given what our cultures teach us. It's also safe to say that John would not be attending a prosperity-teaching church.

For the record, John was one of Jesus' closest friends and followers, was at the cross when Jesus took his last breath, saw the empty tomb with his own eyes, and hung out with Jesus after he rose from the dead. The letter containing this verse was written more than fifty years after the resurrection, after John had had plenty of time to validate the teachings of Jesus.

Remember, the outward circumstances for the early followers of Jesus did NOT improve after the resurrection but got demonstrably worse. After the resurrection, their perspective on their lives and their circumstances was seen through the cross of Christ, and first-hand experience (*epignosis*) with a dead man walking. Paul said it this way: "What is more, I consider everything a loss because of the surpassing worth of knowing Christ Jesus my Lord, for whose sake I have lost all things. I consider them garbage, that I may gain Christ" (Philippians 3:8).

"All things" (circumstances) would now be viewed through what Jesus *had done, was doing* (through the Spirit), and *had promised* to those who place their faith in him.

What had Jesus done? He had fulfilled the righteous requirements of the law and the prophecies from the Hebrew scriptures, satisfied God's wrath, atoned for sin, and installed a new system of love and grace through which believers may have a personal relationship with him. Everyone was equally loved and valued regardless of their past or present performance.

What was Jesus doing? Jesus was actively working in the lives of the first-century believers so they would bear fruit and live out their created purpose through the person of the Holy Spirit.

What had Jesus promised? Well, lots of things, but most importantly to that first group of followers, that they would spend eternity with him. In addition, everything about their lives now would have meaning in the kingdom of God, and no matter what the difficulty, even intense suffering and persecution, God would bring them through it.

Think about it. How could any of his followers view their circumstances any other way than through the frame of Jesus' life, his words, his death, and his resurrection? How else can we explain how Stephen, while being stoned to death, asked God to not condemn those who were killing him?[4] People die all the time for something they believe to be true, but never would someone die for something they know to be a lie. Stephen would have known if Jesus were alive or not. He had the ultimate perspective on his circumstances, even at the point of his death. Fortunately for us, we may also view our circumstances in the same way and receive a great benefit—joy.

WHEN THE LOCKDOWN HIT OUR STUDENTS

For those of us who grew up in youth groups and high school ministries, we are very familiar with the youth camp "high." Unfortunately, we are also familiar with what often happens when the students come down from that high and start dealing again with the real circumstances of the real world. It is only by God's grace that I didn't become cynical because of such things. I did, however, become cautious with how I thought about the spiritual experiences I witnessed with teenagers in the States, especially when I didn't see much confirming fruit. The New Testament is very clear that there will be fruit in the life of a true follower of Christ.

I moved to Uganda with this somewhat-skeptical posture. Since we are a boarding school and we have the students with us 24/7 for thirteen weeks at a time, the breaks between terms become the barometer for the authenticity of their faith. During the holiday periods, our Family Mentors visit the homes of their students to invest in relationships, and to check on them. Most of the time we receive positive reports about the students. In many cases, the appraisals are so positive they are hard to believe. It is not uncommon for a parent or guardian to say, "I don't recognize my child!" (in a good way).

When COVID-19 hit and it became clear that our kids would be back home for an extended period, I was extremely nervous. Would the faith of our students survive what would become the worst circumstances of their lives? Pastor Daniel, our Campus Pastor, is fond of saying, "A faith that hasn't yet been tested is a faith that can't yet be trusted." I'm not sure if that's an original saying from him or not, but regardless it's 100 percent correct. As it relates to the authenticity of their faith, this would undoubtedly be the most trying test of our students' lives.

After Uganda's President Museveni closed schools and locked the country down, there was some initial optimism that students would be back on campus in a couple of months. But as time went on, hopelessness and despair overtook the country, and this was especially felt by the young people. News programs were reporting youth pregnancies and dropouts in terms of *percentages* instead of simple numbers. The statistics were staggering, but who could really expect anything different? For teenagers in the US, the consequences of the lockdowns were found in alarming mental health statistics.[5] Regardless of the locale, students were having a tough time.

After a few months, the President started lifting restrictions about movement, and we quickly started visiting our students again. Since it didn't look like they would be back in school anytime soon, the strategy was to bring Mentors and Teachers to the students, on an almost-daily basis, for consistent learning and discipleship. At least on those days, the students seemed to be responding to their circumstances with a positive attitude and in most cases, with joy. But what about when nobody was watching?

I remember where I was sitting when I learned about a service program our students started during this season, completely on their own, without outside support or funding. I was completely shocked at the news. Apparently, a group of thirty to forty students (depending on the day) were spending their Thursdays and Saturdays serving the most vulnerable in their own communities. Remember, these students are part of families that would also be considered among the most vulnerable, so to hear of their selfless service was emotionally overwhelming to me.

On one Saturday, I was invited by the students to tag along. The recipient of the effort that day was an elderly *jaja* (grandmother) who lived by herself, deep in the village, in a six-foot-by-six-foot mud house. When we reached the place, I was struck by how remote her location was and the lack of any amenities. At one point a student asked her about COVID and she replied, "What's COVID?" She didn't even have a garden because she was too frail to dig. I looked at the small patch of overgrown land and wondered, *What are these students going to do?*

Within ten minutes they were all working their assignments. To this day, I still don't know how they mapped out their plan. One group of boys was digging a latrine while another was building a foundation for a small kitchen. Some of the girls were cleaning whatever clothes the *jaja* had, and others had built a fire to cook her enough food to sustain her for a week or so. Boys and girls worked together to slash the land and apply new mud to the walls of her little home. The most amazing part, however, was watching how the students spent time with the *jaja*. For almost four hours she was never left without multiple students chatting with her.

They listened to her stories from long ago and asked questions about her life and family. Some of the girls playfully teased her and brought out some much-needed laughter. Above all, the woman was shown love, in the name of Jesus, and given a dignity she hadn't experienced in a long time.

When the work was finished for the day, I had to ask, "What's next for her?" I was told a smaller group would be back to finish the projects on her property, and that moving forward, students would take turns checking on her. Amazing.

These same students didn't know where their next meal would come from during that season. There was sickness, death, and despair all around them. They had no idea when they would be back to school and were seeing, in great numbers, their friends from other schools giving up on life. Some pastors in their community were pushing false teachings and using the people's hopelessness to enrich themselves. I would not have been surprised if our students had fallen prey to the difficulties they were facing. Who could survive such circumstances with their faith still together?

I will always believe God graciously provided special protection for our students in that time of great trial. Apart from him, there is simply no explanation. Their response to this great test, however, provides a window into their perspective of their circumstances. God had matured their perspective in a way that allowed them to see their circumstances through the lens of what God *has done, is doing,* and *has promised*—just like the first-century Christians. Their response? Gratitude. And the outcome, even in that difficult season, was peace, joy, and contentment. After more than a year out of school, having faced the worst this broken world had to offer, all but two of our students returned. Again, amazing.

Or maybe not. Maybe it's the response we should expect when we have the correct perspective of our circumstances. In light of what was accomplished on the cross for us, and what it means for us in this life and the next, how can we let negative circumstances steal our joy or make us question the person of Jesus? How can we allow positive circumstances lead us to pride or a distortion of God's grace? In addition, the right perspective will allow us to acknowledge that sometimes trials come so the genuineness of our faith can be proven.[6] If you want to know if you are moving toward the correct perspective, just look at how you typically respond to the ups and downs of life.

God has used our students in Uganda to mature my perspective. Their response to difficulty and poverty has contributed to my certainty about the truth and wisdom of Scripture. I'm even confident that I could now face the brick oven with a grateful heart and a smile on my face.

> **Something to Remember:** Only through a right perspective on the cross, framed by grace, can we respond to circumstances with the gratitude and humility that will point others to Christ.

Learning to view circumstances through what God *has done, is doing,* and *has promised* is hard because it's unnatural and against our performance-driven cultures. In the same way, it's extremely difficult to view *God's rules* with the right understanding, framed by grace.

CHAPTER 13

PERSPECTIVE ON GOD'S RULES

Christ is the end of the law for
righteousness to everyone that believeth.

Romans 10:4 (kjv)

The official language of Uganda is English, so when I was brainstorming what the Student Life ministry would look like at TAS, I didn't think we'd have a language barrier to overcome. I was wrong.

When our first students arrived, their ability to comprehend the English language was significantly lacking, and they had little desire to improve. In the primary schools they had come from, the goal was memorization, not comprehension. Additionally, there was a cultural aversion to English because it was the language most associated with white people. We had a big problem on our hands.

One issue had to do with the students understanding their teachers, who were only speaking English. Another was that I had to figure out how to lead a relational discipleship program with students who knew English words but for the most part, could not coherently speak the language. As a starting point, we implemented a rule prohibiting speaking "vernacular." We told our students not to speak their local languages. As you maybe have guessed, the rule was not received very well (understatement). To make it worse, the students didn't yet know my motivation and couldn't understand the purpose for the rule. Their perspective led only to resistance and a consistent negative response.

Among the staff—and especially among our Ugandan teachers—we had complete unity on the importance of mastering English. The head of the English and Language Department, Ms. Joanita, was probably the fiercest proponent of making sure we did everything we could to help our kids learn. It was (and is) her assertion that the only way our students can compete in a culture with limited opportunity is to master the English language. Our motivation was in the best interest of the students, and the purpose for the English-only rule was to help our students succeed. It took almost two years for the students to accept the idea of intentionally and consistently practicing their English. Everything finally came together in 2018.

Debate competitions are a big deal in Uganda. With the honor/ shame dynamic alive and well, every secondary school that wants to be taken seriously will submit teams to compete at the district level. A good performance earns a spot at the regionals and then, possibly, at the national competition, held at the end of the year. The Amazima School debate team in 2018 consisted of six of our Senior One (S1) students, who would be competing against students who were at the "college" levels of secondary school (S5 and S6), and representing some of the most well-known and respected schools in Uganda. Nobody expected our kids to compete well. This first year of competition was to just be for experience and exposure—or so we thought.

From the district event, our six students (two teams of three) all qualified for the regional competition. I have always felt uncomfortable watching any of my students compete (at anything) but since we were at that point only there for the learning experience, I decided to attend. Throughout the morning our teams performed well, and one of them, a team of three girls, made it to the semifinal round. They were to face a regional powerhouse, and honestly, I was nervous for them.

Their debate was against a school called Kiira College Butiki which, in addition to having great debaters, were known for their signature green blazers. The three young men on their team had certainly never heard of TAS, and maybe had taken part in the ridicule our students experienced earlier in the day. Whenever TAS students compete in anything, they are made fun of for being from poor villages and are often called orphans, which is about as hurtful a thing as one kid can say to another in Uganda. Our students were undeterred, however, and ready for the challenge.

I remember, in great detail, most of that semifinal debate because of the person I was standing beside. It wasn't on purpose (or maybe it was), but I found myself next to the head of the National Debate Council (NDC), who was also the coach for the Kiira College team. As the debate got going and the TAS girls began to show why they had made it to the semis, the NDC guy started asking me questions.

"What level are these students?"

"Senior One," I replied.

"Are you sure?"

"Very sure."

"What is happening at this school to have S1 girls debate like this?"

"Well, for starters, we teach students *how to think* rather than just *what to think*."

Our team beat their opponent and qualified for the national competition that would bring together the top sixty schools in the country.

The national debate competition that year would prove to be a great experience for our three students and served to validate our tireless push to have our students master English. The students recognized that their progression in the English language was one of the key reasons for their success. In other words, they finally understood the *purpose* for the rule. At the same time, they also developed a trust for the rule-givers who consistently and tirelessly enforced the rule against speaking local languages.

Soon after, the students changed their perspective on the whole structure of rules given to them. Because their perspective had changed, their response was now (mostly) positive, and collectively they began to thrive. The intended benefit was finally being realized. By the end of the following year (2019), not a single student in the entire school failed math or English. Not one.

Oh, and that same year our debate team made it back to the nationals in Kampala and beat the defending champions before falling in the semis, after a controversial 2-1 ruling. Their unlikely success became a national story. Two of the major news outlets reported on how three S2 girls from a little-known school in Jinja took down the champs and almost made it all the way.

WHO NEEDS RULES?

Laws and rules are fundamental to every aspect of our lives. We need rules for order and safety as we interact with each other and the environment around us. Without rules, there could be no games or sports. Ethics can't exist without laws and structure. The basic idea of fairness can't operate without laws to legislate activity. Even the concepts of good and evil disappear without a moral law. Given all this, why do we so often resist the rules and laws we are given?

Well, nobody likes to be told what to do, and for some reason, many of us enjoy breaking the rules. Even the Dalai Lama is credited with saying, "Know the rules well so you can break them effectively." We all hold strong opinions about which rules we will follow, and in many cases, even stronger opinions about which rules *others* should follow.

Our Ugandan students are no different. We have rule-followers, rule-breakers, and the never-popular rule-enforcers. Our kids come from environments where there is very little structure, so when they first come to school, it is jarringly different from anything they've experienced before. In terms of age, some of our students are adults, which only adds to their resentment against rules and structure. When we began, our first students would say they "hated" the school for the first few months, and their negative responses to our rules made that posture perfectly clear. Their responses were completely determined by their perspective on the rules given to them.

Just like with our *circumstances*, our perspective on God's *rules* will largely determine our response to them. Think about this: Jesus established the new covenant almost 2,000 years ago. The rules for the New Testament church haven't changed at all since that time. And yet today we see a full spectrum of responses, varying from hyper-legalism to a reckless, "do anything you want" misunderstanding of grace. Even if we allow room for exegetical and theological differences, there shouldn't be such a wide range of responses, because God's guidance is not ambiguous.

In order to respond appropriately and to experience the full benefit of the rules God has given us, we must pursue understanding. To get a right perspective on any rules first requires an understanding of the rule-giver and the purpose behind the rules.

MOTIVATION GOOD AND BAD

Our perspective on the rules we are given is heavily influenced by how we view the person who creates or enforces them. Whether or not we trust the rule-giver frames how we think about the rules we are expected to follow, and how we respond. In simple terms, if we trust the person or institution telling us what to do, we will generally follow. When we don't trust, there is division, doubt, fear, and a higher likelihood of noncompliance. There are two things about a rule-giver that we consciously or subconsciously evaluate when deciding whether or not to trust and follow: *motivation* and *credibility*.

When I arrived in Uganda, I had no *credibility* with the community, and because I was a foreign national with white skin, my *motivation* was called into question by default. For one thing, foreign missionaries don't exactly have an exemplary track record in East Africa, and let's be honest, they can be a little (or a lot) strange sometimes. I was also atypical as a missionary, given my background in business, and my role was to develop a never-before-tried student life/discipleship program at a school with a never-before-tried model of education. Oh, and my constituents were among the most disadvantaged in all of Uganda. Fun times.

While it was certainly going to be a significant challenge to prove my motivation and establish credibility, it absolutely had to happen if there was going to be any hope of earning the trust of the community and the trust of the students. My strategy was to first focus on *motivation*.

A.W. Tozer, one of the most influential and effective ministers for the gospel in the twentieth century, said this about motivation: "It is not what a man does that determines whether his work is sacred or secular; it is why he does it. The motive is everything. Let a man sanctify the Lord God in his heart and he can thereafter do no common act."[1]

Maybe you'd say he was overstating, but I don't think so. If our motivation isn't right, the good we're trying to do is no good at all. Instinctively we know this to be true whether we are followers of Jesus or not. Before we give the trust required to follow the rules put in place for us, we must first know and accept the motivation of the rule-giver. A good way to understand motivation is to simply ask, "Does this person have my best interests in mind?"

This concept is most obviously seen in how teenagers question the rules and restrictions given to them by their parents, especially in the realm of technology and social media. There is no debate about the massive dangers and severe consequences of prolonged screen time, especially with social media apps. The motivation of parents who limit their children's access to technology is unquestionably about protection. They feel strongly it's what's best for their child's mental health and well-being. Moreover, in my experience with American teenagers, students who are less connected to their phones are happier and more relationally successful, 100 percent of the time.

In spite of clear evidence in support of limiting access, teenagers still often struggle to trust the motivations behind the restrictions, and as a result question all the rules given by their parents. Again, if the motivation of the rule-giver is not accepted and trusted, the rules won't have the intended benefit.

With people, it can be difficult to assess someone's motivation. With Jesus we don't have that tension.

> Therefore Jesus said again, "Very truly I tell you, I am the gate for the sheep. All who have come before me are thieves and robbers, but the sheep have not listened to them. I am the gate; whoever enters through me will be saved. They will come in and go out, and find pasture. The thief comes only to steal and kill and destroy; I have come that they may have life, and have it to the full" (John 10:7-10).

After talking about the sinister motivation of "thieves and robbers," Jesus clearly stated his own motivation: he came so his "sheep" may have life to the full. We can know, with absolute certainty, that Jesus has our best interests in mind.

Establishing motivation makes it far easier to build trust and will also usually make room for the grace that rule-givers need, since we all make mistakes. In many situations, though, the motivation of a rule-giver is not easy to see. In the absence of known *motivation*, the perceived *credibility* of a rule-giver will largely determine how the recipients of the rules accept and follow them.

A SURFING LESSON

America is in a season of struggle with following the laws of the land, or with following any rules at all. The tepid and often negative response to COVID restrictions had everything to do with distrust of the people who were making the rules, and not necessarily with the rules themselves. There is an ever-eroding lack of trust with our elected officials, media outlets, and unfortunately, leaders in the faith community.[2] In other words, there is a lack of credibility for the people who are directing our society. It also doesn't help that laws are selectively enforced based on politics and emotions. But when a leader has credibility, we're far more likely to follow the rules, even if we don't yet understand the motivation or purpose.

In *The Karate Kid*, Daniel (played by Ralph Macchio) was given a strange set of rules and activities to follow from his sensei, Mr. Miyagi (played by Pat Morita). As part of his karate training, he was asked to do things like wash cars, paint fences, and sand floors, with "no questions asked." Even though the tasks made no sense to him at the time and were frustrating, he did them anyway because Mr. Miyagi had earned credibility with him. Earlier in the film, Miyagi had rescued Daniel from getting beaten up, by single-handedly besting a group of bullies from the rival dojo, Cobra Kai. From that point, Daniel willingly, although sometimes begrudgingly, followed the rules and direction given to him.

I had a brief but memorable experience with this same concept in the warm waters of Hanalei Bay, Kauai, Hawaii. As a baseline, you should know that I am overly competitive with athletic challenges and especially board sports, and I've always struggled to take instruction from others. Embarrassingly, it's usually because of prideful thoughts that tell me I am more talented, so therefore nobody can teach me anything meaningful. That posture changed dramatically when I found myself surfing the same wave as Laird Hamilton.

Danlyn and I had seen him and his wife (Gabrielle Reece) in

a restaurant the night before, where I had successfully restrained myself from "fangirling" all over him. I will admit that when I went out surfing the next morning, it was with the hope that the king of big-wave surfing would be out there. For those of us who grew up in the 1980s, Laird Hamilton was well known for his villain role in the classic film *North Shore*, so naturally my instinct was to call out to him by the name of his character in the movie. "Hey, Burkhart!"

As soon as the words left my mouth, I realized I must have sounded like quite the moron. He graciously smiled and asked me my name and where I was from. His reply was, "Okay, Georgia, let's see what you got." He directed me to catch a wave while he watched. This would be like having Jack Nicklaus watch you hit a drive at the Augusta National Golf Club. I was mortified. Even so, I paddled out, caught a decent wave, and was able to ride it to the end. When I made it back, he said, "Are you a wakeboarder?" Surprised by the question, I replied, "Yes. Why do you ask?"

"Everything is wrong about the way you ride, and it's obvious you're used to riding differently."

I won't lie—that one stung a bit, especially for a guy with pride issues. He then asked if I wanted some pointers to improve my surfing and better enjoy the experience. Usually when someone offers to tell me how to do something, I don't say, "Yes." But this was Laird Hamilton. I didn't know his *motive* but because of his *credibility* as a legendary surfer, I was happy to do whatever he said. His tips paid immediate dividends and I've never forgotten what he taught me. But that kind of positive response to advice or direction is somehow more difficult when it comes to matters of faith.

Credibility in the area of faith can be a tough topic because there is no faith system, aside from Christianity, that has any real credibility in its founding or its development. As a result, the unassailable credibility of Christ, and the growth of his movement, can be controversial or offensive to outsiders. Even Christians are sometimes hesitant, instead of enthusiastically embracing the credibility of Jesus and his teachings. While I can only guess at the source of that resistance, I do know that if we fail to pursue an understanding of Christ's credibility, it limits our acceptance of him as a rule-giver, and of the rules and guidance he gives us to live "full lives."

Given the pure and selfless *motivation* of Christ, combined with his inarguable *credibility* because of the resurrection, we can trust him as a rule-giver like nobody before or after in history. But to have the best perspective on God's rules we also must have the correct view of his *purpose* for the law and the guidance he gives to us.

WHY ALL THESE RULES?

Although God's *purpose* in giving the Old Testament law and the New Testament commands is very clear in Scripture, there is still some confusion in understanding because of the question of how the Old Testament law should be applied in our era, after the resurrection. Before the law was given to the Israelites on Mount Sinai, God made a promise to Abraham to bless all the nations of the world through him and his family.[3] In doing so, God also revealed the means by which he would restore the broken relationship between himself and humanity. He was going to use covenants with human beings to accomplish his redemptive work.

The covenant relationship God had with ancient Israel included more than 600 laws. This was to establish a structure for holy living by which God's people would be unique and set apart from other nations. The law highlighted sin and provided the basis for obedience in the covenant relationship between God and Israel. It was much like a contract. If they obeyed, God would bless them, and if they didn't obey, God would respond accordingly.

Even though God's people lived under that contract for more than 1,500 years, they still missed one of the key purposes for the law, which was the need for a Savior to satisfy the contract once and for all. Because this was such a big miss, they struggled to understand how the application of the law changed after the coming of Jesus.

This confusion created a lot of tension and disagreement amongst the first-century followers of Jesus. Jewish Christians were struggling to let go of the law as the basis for their relationship with God and were wanting non-Jewish believers to follow the old rules as well. As a result, the leaders of the early church devoted a lot of their time and teaching to making sure all believers knew the truth about this new paradigm. Paul characterized it this way:

> For what the law was powerless to do because it was weakened by the flesh, God did by sending his own Son in the likeness of sinful flesh to be a sin offering. And so he condemned sin in the flesh, in order that the righteous requirement of the law might be fully met in us, who do not live according to the flesh but according to the Spirit (Romans 8:3-4).

Throughout the book of Acts we see this struggle continuing to play out. In addition, Paul addressed this conflict in many of his letters, including an entire chapter in his letter to the church in Galatia. In chapter three, after reminding Jewish Christians they received the Spirit only through belief and not by "the works of the law," he called them "foolish" and admonished them for continuing to try to earn righteousness by works.[4] He doubled down by saying:

> For all who rely on the works of the law are under a curse, as it is written: "Cursed is everyone who does not continue to do everything written in the Book of the Law." Clearly no one who relies on the law is justified before God, because "the righteous will live by faith" (Galatians 3:10-11).

The laws of the old covenant still had great value to those early Jewish believers, but they were not (and are still not) the means of justification and salvation. Two thousand years later, we are still struggling to understand how to apply the laws given to ancient Israel, in the context of the grace of Jesus. As a result, there are many Christians (and churches) focused on following rules for the wrong reasons. In doing so they miss the benefits intended for New Testament believers.

Fortunately for us, Jesus clarified the purpose of the law, and at the same time harmonized the rules of the old and new covenants. An expert in the law asked him which was the greatest commandment, and he replied, "'Love the Lord your God with all your heart and with all your soul and with all your mind.' This is the first and greatest commandment. And the second is like it: 'Love your neighbor as yourself.' All the Law and the Prophets hang on these two commandments" (Matthew 22:37-40).

Jesus was saying that loving God and loving others best summarizes the old law, and since his new commands also centered on those same big ideas, we can be certain about their purpose and application to us as believers.

God's rules serve to guide us, in wisdom, on how to live and how we are to bring him glory through loving service. The nature of God and his will can be known through looking at the rules he has given to his people. The Old Testament law set the table for the grace of Jesus and the new application for believers in him.

The practice of *comparison*, when it uses the law as a basis for judgment and rewards, ignores what Jesus did to fulfill the requirements of the law, and fosters legalism, with its inevitable and devastating consequences. The person who has a distorted perspective, who misunderstands the purpose of the law, or who misapplies it, will miss out on the benefits that come with faithful discipleship.

In Uganda, it took almost three years before the staff, the students, and the community trusted my motivation for being there and granted me the credibility to build the Student Life program. It was a painful process, and I almost gave up many times, but it was absolutely necessary if I were to effectively implement a new and very different approach to discipleship with our students.

Gratefully, and only by God's grace, the students came to have a confidence in me, and a belief that I was working for their best interests. This, together with a gracious understanding of the purpose of the structure, meant there were few obstacles to guiding our students in meaningful, life-changing activity.

Something to Remember: Because of God's unquestionable *credibility* and his good *purpose* for the rules he gives to us, we can let go of the pressure of performance and view his guidance as a gift of grace.

God doesn't ask us to do anything that *isn't* good for us, nor does he ask us to avoid anything that *is* good for us. The correct perspective on God's rules will eventually result in a consistent response: *joyful obedience*.

CHAPTER 14

JOYFUL OBEDIENCE

Blessed rather are those who hear
the word of God and obey it.

LUKE 11:28

The first time I met Akim, I was struck by his intensity. He was proud of his Muslim faith and was ready to challenge the idea of Jesus as the only Savior. Even before our friendship had developed, he would ask me questions about Islam and Christianity that basically dared me to talk badly about the only faith he'd ever known. As with others who tried the same strategy, I didn't take the bait. Our conversations were cordial but purposeful. Consistent with our discipleship strategy, I asked him why he believed what he believed, and then also casually asked what he knew about Jesus.

Like almost every Muslim I've ever met in Uganda, Akim's faith was not really his own, but was instead the faith of his family and community. He'd never tested his faith in any way, and certainly had not considered the person of Jesus before coming to our school. For a Muslim, becoming a Christian can mean losing your family, and in some cases, your life. His consistent position was, "I have no desire to know about Christ."

Because he was frequently challenged to develop a faith of his own, Akim was eventually drawn to the message of Christ. As he struggled with what to do with what he was learning and how he was feeling, Pastor Daniel specifically told him to be patient, and to seek an understanding of grace before making any kind of decision, because if he decided to place his faith in Christ, his life would dramatically change. He would be called to a different kind of *obedience*.

Akim knew the gravity of the decision, having grown up in a community where there were no Christians. Despite the trouble that would inevitably come his way, he eventually said *yes* to God's calling and placed his faith in the finished work of the cross and resurrection. One day when he was back at home, in the midst of his Muslim community, Akim got on his knees and surrendered to Christ.

In the days that followed, his community rejected him, and his own family told him he'd have to find a new one. Akim described his parents' reaction to his conversion as "furious quiet." When his father finally broke the silence, his first words were, "Why did you leave us?" Akim's perspective had changed; he now viewed everything differently. Even the dramatic rejection of his community would not deter him from joyfully obeying what Jesus had asked him to do. So after being rejected he prayed: "Give me the strength I need to shine you out, and to do what you taught us to do, so I can help the rest to know you."

As I type these words I'm amazed again at the maturity of his prayer. If I wasn't there to hear it, I probably wouldn't believe it. How could a Ugandan teenager so readily understand the gospel and accept the call to obedience, for the right reasons? Akim was fond of quoting the Great Commission, but more than that, he lived it out authentically and with joy. He understood the need to model what it looks like to be a follower of Jesus, with the goal of leading others to him.

Unafraid of what might happen to him personally, Akim lived out his faith in his community for all to see. Eventually, people started asking him questions, and God graciously allowed him to share his faith in a meaningful way. At the time of this writing, ten of the eleven members of his family have become Christians, and the entire community around them is changing. Even in this difficult season, there is a hope in his village that was not there before, and a joy unexplainable apart from Jesus.

Cultural norms, deep traditions, and the general pressure to conform sometimes can make even the wisest decisions seem impractical and unreasonable. Even though Jesus offers a certain path to complete joy (through obedience), we can carry a wrong perspective that limits our ability and willingness to obey. Subsequently, we may unnecessarily live a life lacking in real happiness, and instead follow the same approach that has failed every generation. Unless our view of obedience is in alignment with God's Word and rooted in his grace, we will not experience the promised joy.

Mature perspectives about God, ourselves, and his rules will lead to better choices and happier outcomes, but we can't simply change our perspectives by just deciding to do so. Our knowledge of the right thing to do, no matter how correct and well developed, is not enough. So what are we to do? What is our role in pursuing the right understanding and the right perspective?

Simply stated, we are to *apply* what we learn in Scripture and *obey* his commands. Continued growth to mature perspectives requires decisive actions and willful obedience. Our job, as believers in the one, true God, is (and always has been) to apply God's wisdom and obey his commands—even when we don't understand. We're to obey when things are going well, and obey when we are suffering or being persecuted. If we trust God we will do what he guides and commands us to do. There can be no authentic trust in God without willful actions and obedience.

Let's start with looking at what Scripture says about the idea of *application*.

DON'T JUST LISTEN

If you struggle with applying what you learn, even as you grow in understanding through Scripture and experience, you're in good company with the first-century Christians. The early followers of Christ struggled mightily with application, even though they were eyewitnesses to the miracles of Jesus. The Jewish Christians also had the additional wisdom of God's Word in the Hebrew Scriptures (the Old Testament). Unfortunately, like most of us, they were "hearers only" and not "doers of the word."[1] Jesus knew this and made sure to encourage his followers to apply his wisdom.

> As for everyone who comes to me and hears my words and puts them into practice, I will show you what they are like. They are like a man building a house, who dug down deep and laid the foundation on rock. When a flood came, the torrent struck that house but could not shake it, because it was well built. But the one who hears my words and does not put them into practice is like a man who built a house on the ground without a foundation. The moment the torrent struck that house, it collapsed and its destruction was complete (Luke 6:47-49).

In this context, Jesus was not talking about belief and nonbelief. He was also not (directly) addressing the concept of obedience. He was specifically talking about the issue of his followers not applying the wise instructions he had given to them. The message is clear: applying his Word prepares us for the inevitable storms of this world, and not doing so leads to complete destruction. James, the brother of Jesus, illustrated the same principle by saying,

> Do not merely listen to the word, and so deceive yourselves. Do what it says. Anyone who listens to the word but

does not do what it says is like someone who looks at his face in a mirror and, after looking at himself, goes away and immediately forgets what he looks like. But whoever looks intently into the perfect law that gives freedom, and continues in it—not forgetting what they have heard, but doing it—they will be blessed in what they do (James 1:22-25).

In the second chapter of Romans, Paul joined Jesus and James in teaching about the difference between hearing and doing, and went even further by calling out his fellow Jews who were proud of their knowledge, but did not put it into action.[2] It's important to note that in all three examples, the benefits of applying and obeying the Word, or the consequences of not doing so, come as natural outcomes and not direct judgments from God. We are not expressly rewarded or punished on the basis of our performance in applying and obeying the Word or not.

Jesus, James, and Paul are making an appeal for believers to apply the wisdom of what the Word says, because doing so greatly benefits us, strengthens our faith, brings blessing, and protects us from spiritual dangers.

THE JOY CONNECTION

For many reasons, it's not easy for Christians to obey God. If you're reading this and you call yourself a Christian, you probably agree. At the most basic level, the sheer volume of rules and commandments in the New Testament can be overwhelming. Even if we have gained the right perspective of the rules, it's difficult to know where to begin or how to obey everything.

You know the saying, "Actions speak louder than words." The best-case scenario, however, is when actions are in harmony with words. Jesus was so devoted to teaching and modeling obedience that we should have no confusion about the critical importance of it. At key moments throughout his ministry, he repeatedly taught about the significance of obedience, and he consistently commanded his followers to obey him.

The apostle John, who was in attendance, documented for us what Jesus said at what is commonly known as the Last Supper. What Jesus said that night, the night before he was to be tortured and killed, were the most important words ever spoken in all of history. As part of his farewell discourse, Jesus emphasized the centrality and importance of obedience. He taught that obedience is the proof of love— that the person who obeys him is the person who loves him. He also taught that the person who obeys him will receive the Holy Spirit. "If you love me, keep my commands. And I will ask the Father, and he will give you another advocate to help you and be with you forever—the Spirit of truth" (John 14:15-17).

A few verses later, Jesus reinforced this idea by saying, "Whoever has my commands and keeps them is the one who loves me. The one who loves me will be loved by my Father, and I too will love them and show myself to them" (John 14:21). After Judas (not *that* Judas) asked a question, Jesus continued his teaching about the close connection between love, obedience, and saving faith. "Anyone who loves me will obey my teaching. My Father will love them, and we will come to them and make our home with them. Anyone who does not love me will not obey my teaching. These words you hear are not my own; they belong to the Father who sent me" (John 14:23-24).

There is not much wiggle room in this passage. If we are consistently choosing to disobey God's commands we probably don't have saving faith, because according to Jesus, obedience is the *evidence* of love. If we authentically love him, we will obey him by loving God and others. If this sounds narrow or harsh, consider these words from the apostle John:

- "We know that we have come to know him if we keep his commands. Whoever says, "I know him," but does not do what he commands is a liar, and the truth is not in that person. But if anyone obeys his word, love for God is truly made complete in them. This is how we know we are in him: Whoever claims to live in him must live as Jesus did" (1 John 2:3-6).

- "This is how we know that we love the children of God: by loving God and carrying out his commands. In fact, this is love for God: to keep his commands" (1 John 5:2-3).

This does not mean we have control over God's love, his favor, or our salvation, based on our obedience. Obedience that comes from a feeling of obligation, or from a desire to earn God's favor, is not meaningful in this context. It does not glorify God or please him. The right kind of obedience, that confirms we are in him and he is in us, is sincere and willful obedience, flowing out of gratitude and love for him.

We all know the difference between selfish, obligatory, or forced obedience and sincere, willful, or joyful obedience. If we are honest, we can see the difference by simply thinking about our attitude toward obedience in our own lives. Here is what the wrong kind of obedience might look like with a teenager and his dad:

"Before you go out tonight, I would like for you to wash your car."

"Come on! It's not that dirty, and I was going to watch a movie this afternoon."

"I understand this request was not in your plans, but I would appreciate it."

"Maybe I'll just stay home then. It's not fair that you're asking me to do this on short notice."

"Okay. If that's your decision, I understand."

"FINE. I'LL DO IT."

You can guess what happened next, right? The dad was so beaming with pride at the obedience of his son that he texted his buddies to brag about it! (That's sarcasm, in case you missed it.)

Early on, this sort of obedience was typical from our students in Uganda. They'd obey the rules out of fear for losing their scholarships, to gain favor with staff, or to be seen as better than their fellow students. Not surprisingly, their poor attitudes about obedience revealed their lack of sincerity. Selfish, obligatory, or forced obedience is not the type Jesus is asking for. Fortunately for us, we don't have to guess or make any assumptions. Jesus told us what he wants from us: *joyful obedience*.

Later in the conversation in the Upper Room, Jesus used the metaphor of a vine and branches to teach about living joyful, loving, and God-glorifying lives. He taught about how obedience confirms our faith, and about how keeping his commands is how we stay connected to him and produce fruit. Jesus, "the true vine," is the only source of the life-giving fruit of love and joy.[3]

Jesus taught that real "fruit" (which includes joy) is only produced when we abide in him.[4] The Greek word that is most often translated "abide" means to stay, remain, or wait. Since John uses the word over fifty times in his writings, it's easy to discern his intended meaning. In this case, a good working definition for "abide" is "active fellowship" or "connection."

> As the Father has loved me, so have I loved you. Now remain [abide] in my love. If you keep my commands, you will remain [abide] in my love, just as I have kept my Father's commands and remain [abide] in his love. I have told you this so that my joy may be in you and that your joy may be complete (John 15:9-11).

You could read this passage in a legalistic way, but remember that the idea of earning God's favor through obedience was canceled through Jesus. Obedience is not the means to a saving connection (abiding) with Jesus. As it relates to salvation, there is no back-and-forth swing of disconnecting and reconnecting to Jesus based on how well we obey. Obedience comes from a connected, active fellowship with Jesus, and it's also what allows the believer to produce fruit.

Active fellowship with Jesus will produce a sincere desire to obey, out of love and gratitude. If we are willfully obeying, then our connection to Jesus in a divine, loving relationship will result in complete joy, including effective and joyful obedience. What could be better?

According to Scripture, when we choose to obey, we produce good fruit, especially the fruit of love and joy. Even with this understanding, God's people have always had a tough time obeying him; that has made consistent, joyful obedience elusive.

In our flesh, obedience is not natural, which is why we need the help of Jesus in order to obey him. In fact, we often go beyond simply not obeying and instead, willfully disobey. We need to become aware of our disobedience, acknowledge it, and deal with it, if we hope to grow in our relationship with Jesus and find our way to joyful obedience.

FOMO AND EMO

Disobedience is ugly, and almost always results in serious consequences. All the harm done by Christians and churches, for the last 2,000 years, has come from a place of disobedience. No teaching from Jesus leads to devaluing or harming another human being. Somehow, though, Jesus still gets the blame when professing Christians do damage through their disobedience.

In our own lives, the worst times and outcomes we've experienced can often be traced back to disobedience. Probably everyone reading these words has stories of regret resulting from disobedience. I'm confident of this because history tells us that human beings are naturally and universally disobedient. Unfortunately, God's people, from ancient times to the present day, are not exempt from this reality.

Way back in the beginning, when everything was still good, God gave a guy named Adam free reign over a pretty awesome place, but he also asked him to not eat from just one specific tree. Instead of accepting the rule and just enjoying the beauty and richness of all that God had given him, Adam and his wife decided to disobey God and eat the forbidden fruit.[5] The consequences of their disobedience were existentially catastrophic. If you're looking for someone to blame for your sin nature, you can start with Adam.

Things only got worse over time. Ancient Israel's overall relationship with God could best be described as disobedient. In an unfortunate pattern, God proved his faithfulness and graciously gave them rules to follow, but then they would whine and disobey. Still, God never abandoned them and remained faithful to them, even when they suffered the consequences of their disobedience.

Israel's reputation for disobedience was so strong that at a key moment, Moses gathered all the people together in a grand event, to remind them of God's faithfulness, the promised blessings for obedience, and the promised consequences of disobedience to the rules of the covenant. As he passed leadership to Joshua he pleaded with them to honor the covenant. Unfortunately, they didn't listen. Almost 1,500 years later, Stephen was seized and brought in front of a group of Jewish religious leaders, the same group that had Jesus killed. Before being stoned to death Stephen made a remarkable speech in which he reviewed the history of Israel, highlighting their continual rejection of Moses' plea.[6]

Disobedience by God's people has persisted through the ages, although now it looks differently. Today's church doesn't give much attention to the topic. Maybe it's because our right standing with God no longer depends on keeping the Old Testament laws. Maybe it's because our disobedience is harder to measure since it's hiding (in plain sight) in the way we treat people, how we manage our finances, the entertainment we consume, or our priorities. Regardless of how it manifests today, it's still a huge problem, and it can prevent us from a growing fellowship with Jesus.

Obedience to God shouldn't be that hard. In Christ, we don't have to follow the Law to be in a right standing with God, and there are no sacrifices, rituals, or ceremonies we have to navigate when we fall short. In the new covenant, we get to shave, have tattoos, and eat whatever we want, and we don't get executed for sexual immorality. Although there are fewer rules, fewer direct punishments for disobedience, and great benefits for living according to the teaching of Jesus, we somehow still resist God's call to obey him. My question to you is the same one I used to ask my students in the States when they were disobeying God:

How's that working out for you?

How often do you go with your gut or follow your heart when there are clear commands from Scripture to guide you in a better direction? If obedience means trusting God, then disobedience means trusting ourselves. We tend to look for inward guidance because our current post-truth, post-fact culture stands against the basic idea of personal obedience. If each of us can have our own truth, and with that have our own rules, then disobedience doesn't effectively exist as a real concept. If our culture is rooted in this mindset, it's difficult to approach God differently.

In addition to cultural pressures, social dynamics have an enormous effect on how we view disobedience. When a society, directly or indirectly, celebrates disobedient and dangerous behavior, obedience becomes unpopular and offensive, and people are hesitant to follow even the wisest of God's rules, regardless of the obvious benefits.

There are benefits to obedience, but also this: Jesus said that following him will cost us greatly, so obeying him inevitably means trials and suffering. Fear of missing out (FOMO) is one thing, but willful obedience to God is more like *embracing* missing out (EMO). Joyful obedience probably doesn't attract likes or followers on social media. My strong suspicion, based on watching students for a long time, is that we struggle with disobedience mainly because we don't fear the consequences that come with it.

That's a curious thing, since there's not a lot of mystery about the likely outcomes for most questionable actions. There are also thoughtful warnings and reminders we somehow miss or ignore. Maybe the desire to be known and accepted is a stronger force than the fear of consequences. Because the internet can give visibility to just about anyone who wants it, the lure of fame usually overrides any idea of caution. This is especially true through social media. I've known American teenage girls to remain in abusive relationships so they can continue to post about their boyfriends on Instagram. The current generation has grown up with social media practices that are sometimes dangerous or even fatal.

THAT VERSE IN 3 JOHN

As I've written earlier, I've had the great blessing of seeing God's wisdom in the truth of Scripture validated through experience. Since many of these life-changing experiences have been with the remarkable students of TAS, I drew on 3 John 1:4 for what would end up being my final sermon at the school. Here is what the apostle John wrote to a beloved friend named Gaius: "I have no greater joy than to hear that my children are walking in the truth."

Since 2012, long before there was any talk of moving to Uganda, this verse hung above our bed at our home in Georgia. We commissioned an artist to create a unique painting incorporating that verse together with the signatures of all the students we had done life with. Recently I've been thinking about that verse more than ever.

The first thing that strikes me is the "no greater joy" part—especially for the apostle John. Really? What about seeing Jesus rise from the dead? What about the saving and sanctifying work of the Spirit? Didn't John look after Mary the mother of Jesus after the resurrection? Apparently, whatever he meant by "children walking in the truth" was his greatest joy.

In this case, when John said "children," he was talking about people he had led to Christ and for whom he had a deep affection. Because of his close relationship with his spiritual children, he surely wanted the best for them, and would have taught them about the impact of obedience and the wisdom of Scripture. With this understanding, let's look more closely at the entire verse: "I have no greater joy than to hear that my children are walking in the truth" (3 John 1:4).

The Greek word for "walking," *peripateo,* in this context is more accurately translated "walking around." *Peripateo* can also mean "actively living" or "conducting one's life." So in this verse John is saying that his children are gladly choosing to live their lives according to "the truth." If their obedience was selfish, obligatory, or forced, it's not likely John would be excited about their actions. It's also important to note that in this case John was not referring to a saving knowledge of the gospel when he said, "the truth." Rather, he was talking in a general sense about the infallible and life-giving teaching of Jesus. So the source of John's greatest joy was a group of "students" who willingly and joyfully organized their lives around Jesus.

Studying this verse allowed me to realize why my experience here in Uganda with the students of TAS has resulted in such an unexpected joy for me. I love them deeply and would do anything for them to know Jesus and the abundant life he offers. I want them to enjoy the life-giving fruit of the Spirit and have mature perspectives. Watching my Uganda "kids" obediently embrace the teaching of Jesus and grow in joy, regardless of their circumstances, in a culture that is so often at odds with his guidance, has been the most encouraging experience of my life.

After preaching that last sermon and further reflecting on the remarkable and unlikely joyful obedience of our students, I said to Danlyn that I couldn't be more certain of Christ even if I'd been alive to see the resurrection. Scripture says that if we love him, we'll obey him, out of gratitude. When we obey, we're in an abiding relationship with Christ, which produces life-giving fruit, including joy—a joy unaffected by the difficulties we face or the culture we live in.

In Uganda, I have seen this teaching from Jesus play out in the most dramatic and confirming ways. These recent experiences have also helped me see that it was also happening throughout my time in student ministry in the States. I just needed the right perspective to view God's call to obedience as evidence of his gracious love.

> **Something to Remember:** According to Jesus, organizing our lives around his teaching, through sincere obedience, leads to complete joy.

So obedience leads to joy. The next question is, Where do we focus our obedience? Where do we begin?

CHAPTER 15

WWJ(HU)D?

Don't pity the dead, Harry. Pity the living,
and above all, those who live without love.[1]

ALBUS DUMBLEDORE

I n 2013, I led my first student trip to Uganda, with a special group of high school graduates I had grown to love deeply. They courageously and faithfully lived life differently than most of the kids their age and were a source of great encouragement and joy to me. All of them had been on short-term trips before and were excited to apply their experience and gifts to serve the people of Uganda. Our goal was simply to come alongside Champions United, who uses soccer as a tool of discipleship, and shows the love of Christ through programs designed to give dignity to young people.

The days were long and tiring. We spent most of the time with local kids, under the warm Ugandan sun, with few breaks. There was always some time allowed at the end of each day to take a deep breath and relax a bit before dinner. But some of the students had an excess of energy and looked for more to do. They asked the Ugandan coaches what they might do that would be helpful to the community in their afternoon spare time.

The coaches suggested they visit the local well and offer help in carrying water back to homes. In the late afternoons there was typically a large gathering at the well, mostly women and children, who queued up to fill their jerry cans for the evening. Once filled, the jugs were extremely heavy, so an offer to help carry them would be a welcomed gift. It sounded like a good idea, so a few students set off for the well with some coaches, ready to help anyone who would appreciate it.

When they returned, those who participated had good things to say. The Ugandan coaches, even more than the students, were amazed by how this simple task created opportunities for conversation between people who hadn't previously met. The following afternoon, the same group, with some new additions, went back to the well to again help with carrying water. As the effort grew, so did the number of meaningful conversations. Students and coaches were often invited into homes for fellowship, and sometimes were given the opportunity to explain why they were so different from everyone else.

One person didn't like what she was seeing. Hajara lived directly across the street from the well. She had been watching every afternoon and felt a growing frustration. After the third day, she'd had enough. She sent her brother over to the well to talk to the students. "Excuse me. My sister is bothered by what you are doing. She wants to know why you are helping carry water for these people. What are you gaining?" Brice, one of our students, saw her standing across the dirt road and said to the brother, "Let's go talk to her." Brice, the brother, and two other students walked across the street to meet her.

"Your brother said you were curious about why we are helping carry water?"

"Yes," she said. "People don't help people without wanting something in return. You are surely exploiting them, somehow."

Brice replied with, "What do you know about Jesus?"

A bit taken aback, she said, "I'm a Muslim; I know nothing about Jesus."

"Would you like to hear about Jesus? He's the reason we're help-ing carry water."

For some reason, she decided to listen. After talking with her about Jesus for thirty minutes or so, it was time for our students to head back. Before they could leave, Hajara asked if they would come back again. That evening, the guys told me about the conversation and asked for help with what they should share the next day, if they were to see her again.

I suggested they talk with her about grace, the grace that only exists in Jesus. The grace that shapes our perspectives. The grace that frees us from the shackles of shame. The grace that says we don't have to be "good enough." The grace that says we are loved unconditionally, regardless of our past. The grace that says that she, a woman born into Islam, has equal value.

The next afternoon, our whole team was at the school where the well was located. Many people came as before to fetch water, but there were also many who came just to continue the conversations that had started on the previous days. Hajara was also there, and ready to hear more about Jesus. The guys started with the parable of the prod-igal son and spent a couple of hours with her talking about God's incredible grace. When we gathered as a team that night, we listened with amazement as they shared about what had transpired. Unbeliev-ably (or not), Hajara had asked for them to come again the next day.

I remember standing across the road when I saw them praying together. Our three students, Hajara, and her brother were all hold-ing hands as one of the students prayed. The team had been also praying, both individually and together, for God to use their con-versations to bring Hajara to faith in him. When they were finished and had dispersed, I waited for the guys to cross the road and tell me what had happened.

"How'd things end up?" I asked.

"Brice just simply asked her what she thought about Jesus now."

"Well, what did she say?"

With the biggest grin I'd ever seen on his face, Brice replied, "Hajara said, 'I think I love this Jesus.' She then asked how to become a Christian, so we guided her to pray, in her own words, to receive Christ."

Given the cynical nature of Western culture, maybe you're doubting the authenticity of her conversion, and in general, the significance of this story. That would be a mistake. We provided a Bible for her in the local language so she could begin to study God's Word on her own. The coaches would check in with her from time to time, and a couple of our students stayed in contact through Facebook. Hajara ended up moving out of the country to be with some family in a place where she hoped to get a job. When her relatives found out she had become a Christian, they gave her an ultimatum: reject Christ or leave the family. She chose to leave the family. Her relationship with Jesus was real, and even the uncertainty of facing the future after losing her family couldn't change her decision.

For me, this experience confirmed my understanding (*epignosis*) that if we do what God asks us to do, we will see what is true about God and the world he created. If willful obedience is that important and valuable, where do we prioritize or focus our obedience? More specifically, which commands are most important? Which guidance, when followed, will lead to the closest connection with Jesus and the joy he promised? In addition to being the author and perfector of our faith, Jesus is the source of our call to obedience, so we would be wise to pay close attention to what he taught on this topic. In other words...

WWJHUD

The WWJD bracelets have been around a long time, and I've always been a fan. They're certainly a great reminder to pay attention to our actions, but let's face it, we ain't Jesus. We can't do what he could do, at least not in our own strength. The better way is to try to understand what he would *have us* do and go from there. Unfortunately, we often prefer cherry-picking the commands we think are easier to obey, or that can be used to put down or judge others. Ironically, Jesus commands us to not judge in that way.[2] At the same time, we typically avoid the commands that are difficult or inconvenient.

It's the difficult commands, however, that are often the most critical to personal growth and our relationship with Jesus. By my count, there are about fifty direct commands from Jesus recorded in the four accounts of his life (the Gospels). I'm going to focus on the few that I've seen to have the greatest impact on my life and on the lives of the young people I've had the privilege of leading. Logically, we should start with the commands that Jesus said were the most important. Love God. Love Others.

THE GREATEST

"'Love the Lord your God with all your heart and with all your soul and with all your mind.' This is the first and greatest commandment. And the second is like it: 'Love your neighbor as yourself'" (Matthew 22:37-39). Jesus said this after being challenged by a Pharisee (teacher of the law) who had asked him which of the commandments in the Law was the "greatest." Jesus responded with two laws, from Deuteronomy and Leviticus,[3] which together teach us to love God with everything, and to love our neighbors.

If this was all Jesus ever said on the subject, it would be enough to confirm that love is the supreme ethic of Christianity, and the command we should take most seriously. This idea is so important that Jesus repeatedly emphasized it in his teaching, and consistently modeled it for all his followers to see. In Luke's Gospel, these same two "greatest" commands were (correctly) given, by a Pharisee, in answer to Jesus' question about what the law says on how to inherit eternal life. The teacher, however, pressed Jesus about who constitutes a "neighbor." Who should be the object of our loving actions? Jesus replied with a story:

> A man was going down from Jerusalem to Jericho, when he was attacked by robbers. They stripped him of his clothes, beat him and went away, leaving him half dead. A priest happened to be going down the same road, and when he saw the man, he passed by on the other side. So too, a Levite, when he came to the place and saw him, passed by on the other side. But a Samaritan, as he traveled, came where the man was; and when he saw him, he took pity on him. He went to him and bandaged his wounds, pouring on oil and wine. Then he put the man on his own donkey, brought him to an inn and took care of him. The next day he took out two denarii and gave them to the innkeeper. "Look after him," he said, "and when I return, I will reimburse you for any extra expense you may have" (Luke 10:30-35).

This story is where we get the idea of a "good Samaritan" in our Western vernacular. Samaritans and Jews hated each other. The suggestion that a hated Samaritan was following the law while two esteemed Jewish leaders were not was a dramatic illustration, and undoubtedly hammered home the point Jesus was trying to make, that our love for others must be indiscriminate. As Bob Goff says, if we want to love God, we have to "love everyone, always." After all, Jesus commanded us to even love our enemies, and to do so with demonstrable, loving actions toward them.[4] Perhaps the most difficult part of the teaching is what comes next. "If you love those who love you, what credit is that to you? Even sinners love those who love them" (Luke 6:32).

That one stings because it hits so close to home. I won't project onto you, but I really struggle with loving people who aren't "my people." Still, I don't let myself off the hook in this area of obedience. It's just too important.

Jesus said this to his disciples, about loving one another: "A new command I give you: Love one another. As I have loved you, so you must love one another. By this everyone will know that you are my disciples, if you love one another" (John 13:34). Now, this wasn't a new command in and of itself, but rather, "new" in the sense of loving like Jesus loved, and in its increased level of importance. From that point forward, Jesus followers were to be *known* by their love for each other.

The apostle Paul, maybe as much as anyone in history, lived his life by the "new command," and consistently used strong and dramatic language to remind believers of how critical it is to live in joyful obedience to Jesus. In his first letter to the believers in Corinth, Paul said that even if he had been given the greatest of spiritual gifts, had mountain-moving faith, and lived a truly selfless life, without love all of it would be completely worthless.[5] Maybe it's because I also tend to speak in absolutes, but I'm a big fan of how Paul talked about important stuff. From what he wrote, here's my favorite as it relates to love: "For in Christ Jesus neither circumcision nor uncircumcision has any value. The only thing that counts is faith expressing itself through love" (Galatians 5:6).

If we are going to organize our lives around the commands of Jesus, love for others is the place to start. Obedience to other commands doesn't matter if we don't nail this one. Also, most of Jesus' commands directly support loving God through loving people. We all know this, right?

If you've been a Christian for any length of time, you've heard all this teaching about loving one another. Even now as I write, it seems rudimentary, and feels like it should be simple to obey such obviously important teaching. For those who've experienced the fruit of joy that comes from doing what we're created to do, it *is* simple. Our founder at Amazima, Katie Davis Majors, is fond of saying, "Just love the one in front of you." For her, it's a choice that comes naturally, from years of faithful obedience.

But for most of us it doesn't (yet) come naturally, nor would we say it is simple. Moreover, we can't just flip a switch and all of a sudden start loving people well, even if we sincerely want to. We can, though, rest in the promise that loving others becomes easier as we mature in perspective and abide in Christ through obedience. We are also able to look to Jesus for his example and his help, so we can consistently do loving actions and guard against doing the right things in the wrong ways. By simply choosing to put the needs of others before our own, we are far more likely to grow in faith and live as effective witnesses for Christ.

ENCOURAGE DAILY

One of the most effective ways to develop an others-first mentality is to treat people as if they are better than ourselves. This approach is an easy place to start, because realistically, we've all had lots of practice. Think about how you act on a first date or in a job interview. What about when you've had the opportunity to meet somebody famous, or maybe a person you admire? Maybe you've never thought about it in these terms, but if you're honest, you have examples of treating people better than you otherwise would have, because of an advantage they represented to you.

As a software executive whose job performance relied on my ability to influence people and gain trust, I became an expert in treating people as if they were better than me, even if it was for the wrong reasons. My favorite steak house in all the world is Del Frisco's in Manhattan. Because many of my clients were based in New York, I was fortunate to be able to host many dinners there during my career. On one particular summer evening I was there with a key executive of one of the largest financial institutions in the world, celebrating a deal that had been signed earlier in the day. From a business-world perspective, this was the most well-known and important person I'd ever had dinner with. With the way I prepared myself and acted, you would've thought my life depended on this meal.

I wore my best-tailored suit, matched it with a killer tie, a fancy shirt, and an even-fancier pair of shoes. I also broke out the expensive watch and pen to complete the ensemble. After getting a little sun at the hotel pool, I got a haircut, a hot shave, and a manicure, to ensure I would look my best. I arrived early at the restaurant to negotiate for the best table and tipped the wait staff, ahead of time, to make certain my guest would be treated as if he were the most important person in the room. There was a lot of information about him online, so I also did the requisite research to prepare for an engaging conversation.

Not surprisingly, it all worked extremely well. My dinner companion certainly felt special that evening, and I gained a position of influence, at least for a season, by simply treating him with the utmost care and respect. Did he deserve it? Not really, but who does? The point is not whether or not he deserved it but rather, how effective is it to treat people this way? In my experience, it's extremely effective, and even more so when we're doing it for their benefit and not our own.

The apostle Paul described the same principle, with the correct perspective, in this way: "Do nothing out of selfish ambition or vain conceit. Rather, in humility value others above yourselves, not looking to your own interests but each of you to the interests of the others" (Philippians 2:3-4).

Jesus modeled this perfectly. Even though he was God, his loving actions toward an undeserving people were for our benefit, and ultimately gave him tremendous influence for his message of salvation. As I said earlier, we are not Jesus, so it's not natural for us to put the needs of others in front of our own. We can start by *choosing* the loving actions that will have the greatest impact on those who would receive our love. In my experience, and in light of the culture of criticism in which we live, the most effective others-first action is to intentionally use *words of encouragement.*

More than any other loving action, encouragement has had the biggest impact, both individually and corporately, on our students and staff in Uganda. Why? In my view, it's because there is such a desperate need, given the complete absence of encouragement in the local culture. The honor/shame dynamic rejects the very idea of encouragement, leading to a low sense of self, which makes it difficult to stand up to self-defeating cultural norms.

In Student Life, our students are taught a kingdom-culture mindset that guides them to prioritize what God says over what their culture or tradition says, so there is some pushback from their communities, that generally have different values and different ideas about God. Because of this, it wasn't surprising to see our students (and staff) get discouraged as they began to understand that what they'd grown up believing about themselves and God wasn't necessarily true.

Similarly, in the first century the way of life for believers completely changed as they transitioned from the temple/sacrificial system to the Jesus way, and in doing so they had to deal with many of the same challenges now facing our students. In that season, the apostle Paul consistently used encouragement as a way to put the needs of others before his own. In every recorded letter he wrote to Jesus followers, encouragement was a critical or dominant theme. In his letter to the church in Ephesus, Paul wrote, in the context of Christian living: "Do not let any unwholesome talk come out of your mouths, but only what is helpful for building others up according to their needs, that it may benefit those who listen" (Ephesians 4:29).

We sometimes read "unwholesome" to mean loose talk or maybe bad words, but that's not what Paul was saying here. It's better translated "unhealthy," and in the context of the rest of the verse, it means any words that are not specifically helpful for the benefit of others.

Words that "build others up according to their needs" are simply words of intentional encouragement. In practical terms, Paul is telling us to discern the needs of others, and to lovingly use words to encourage them, for their benefit.

Based on the wisdom of Paul's consistent teaching and considering the similar environment we serve in in Uganda, I decided to make encouragement part of the DNA for the Student Life program. The effort, however, was met with confusion, and at times, full-on rejection. I had been doing my best to model encouragement for my team, but unfortunately, about six months after the school opened, I realized I wasn't seeing the results I had hoped for. My loving actions were being received very negatively by the Ugandan staff. So much so, they called a meeting to tell me to stop encouraging them, and to make their case as to why Christians shouldn't need to be encouraged.

As we all agreed later, their cultural perspective and initial distrust of me was not allowing them to accept my encouragement as genuine. Because I was certain of the principle, and because I knew my motivation was for their benefit, I was undeterred, and doubled down on my efforts to encourage them. Eventually, love won, and the team fully embraced the idea of encouragement because of how valued they came to feel when receiving it. From that point forward, all meetings, whether with staff or with students, started with what were called "encouragement deposits." Participants would deposit to the "accounts" of others in the meeting, by simply sharing encouraging words, based on what they'd seen or heard recently.

After seeing the power of encouragement play out in real life and in real time, I understand why Paul so consistently encouraged others in their faith in Christ. We all need to be encouraged in order to fight against the lies of the enemy. As the writer of Hebrews wrote, we should "encourage one another daily" (Hebrews 3:13). In America, encouragement has been replaced by hair-trigger criticism. Even in the broader Christian community, the idea of others first, of working for the benefit of others, has all but disappeared. After spending almost five years in Uganda, my feeling is that we need to choose encouragement, no matter the cultural pressures around us.

Encouraging others is a practical and effective way to obey the "new command" to love God by loving people, but there is no better example of where our obedience and another person's benefit comes together as with Jesus' call to share the gospel and make disciples.

> Therefore go and make disciples of all nations, baptizing them in the name of the Father and of the Son and of the Holy Spirit, and teaching them to obey everything I have commanded you. And surely I am with you always, to the very end of the age (Matthew 28:19-20).

In this passage, known as the Great Commission, Jesus again reminded his closest followers of the critical importance of obedience to his commands. In that moment, Jesus commanded them to make disciples, which of course includes sharing the message of the gospel. While there is no debate about the *what* of Jesus' command, there has always been tension about the *how*. If we are serious about obeying Jesus and making disciples, we should desire to know how to be as effective as possible.

No matter where I've lived, there has always been that person who holds up a sign about repentance and screams something about accepting Jesus or going to hell. For some reason, preachers in church sometimes do the same thing (without holding up the sign). You're probably not surprised to learn I'm not impressed with these tactics. Reason being, they most often fail to produce the desired outcome. It may seem unfair to criticize people who are genuinely wanting others to know Christ, but as I wrote earlier, sometimes we inadvertently do the right thing in the wrong way.

There are two primary ways to share the gospel and make disciples, and depending on the context and audience, both can be effective. The obvious and most common way is through words. Whether from the pulpit or through intimate conversations, the Good News of Jesus is powerful, and God certainly uses the words of people to accomplish his work of salvation. In Christian churches and at events all over the world, millions of people have placed their faith in Christ, and have gone on to be faithful disciples, after hearing a moving message. But we aren't all gifted preachers or presenters, so maybe there is more than one way to effectively share the gospel and lead people to faith.

It's been said (by many), "Preach the gospel at all times, and when necessary, use words." Regardless of who coined the statement, the point is that we all are capable of sharing the gospel with how we live, and more specifically, with how we treat people. When it comes to making disciples, modeling what it looks like to live in obedience to Christ is by far the *most* effective way. A changed life is the best witness for Christ, because a fruit-bearing Jesus follower looks different, and people take notice. If the apostle Peter were to redraft this statement, he might say, "Share the gospel at all times, and when asked why you live the way you do, be ready with your words."[6]

Words will always be necessary, but in my experience they're much more effective when they come in response to questions from someone who has watched a person joyfully live out the gospel, regardless of the circumstances. The leaders of the first-century church knew this and consistently taught believers to model their faith for others to see and be challenged.

- "Follow God's example, therefore, as dearly loved children and walk in the way of love, just as Christ loved us and gave himself up for us as a fragrant offering and sacrifice to God" (Ephesians 5:1-2).

- "In everything set them an example by doing what is good. In your teaching show integrity, seriousness and soundness of speech that cannot be condemned, so that those who oppose you may be ashamed because they have nothing bad to say about us" (Titus 2:7-8).

- "Be shepherds of God's flock that is under your care, watching over them—not because you must, but because you are willing, as God wants you to be; not pursuing dishonest gain, but eager to serve; not lording it over those entrusted to you, but being examples to the flock" (1 Peter 5:2-3).

- "You became imitators of us and of the Lord, for you welcomed the message in the midst of severe suffering with the joy given by the Holy Spirit. And so you became a model to all the believers in Macedonia and Achaia" (1 Thessalonians 1:6-7).

When people see us living differently and obediently in love, those actions and the inevitable words that follow should point people to God. Jesus said it this way: "Let your light shine before others, that they may see your good deeds and glorify your Father in heaven" (Matthew 5:16). Jesus commands us to live a life that is different, a life that grabs the attention of others, but also one for which God gets all the credit. Live a life where God's powerful, beautiful, and disruptive grace is on display, a life through which the gospel is shared.

Based on my experiences in responding to What Would Jesus Have Us Do? (WWJHUD), and the success of the first-century Christian leaders in doing the same, we made the easy and obvious decision to build our discipleship strategy around modeling joyful obedience to the commands of Jesus, with a focus on grace. We are committed to willfully and joyfully doing what Jesus has asked us to do, for our students to see. At the same time, we are always ready to answer questions about why we are living so differently from the rest of the culture.

Something to Remember: Jesus is clear about where to prioritize our obedience: Love him by loving others. Share the gospel and make disciples.

God is clear about the most important commands for living the fullness of the Christian life. There is an abundant gift of grace for this: he also gives us the power to accomplish his will and fulfill our created purpose.

SECTION FOUR

THE "REAL HOW"

So far, we've been exploring how important perspectives, framed by brokenness and grace, create an environment of freedom and confidence to embrace obedience. Now we have to deal with the fact that we can't *perform* or *achieve* our way to the full life God has promised. Contrary to what our parents (and others) tell us, we can't really "do anything we put our minds to," nor can we "be anything we want to be." This is particularly true for growing in Christian maturity.

With great effort and a little luck, we can certainly earn most of what the world has to offer, but as Jesus famously said, "What good will it be for someone to gain the whole world, yet forfeit their soul?" (Matthew 16:26). Whether you've heard it said many times or experienced the disappointment yourself, the things our world has to offer will never fully satisfy or lead to contentment. Because God loves us and created us for a purpose, he wants something better for us than "the world." He wants us to experience the complete joy that only comes from walking closely with him.

He doesn't just want this for us; he directs us toward the goal by being very clear about what to do (sincere obedience), and how to do it (loving actions toward others). We have yet to explore, however, the "real how" in accomplishing all he has asked us to do. There is one frame of *awareness, understanding,* and *perspective* left to unpack. And it might just be the most important one.

Maybe you've seen this coming. Throughout this book, I've mentioned the idea that there are important and meaningful things we can't fully accomplish in our own strength or apart from the Holy Spirit. Now we have to deal with it directly. If we truly want to grow or see the changes we desire for the world, we'll have to accept that God provides the strength and power to help us fulfill our purpose and accomplish his will. In other words, the real how is from God.

For the rest of this book, we're going to take a deep dive into the real how and the outcomes promised to those willing to fully depend on God. I'm praying for God to make us keenly aware of our motivations to do good things, and that we'll be open to trusting him for the results of our efforts. My goal is for you to understand how our efforts, in concert with his, can lead to a contented and full life characterized by extraordinary joy.

CHAPTER 16

THE "REAL HOW" IS A "WHO"

The Spirit gives life; the flesh counts for nothing.
The words I have spoken to you—
they are full of the Spirit and life.

JOHN 6:63

All of us, regardless of culture, will sometimes struggle to comprehend the Holy Spirit, how to engage with him, and how to live in his strength. In Uganda, this challenge is compounded by the honor/shame culture most of our staff and students grew up in. I didn't realize the extent of the problem until the day before I was to preach my first message in a series about the fruit of the Spirit.

It was late afternoon on a Saturday, and I was sitting outside, on the veranda of our little house, polishing off my sermon for the following morning. I was ahead of schedule (for a change) and feeling very good about my message. Muggle, the school dog, was sitting on the couch with me, while in the background there were the usual sounds of village life, including that of a cow giving birth in the distance. Suddenly, these familiar sounds were interrupted by strange noises that seemed to be coming from the Family Mentor house for our single female staff.

As I focused my attention, I quicky realized that the loudest voice was definitely not female. A man was chanting loudly in the local language, and every so often I could hear him say, "Fire! Fire!" in English. Because I had no idea what to do, I quickly called Pastor Daniel, who happened to live next door to the Mentor house, to make sure this wasn't a dangerous situation. He had heard the same loud screaming but assured me that everyone was safe. Apparently, the male voice belonged to a "spiritual advisor" and what I was hearing was not uncommon in Uganda. Although it all was a little strange and I was a bit shaken by it, I chose to trust my friend.

A couple of hours later, Daniel came up to my house and asked if he could have a word with me.

"Uncle Kelly, you have to change your sermon for tomorrow."

"Why?" I asked.

"You can't teach about walking in the Spirit until everyone understands the person of the Holy Spirit. Our churches sometimes teach a confusing and wrong view, which makes it difficult to talk about how to authentically walk with him. It's why there was an 'advisor' on campus today."

My initial reaction was an overwhelming sense of dread. This was not because I thought teaching about the Spirit was a bigger challenge in Uganda than in the States. The Western church certainly has many of the same issues and misunderstandings about the Holy Spirit. The way these problems present in Uganda, however, is very different than I had personally experienced before. For example, the Spirit is available *for sale* here in various forms and viewed more in a magical sense than as a member of the trinity, as God himself. I knew it was a large-scale issue, but for some reason I had just assumed our staff had grown beyond those cultural teachings. Never did I think I'd be given the task of blowing up what most of them grew up believing.

One of the biggest challenges with preaching or teaching in a developing country is that wrong perspectives are anchored in the idea of *fairness*. Come to think of it, it's a problem everywhere, since cultures and social structures always tend to be built on a concept of fairness, rewarding effort and performance. All of us have a "fairness gene" that influences much of our actions and attitudes. Regardless of age, experience, or situation, we seem to want, and work toward, a world that we hope will be, at its core, fair. But by any measure, if true fairness is the goal, we continue to fail miserably.

Not surprisingly, we often approach our faith in much the same manner, and (predictably) experience the same poor results. We do our level best to be good, be obedient, and love others, but the joy and contentment we expect, based on our efforts and the idea of fairness, doesn't materialize. We work to improve ourselves, but the positive changes that may come as a result are either short-lived or inadequate. We can manage to do self-help or self-care, but can never do true self-transformation.

We certainly keep trying, though, no matter how many times our efforts fail to get us there. So what's the problem? Why can't we transform ourselves into the people we desire to be? As it turns out, we're our own worst enemies. Our pride, and the cultures we grow up in, combine to fight against the idea that we can't transform our lives or our faith by our own works. The way we see it, if things are fair, then our efforts should logically lead to the results we want for ourselves. Despite experiences to the contrary, our desire for control and independence makes it difficult for us to accept what I am calling the "real how."

This concept played out very specifically in one of my weekly Prefect (student leader) meetings. After everyone had been given their tasks for the week, I asked the group a question: "How many of you would be offended if Uncle Kelly offered to help you with your items?" Twelve of the fourteen students raised their hand. Regardless of the reason, most of us would rather succeed on our own than ask for help. For Christians, this would mean ignoring God's system of grace, and instead pursuing the way of fairness and performance as if we're still under the law.

GRACE AND FAIRNESS

Life is not a game, but if it were, we are playing checkers and God is playing chess. Grace and fairness are completely incompatible, at least in the way we view things. In fact, I would say that God's system of grace is so incredibly and universally *unfair* that it's *perfectly fair*. We don't see it that way, though. It's why there is such a resistance to God's system of grace, and why we struggle to accept our inability to do anything good in our own strength, apart from the "real how."

God understands we have a hard time accepting this truth, so he's made it obvious, if we are willing to pay attention. Have you ever wondered why God asks us to do the impossible? Why he sets unreachable standards we have no chance of consistently meeting? Love our wives as Christ loved the church? Pray continually? Give thanks in all circumstances? Rejoice in suffering? Give me a break!

He does this for the same reason he gave Israel more rules than they could possibly follow—so we will realize we need him and his power to accomplish what he asks of us. In other words, it's all about God's grace, and it always has been.

So where do our efforts intersect with God's grace? I agree with Dallas Willard when he wrote, "Grace is not opposed to effort; it is opposed to earning."[1] If our efforts come only from our own strength, then our motivations, even subconsciously, are likely rooted in whatever benefit we think we can earn. For our efforts to play a positive role in God's system of grace, we must learn how our actions work *together* with the Spirit to accomplish what God has asked us to do.

Before we can go there, we need to wrestle with the hard truth that we can't really do anything good or accomplish anything meaningful on our own, without the real how, which (in case you haven't figured it out yet) is the Holy Spirit.

Let's start by admitting that it's hard to accept it when our efforts don't yield the results we expect, or the acknowledgment we think we deserve. It can be even harder when we see others celebrated for similar or lesser achievements. In these moments, our response is governed by how we deal with the tension of fairness and grace.

In my experience with students on this topic, the big "Aha!" moment comes when they realize their efforts don't earn anything with God, and there is no such thing as fairness in God's economy—at least not the kind of fairness we think we deserve. Only then do they begin to understand that God's grace is in everything and permeates every aspect of our lives.

God's economy of grace is a stark opposite to Uganda's culture of honor and shame. Because of this we had to figure out how to have the tough (but needed) conversations about effort, fairness, and grace. So, with our first class of students at TAS, we tried a simple experiment. We assigned a monetary value to yellow and blue poker chips, that could be used as currency at the school's canteen. The Family Mentors handed out chips at their complete discretion, and there was nothing the students could do to earn them. As you can imagine, the whole thing played out in dramatic ways.

Sometimes a group of students would all be doing the same task, and some would be singled out to receive a chip. The other students in the group would then question why they didn't get a chip for the same work. Sometimes chips were given without a specific explanation, and the recipient was told not to tell anyone about it. Often, a student would be given a chip for a specific act of kindness or service, and then repeat the same deed again, expecting another chip. When they didn't get another chip, they would ask, "Why not?" Initially, our kids were confused by the whole thing, but every time they asked a question it led to an intentional conversation about God's economy of grace. The illustration was so successful that it persists to this day.

The chips program has evolved over the years, but the goal remains the same: to help students understand the difference between the world's economy of fairness and performance, as against God's economy of grace. Even better, it has led to conversations about what is even harder to understand: that we are incapable of doing what God has called us to do, in the way that *most* glorifies him and *most* benefits us, without his power.

COMPLETELY INCAPABLE

Wait—am I saying that God asks us to obey him, but without his help we can't do it in the way he commands? That's exactly what I'm saying. Fortunately for my argument, Jesus said the same thing about our inability to produce (good) fruit by ourselves without the power of the Spirit: "Those who remain in me, and I in them, will produce much fruit. For apart from me you can do nothing" (John 15:5 NLT). This is important, because if we can't accept the need for the Spirit, we will never be able to properly engage the Spirit.

We are made in the image of God, we co-reign with him, and we are created for a purpose—to do good works for the benefit of others and for his glory. But we can do good and helpful things that are, at the same time, not good in God's eyes, and not spiritually beneficial. If this is true (and it is), how do we know if our good is actually good? How do we know if our actions are actually helping us grow in faith, and helping us grow more mature in our perspectives? It centers on our motivation.

If our motivation has to do with our own benefit and our own glory, those good works will have no value to our growth in Christ and will not glorify God. We can do things that are seen by the world as good, but at the same time are not the good for which we've been created. On our own and apart from the Holy Spirit, we can only do things from selfish motivations or a desire for glory. On our own and apart from the Holy Spirit we are incapable to doing anything good for others or spiritually meaningful for us.

God has called us to loving actions for his glory and our good, but he also says we can't do it without him, at least not in the way that aligns with our purpose, or that results in the complete joy and life-giving fruit he desires for us. Some will be encouraged and excited to know that God has graciously provided his Spirit to come alongside us to accomplish his will. Others will push back on the idea, will be discouraged at the (apparent) loss of control, and will struggle to let go of the ideas of fairness and comparative performance.

ALL FROM FAITH; ALL FROM THE SPIRIT

The case of the apostle Paul is helpful to this discussion. Of all those who followed Jesus in the first century, Paul would've benefited most from a system of fairness that rewarded effort and performance. Instead, he consistently pointed to God alone as the source of salvation, faith, and any good deeds that truly honor God. The only way Paul would promote a system that didn't offer him an advantage would be if he knew, from experience, that the system of fairness and reward was not from God.

He also shared about how he struggled when he operated in his own strength: "For I know that good itself does not dwell in me, that is, in my sinful nature. For I have the desire to do what is good, but I cannot carry it out" (Romans 7:18). Paul often taught about how incapable we are in our own strength, by specifically identifying actions that require faith and the Holy Spirit. Even our faith itself is a gift of the Spirit and has nothing to do with our efforts. "For it is by grace you have been saved, through faith—and this is not from yourselves, it is the gift of God—not by works, so that no one can boast" (Ephesians 2:8-9).

With this understanding, we know that whenever we act out of faith, we are acting with God's power. This is important because according to the apostle Paul, "Everything that does not come from faith is sin" (Romans 14:23). Ouch. The writer of Hebrews says it's

"impossible to please God" without acting out of faith (Hebrews
11:6). If our good deeds are not motivated by faith and in coopera-
tion with the Spirit, God is not pleased. Ouch again. As we learned
from Jesus earlier, even the salvation-confirming, fruit-bearing, joy-
giving obedience we are called to is a product of our faith. Paul said
it this way: "Through him we received grace and apostleship to call
all the Gentiles to the obedience that comes from faith for his name's
sake" (Romans 1:5).

Like obedience, true righteousness comes only from faith. Paul recognized this when he described his righteousness as not coming from
the law, "but...through faith in Christ" (Philippians 3:9). As I mentioned before, the prophet Isaiah calls the righteousness that comes
from our good deeds, apart from the Spirit, "filthy rags" (Isaiah 64:6).

Is this starting to make sense? Our efforts, our pursuit of righteousness, regardless of the results, don't matter if they are not out of
faith and through the power of the Holy Spirit. Scripture says that
only in God's strength can we do the good works he's prepared for
us.[2] If we are acting in a God-glorifying way according to his purpose, it's because of his power and his work in us.[3] Not convinced?
Let's keep going.

So much of what we've talked about in this book requires the power
of the Holy Spirit to accomplish. Remember the *epignosis* (experiential understanding) God wants for us? Yep. That critical understanding only comes from God: "His divine power has given us everything
we need for a godly life through our knowledge [*epignosis*] of him
who called us by his own glory and goodness" (2 Peter 1:3).

In the last chapter I talked about serving people in such a way that
others will see how different we are, and that that will point them to
God. Again, we need God's strength to do this consistently, in a way
that glorifies him. Here is how the apostle Peter described it: "If anyone serves, they should do so with the strength God provides, so that
in all things God may be praised through Jesus Christ" (1 Peter 4:11).

What about contentment in all circumstances? Contentment is what Paul was referring to when he wrote, "I can do all this through him who gives me strength" (Philippians 4:13). What about overcoming sin? Can we do that on our own? Not even close. Paul wrote, "For if you live according to the flesh, you will die; but if by the Spirit you put to death the misdeeds of the body, you will live" (Romans 8:13).

Most importantly, we've talked about the true gospel and how salvation is never earned or sustained by our own efforts.[4] Even repentance and belief, the means to receiving the gift of the Holy Spirit, are, in fact, gracious gifts of the Holy Spirit.[5] John Calvin, a sixteenth-century pastor and key leader in the Reformation, summarized this idea beautifully: "Now it ought to be a fact beyond controversy that repentance not only constantly flows from faith but is also born of faith."[6]

Hopefully by this point you're ready to let go of your own efforts as the primary means to accomplish God's will or to grow in spiritual maturity.

FRUIT AND FRUIT

Uganda has a lush and beautiful landscape with an abundance and diversity of trees. Even after living here five years, it's hard for me to identify them when it's not a fruit-bearing season. But when the fruit is growing, the easiest tree to identify is the jackfruit tree because of the unique nature of its fruit. Jackfruit, which is very sticky and tastes like blue Fruit Gushers (seriously), is well known for its massive size and strange appearance. Also, since large fruits or vegetables usually grow on vines spread on the ground, it doesn't seem natural for a fruit larger than a watermelon to be hanging from a tree limb.

What is not natural for other trees is normal for the jackfruit tree. Specific trees and vines produce the fruit that is natural to each of them. Oranges don't grow on apple trees and grapes don't grow on thornbushes. Also, a tree doesn't have to be trained to produce its fruit nor does it have to make any effort; it just happens naturally.

You can identify a tree by the fruit it bears, and the fruit itself also has its own distinctive characteristics like size, color, texture, and taste. But none of these variables are consistent within a given type of fruit. For example, avocados in Uganda are larger and higher in quality than what you would typically see in the States. The bananas here are quite a bit smaller but have a sweeter taste. My point is, fruit of the same name can be different in many ways but still be compared by quality.

Why am I talking about fruit in a chapter about recognizing the need to rely on God? Since Scripture speaks of our actions or choices, whether good or bad, as "fruit," thinking about fruit helps us understand "the fruit of the Spirit."

"The fruit of the Spirit is love, joy, peace, forbearance, kindness, goodness, faithfulness, gentleness and self-control" (Galatians 5:22-23). You may look at this list and think, *I've produced this fruit before*, and you'd probably be correct. But in the same way that two pieces of fruit can have the same name but differ in quality, so two actions by us can have the same name but differ in spiritual effectiveness. One action can be the fruit of the Spirit and the other the fruit of our own efforts. They might be called the same thing but are worlds apart.

A good work may not be a good work at all, depending on our motivations. In the same way, the quality of the fruit we produce has a lot to do with why we are doing good and for whom we are doing it. If we desire to be more patient and are somehow able to do it, but it's through our own efforts and primarily for our own benefit, the world may see it as good while God sees it as of no value.

To be clear, we are incapable of naturally producing God-glorifying fruit. What we produce naturally are things like sexual immorality, greed, hatred, selfish ambition, and envy. So when, through our own efforts, we produce fruit that resembles the fruit of the Spirit, we must not be deceived. The only way for the Spirit's highest-quality, most-effective, God-glorifying fruit to be produced is through the work of the Holy Spirit. It doesn't matter how many books we read or how hard we work to become better people. We can't produce the equivalent of the Spirit's fruit any more than a jackfruit tree can produce passion fruit.

I realize this concept pushes hard against our hardwired desire to perform and achieve, but any Christian who wants to experience the life-giving fruit of the Spirit must surrender the notion of trusting in their own efforts to grow and must learn to depend on God.

LET'S CLEAR SOME MISPERCEPTIONS

We don't have to fully understand the doctrine of the Holy Spirit to walk in the Spirit, but we do have to deal with some common misperceptions that limit our ability to grow or contribute to wrong perspectives and unnecessary consequences. Fortunately, when Jesus was at dinner with his disciples the night before he died, he established the truth about the coming of the Spirit.

> I will ask the Father, and he will give you another advocate to help you and be with you forever—the Spirit of truth. The world cannot accept him, because it neither sees him nor knows him. But you know him, for he lives with you and will be in you (John 14:16-17).

1. The Holy Spirit is an equal person of the Trinity.

He is not just a feeling, a force, or an emotional high. As a person of the Godhead, the Holy Spirit is fully God and is equal in nature and glory to the Father and the Son. The Spirit is the manifest presence of God on earth. This is a big deal. In the passage above, the Greek word for "another" is *allos*. In this context, Jesus uses *allos* to mean "another like him." He wanted his disciples to know that the Spirit who would come upon them would continue Jesus' ministry on earth.

2. We have direct access to the Holy Spirit.

We do not need anyone or anything to engage the Spirit. We have ready access, through a personal relationship, because he lives with and in us. The apostle Paul described it as "the fellowship of the Holy Spirit" (2 Corinthians 13:14). The Greek word he uses for "fellowship" is *koinonia,* which denotes an intimate communion. It means our relationship with the Spirit is intensely personal.

3. The Holy Spirit always lives in us and actively works to help us.

If Jesus said the Spirit is in us and with us forever, then the Spirit is...wait for it...in us and with us forever. He is not a temporary visitor. The Greek word here is *parakletos,* which describes his role in helping us live the Christian life. *Parakletos* means advocate, helper, counselor, encourager, intercessor, and comforter. In other passages the apostle John refers to the Spirit as a guide and teacher.[7] The Holy Spirit is also the person of the Trinity responsible for regeneration (new life) and sanctification (growing in holiness).[8]

An abundance of Scripture says the Spirit will help us with just about anything and everything related to growing in Christian maturity and fulfilling our purpose. He helps us with things like prayer, unbelief, understanding Scripture, fighting against the schemes of the enemy, and even what to say when we are witnessing for Christ.[9]

Let this sink in for a moment. The Savior of the world promised to ask the Father to send the Spirit, we can have an intensely personal relationship with him, and he lives in us as a guide and helper, to accomplish the will of God, for our good and for his glory. In the context of the fairness- and performance-driven world we live in, this is one of the most encouraging truths we can ever know.

Just like our sin problem was addressed on the cross by the person of Jesus Christ, our inability to live fully for the glory of God is addressed by the person of the Holy Spirit. We can't do self-transformation, but

Scripture says the Spirit can transform the heart of the believer.[10] The question for you (and for me) is simply: will we settle for the limited love, joy, peace, forbearance, kindness (and the rest) we can produce on our own, or will we embrace the real how and pursue the life-giving fruit that only comes from him?

Something to Remember: None of us can live the Christian life on our own. We need the fellowship and power of the Holy Spirit to grow in faith, maturity, and holiness.

For those of us who choose the grace of the Spirit, it's time to learn to walk.

CHAPTER 17

WALKING WITH THE "REAL HOW"

The Advocate, the Holy Spirit, whom the Father
will send in my name, will teach you all things and
will remind you of everything I have said to you.

JOHN 14:26

When I was thirty-seven, life was going great for me. I was in the best shape of my life and the back and hip were still functioning, which allowed for intense workouts and great results. I was confident in my strength. I felt I was strong enough for anything. For some reason, I also felt motivated to be stronger than any of the high school or college guys I was leading.

This was my mindset when my friend Joel called to see if I would like a free couch from Pottery Barn. His wife, Jenn, was pregnant with their second child, and they needed the couch gone in order to provide space for the makeover of a room. Since it was a sleeper sofa and we were constantly having high school kids at our house, my answer was an easy *yes*. Before hanging up, Joel advised me to bring some strong guys because the couch was "really, really heavy."

The next day I went to Joel's with two of my college guys in tow.

The couch was in an upstairs room with a tricky door/hallway combo we'd have to carefully navigate. I positioned myself at one end of the couch and instructed Bradley and Jacob to work together to carry the other end. After a count of three, we lifted the couch and started toward the door. In my head, I was saying, *Oh no, this is really heavy and I don't know if I can do it.* But because of my pride and ego, my instinct was to power through. I didn't want my guys to see me fail. That posture lasted about thirty seconds until I knew there was absolutely no way I could do it. I just wasn't strong enough.

So I called the strongest student I knew and asked for help. I should have called him in the first place, but because he was much stronger than me, it threatened my ego. I wanted the credit and glory for being the strongest guy in the room.

Nick arrived, came upstairs, and joined me at my end of the couch. "One. Two. Three!" I don't know where my strength stopped and his began, but it was *so* much easier with him alongside me. It didn't matter that I wasn't strong enough by myself because I had Nick's strength to accomplish the goal. This is a simple story, but honestly, God used that moment to teach me a principle that has shaped how I've approached walking with the Spirit.

I had taken on a task I wasn't strong enough to accomplish on my own. Fortunately, there was additional strength available to me. All that was required was for me to acknowledge that I wasn't strong enough, and to choose to ask for the help that was accessible the whole time.

Once we gain the right perspective on the power of the Holy Spirit, we realize it's a grave mistake to not call on it. Will we settle for the fruit of the world and the never-satisfying, limited benefit of our own efforts, or will we yield to the power of the Holy Spirit and experience unshakable faith, extraordinary joy, and the full life God wants for us? Assuming it's the latter, we need to learn how to lean into God in all areas of our lives. The apostle Paul called this "walking in the Spirit."

So I say, walk by the Spirit, and you will not gratify the
desires of the flesh. For the flesh desires what is contrary
to the Spirit, and the Spirit what is contrary to the flesh.
They are in conflict with each other, so that you are not
to do whatever you want. But if you are led by the Spirit,
you are not under the law (Galatians 5:16-18).

Walking in the Spirit requires a daily (if not a continual) acknowledgment that we can't produce God-glorifying, purpose-fulfilling,
faith-building fruit on our own. No real joy. No selfless love. No
lasting peace. Nothing redeeming or good at all.

The Greek word Paul uses for "walk" is the same word the apostle
John used when he spoke of the "greatest joy" he experienced when
his spiritual children were "walking in the truth."[1] As I wrote earlier,
the Greek word for "walk" is *peripateo* which means to organize one's
life around something. When Paul said, "Walk by the Spirit," he was
instructing us to live every aspect of our lives with the guidance and
strength of the Holy Spirit. Here is my version: live life sensitive to,
and dependent on, the guidance and the convictions of the Spirit.

If we fail to do this, we will surely give way to selfish motivations
and desires that are in conflict with the Spirit. We must embrace the
fact that God provides the power and strength for us to accomplish
what he's called us to do. This would seem like an attractive proposi-
tion, but as we all know, our pride often gets in the way. Watchman
Nee, a mid-twentieth-century Christian leader in China and one of
the founders of the underground house church movement, wrote:

The Law requires much, but offers no help in the carrying
out of its requirements. The Lord Jesus requires just as
much, yea more (Matthew 5:21–48). But what He requires
from us, He Himself carries out in us. The Law makes
demands and leaves us helpless to fulfill them; Christ

makes demands, but He Himself fulfills in us the very demands He makes.[2]

To walk in the Spirit is to choose relationship over rules, his strength over our own, and his glory above all else. In doing so, we let go of our independence, and instead choose to depend on him. His strength and power are always available to believers, for kingdom purposes, because he lives in us and with us forever. Our efforts matter when they are connected to his strength. Over time, and as we live yielded to the direction of the Holy Spirit, we become more like Christ and produce life-giving fruit.

To summarize and simplify, especially as it relates to doing good and making meaningful choices, we have to learn to say to God: "I can't. You can. Please help."

This applies broadly—to every challenge we face, every decision we make, and every action we take. The specific kind of help we need will vary depending on the situation. Most often, what we critically need is *wisdom*.

A WORD TO THE WISE

Most people believe they make wise decisions, or at least would say they have a desire to do so. The bigger question is, On the basis of what wisdom are those decisions made? Just like we readily settle for the "fruit of ourselves" instead of the fruit of the Spirit, we most often rely on human or worldly wisdom rather than seeking the wisdom of God.

Maybe this explains why people can get paralyzed when they face a decision. Any wisdom apart from God fails to deliver confidence and peace, because according to Scripture, worldly wisdom is "foolishness,"[3] so we are deceiving ourselves if we believe we are wise. God speaks strongly against being "wise in our own eyes"[4] and goes as far as saying he "will destroy the wisdom of the wise"[5] and "shame the wise" by using the foolish things of this world against them.[6]

Even so, like the ancient Israelites and first-century Christians before us, we stubbornly rely on the worldly wisdom of our culture and experiences for our decisions, and then suffer difficult consequences. The good news is that the help of the Spirit, as it specifically relates to wisdom, is always available to us. Even better, God has *promised* it to those who ask. James, the brother of Jesus, said it this way: "If any of you lacks wisdom, you should ask God, who gives generously to all without finding fault, and it will be given to you" (James 1:5).

Paul said the wisdom of God was "destined for our glory" (1 Corinthians 2:7). Honestly, I'm not completely sure what that means, but this is certain: God desires us to do life with his wisdom. Throughout Scripture, the Holy Spirit has always been the source of wisdom and the one responsible for dispensing it to God's people.[7] To live the fullness of the Christian life, we have to make wise choices. To consistently choose wisely, we have to acknowledge the foolishness of our own wisdom ("I can't"), believe God will guide us ("You can"), and, most importantly, invite the Spirit into our decision-making ("Please help").

When faced with difficult or important decisions, we can ask questions based on the guidance of Scripture, and then ask the Spirit to help us think things through. When Danlyn and I were given the opportunity to leave the only life we'd ever known as a married couple and move to Uganda, we prayed for wisdom and asked the following questions, based on Scripture:

- What is our motivation for maybe saying *yes*? Is this for the benefit of others or for ourselves?

- Is the opportunity a good application of our gifts and experiences, for kingdom purposes?

- Has God prepared us to specifically serve in Uganda at Amazima?

- Given our current situation, is there anything unwise about moving to Uganda?

- Are there any commands in Scripture that would prevent us from saying *yes*?

There are many more wise questions we can derive from God's Word, but you get the point. If we spend time in Scripture, ask questions, and ask the Spirit for help in the process, we will make wiser decisions. As the apostle Paul pointed out, our relationship with the Spirit will also grow: "I keep asking that the God of our Lord Jesus Christ, the glorious Father, may give you the Spirit of wisdom and revelation, so that you may know him better" (Ephesians 1:17).

As our relationship with him grows, and as we become more and more sensitive to his guidance, our decisions (big and small) will be made with more ease and confidence. There is an incredible rhythm we can enjoy with the Spirit when we choose to focus on our relationship with him.

IN FOCUS

Driving in Uganda can be a terrifying adventure but also somehow satisfying once you figure it out. Traffic laws are pretty much unenforced and are largely viewed as mere guidelines. There is rarely a trip to town that doesn't include a *matatu* (taxi van) jumping into *your lane*, creating a head-on-collision scenario. When this happens, it's somehow your responsibility to move onto the shoulder and let the oncoming vehicle pass in your lane. In addition, there are *bodas* (motorcycle taxis) everywhere, all the time, doing dangerous and unnatural things. If all this isn't enough, people meander across the street without much thought of oncoming cars.

The only way to survive, both physically and emotionally, is to keep your eyes completely focused on the vehicle directly in front of you. If you look away, even for a moment, the risk of an accident or of hitting a pedestrian increases greatly. While Danlyn may disagree, I'm an excellent driver, and I have successfully driven thousands of kilometers in Uganda without incident. Even though there is much to see while driving there, I've never allowed myself to get distracted. Focus is literally a matter of life and death.

In the same way, focus is important to walking in close relationship with the Spirit. If we are not focused on God, we will be focused on other things. Jesus lists three categories of distraction that take our focus away from him: "the worries of this life, the deceitfulness of wealth, and the desires for other things."[8] What was true then is true now. Distractions have always been a stumbling block against a growing and healthy relationship with the Spirit. Now the addition of the smart phone and social media has resulted in the most distracted generation in history.

According to Jesus, distractions are like thorns that "choke the word, making it unfruitful" (Mark 4:19). Paul went further by asking, "Are you so foolish? After beginning by means of the Spirit, are you now trying to finish by means of the flesh?" (Galatians 3:3). We may know the truth and how we are to live, but unless we keep our eyes on Jesus, we will settle for our own fruits instead of the life-giving fruit of the Spirit.

There are many reasons why we're seeing such incredible transformation with our students in Uganda, but everything starts with their availability. They don't have phones or access to the internet (for personal use), so they're far less distracted and able to focus on Jesus.

Deep down, we all know social media has little redeeming value, and most of the entertainment, news, and other content we consume is at best unhelpful, and at worst is leading us (far) away from Jesus. If you feel distant from God, pay attention to what has your attention. What are your best efforts devoted to? Are they focused on pursuing or maintaining a certain lifestyle? Why are we so surprised at the weakness of our faith or lack of growth when our focus is on everything but Jesus? The apostle Paul gave us the remedy for the persistent problem of distraction:

- "Finally, brothers and sisters, whatever is true, whatever is noble, whatever is right, whatever is pure, whatever is lovely, whatever is admirable—if anything is excellent or praiseworthy—think about such things" (Philippians 4:8).

- "We demolish arguments and every pretension that sets itself up against the knowledge of God, and we take captive every thought to make it obedient to Christ" (2 Corinthians 10:5).

- "Set your minds on things above, not on earthly things" (Colossians 3:2).

Easy enough, right? Hardly. If it were as simple as just changing what we think about, then I don't think we'd struggle as much as we do. If you're like me, you've had times or even seasons with a strong focus on God. But regardless of the accompanying benefits, we tend to drift away or get bored. My experience leading people tells me that the reason we lose focus so easily is because we end up relying on our own strength. To really focus on Christ and avoid dangerous distractions, the strategy is the same: "I can't. You can. Please help."

I know I sound like a broken record at this point, but again, we can settle for the limits of our own capabilities, or we can ask God to help us focus on all the right things. If we are willing to ask, Scripture says the Spirit will protect our thoughts and keep our focus on him.[9] A consistent focus leads to a healthy relationship with the Spirit, and greatly increases the likelihood we will ask for help, from the Helper, in all areas of our lives.

WHEN WE CAN'T, WE ASK

We started with the idea of practically pursuing *awareness* for what we believe about the world and matters of faith, and why we hold those beliefs. With that knowledge the call is to seek a deep *understanding* of the truth by experiencing God in an intimate way. As we grow in *epignosis* (experiential understanding) consistent with Scripture, God corrects our frames and *perspectives*, which allows us to embrace the *obedience* to which we are called.

While I strongly believe this progression leads us to make wise choices and follow God's will, our efforts alone will fail to meaningfully move the needle if our goal is real transformation. We have to say, "I can't. You can. Please help," every step of the way. Even though we can't control the outcomes—because they always belong to God—we can choose to invite the Spirit into everything.

Failure to apply this principle is why I believe that the myriad of books, videos, sermons, and podcasts are not creating the change we all want and need. As I said before, I believe most Christians live as if the Holy Spirit does not live in them.

Instead, we can ask the Spirit to help us become more aware of our sin, our motivations, our beliefs, and all the rest, and to guide us to better understanding through our experiences. John Calvin, in his commentary on Deuteronomy, made the same point when he wrote, "We learn that a clear and powerful understanding is a special gift of the Spirit, since men are ever blind in the brightest light, until they are enlightened by God."[10]

Framed by brokenness and God's grace, having the correct perspectives about important things is necessary to lead us to a correct worldview. But only with the Spirit can we rise to a level of maturity that impacts every area of our life, which is what we were designed for. The correct perspectives encourage us to embrace obedience, which is the key to complete joy. Boom! Even so, we can't abide in Christ or willfully obey him, with the right motivation, unless we involve the Spirit.

If we acknowledge our inability to fully obey and ask God to show us when we are obeying in only our own strength or for the wrong reasons, we can then ask him to teach us how to obey in the right way. Let's say it together: "I can't. You can. Please help."

Whether we ask for help to better execute this framework, for wisdom for decisions, or for personal growth in faith, God has promised to say *yes* when we ask for help. This is what Jesus actually meant in the so-called name-it-and-claim-it verses.

GREATER THINGS

> Believe me when I say that I am in the Father and the Father is in me; or at least believe on the evidence of the works themselves. Very truly I tell you, whoever believes in me will do the works I have been doing, and they will do even greater things than these, because I am going to the Father. And I will do whatever you ask in my name, so that the Father may be glorified in the Son. You may ask me for anything in my name, and I will do it (John 14:11-14).

If you'll indulge me for a moment, I need to get a bit technical in unpacking these important (and often misunderstood) verses that have serious implications to our discussion about how our efforts work in conjunction with the work of the Spirit. Here we go.

"Very truly I tell you, whoever believes in me will do the works I have been doing" (John 14:12).

The first thing to notice is that this verse applies directly to *all believers*, including us, so we need to pay close attention. Secondly, Jesus indicated an assurance of belief for those who "do the works" he had been doing. The most common question I get from our students in Uganda is, "How do I know if I'm saved?" The best way to know is to experience the evidence of the Holy Spirit in the "works" we do like Jesus. What are these "works" then?

Jesus did a lot of cool things like miracles, healing, and raising people from the dead. Are these the "works" he was referring to in this passage? Definitely not! Since the "works" are associated with all believers, we would expect to see the same kinds of miraculous things from anyone who is in Christ. Have you ever known anyone to walk on water? Feed 5,000 people from one little basket of food? I think we can all agree we haven't seen that.

The apostle Paul also removed any idea that the "works" are in the category of "spiritual gifts" when he taught that believers have different gifts:

> Now to each one the manifestation of the Spirit is given for the common good. To one there is given through the Spirit a message of wisdom, to another a message of knowledge by means of the same Spirit, to another faith by the same Spirit, to another gifts of healing by that one Spirit, to another miraculous powers, to another prophecy, to another distinguishing between spirits, to another speaking in different kinds of tongues, and to still another the interpretation of tongues. All these are the work of one and the same Spirit, and he distributes them to each one, just as he determines (1 Corinthians 12:7-11).

According to God's Word, believers have different gifts, and they are given by God completely of his choosing. Jesus did all these things and more. We don't. Not one of us has all the gifts. So since the "works" Jesus referred to in John 14:12 are a sign of all believers, spiritual gifts are not the "works" Jesus meant. To figure out what Jesus really meant by "works," look back at verse 11: "Believe me when I say that I am in the Father and the Father is in me; or at least believe on the evidence of the works themselves."

Don't miss this. Jesus is saying the "works" are those that help people believe in him. For reference, Jesus used the same concept and Greek phrase in John 10:25 when he answered questions about whether or not he was the Messiah. In both cases, the point made by Jesus was that all believers should be doing the same work he did, in helping others to believe in him. So all believers will do the "works" of Christ by pointing others to him.

With that understanding, let's keep going. "Very truly I tell you, whoever believes in me will do the works I have been doing, and they will do even greater things than these, because I am going to the Father" (John 14:12). Dang it. We figured out the "works" but now we have to do "greater things"? What does it mean to do greater works than the work Jesus did to help people believe? The key is in the last part of the verse. The way to the Father, for Jesus, was through the cross and resurrection. The same work has become "greater" because the work of pointing people to believe in him is now based on the finished work of the cross and a resurrected Christ. In addition, the faith we are leading people to, with our works, is now done with the power of the Holy Spirit. Jesus is doing work through us instead of us doing it in just our own strength!

Now that we've clarified what the "works" are, what they are not, and why Jesus said our works would be greater, let's dig into the idea of name it and claim it. "I will do whatever you ask in my name, so that the Father may be glorified in the Son. You may ask me for anything in my name, and I will do it" (John 14:13-14). Those two verses are similar and say the same thing, for emphasis. As before, let's start with what this can't mean. It can't mean we have the power to control God. God is not a genie that we access by saying magic words like "In Jesus' name." It can't mean that "whatever" means absolutely anything.

To be clear, Jesus doesn't say, "You will have it" but instead says, "I will do it." Also, the "and" at the beginning of the verse brings forward the idea that this is about all believers, so there is no room to argue that really good Christians or special pastors have some unique access to "whatever." Finally, there is no glory for the Father in "whatever." Any thoughtful and prudent understanding of this important passage completely rejects any idea of the name-it-and-claim-it ideas of prosperity teaching.

So, what does it mean then? Jesus is saying he will provide whatever you need, to accomplish the greater works of helping people believe in him, through you and with the power of the Spirit. Asking for something in the name of Jesus is like saying, "In the way of Jesus." The way of Jesus is to do God-glorifying works so others will see and believe in Christ. When we seek to glorify him and ask for help in support of those efforts, he will do it! It's one thing for *me* to say this but who can argue with *Jesus*? The night before he died, he clearly taught that when we ask the Spirit for help to do the works we are created to do, with the right motivation, he will do it.

When I had the privilege of preaching through these verses to our staff, the reaction was unexpected. For most, it was like a lifelong tension had been lifted and they'd been given a free pass to walk away from shame and uncertainty. For many, the work of the Holy Spirit and the opportunity for a relationship with him had been so grossly misrepresented, they'd been living in fear, not freedom. Unanswered prayer requests made in Jesus' name, and a lack of gifts—like speaking in tongues—had led to doubt and hopelessness.

Learning the true meaning behind these verses, and learning about the real purpose of spiritual gifts, seemed to be the keys to letting go of destructive beliefs that were the source of much shame. Empowered with a proper understanding, they were free to pursue a healthy, fruit-bearing walk with the Spirit.

ANYTIME YOU'RE READY

The water isn't safe to drink in Uganda, but because of the equatorial sun, it's important to stay hydrated. The easiest and most efficient way to get clean water is to buy or exchange twenty-liter bottles. On campus, the residents collectively order about forty cans every week that are delivered to my house on Sunday mornings. Later, I deliver the water to the staff houses using what's called a "tri-cycle," a three-wheeled motorcycle with a small truck bed in back. These machines are handy to move stuff around campus and are great fun for the little kids who are always ready for a ride.

In the early days of my delivery service, there were three kids who liked to accompany me on all my runs. At every stop, they would seek to help me by trying to move the big jugs to the back of the trike, so (in theory) it would be easier for me to off-load and deliver them to the house porches. The problem was they were not nearly strong enough to move the water jugs more than a few inches. The jugs probably weighed more than they did! Inevitably, they would realize their limitations, look up at me and say, "Uncle Kelly, you do."

As I was writing this chapter and recalling those precious moments, I couldn't help but wonder if this is how God feels watching us struggle to do the things we aren't strong enough to do, while at the same time we resist the help only he can provide. One thing I know for sure is that trying to do good things, or even avoiding bad things, in our own strength alone, is exhausting, and the results are mostly disappointing. The help we need is always available because the help is a "who" residing in us.

We can choose to focus on Jesus and less on other things.

We can choose to dig into Scripture and seek God's wisdom.

We can choose to do good things and put others first.

We can choose to acknowledge the limits of our own capabilities and ask for help.

Something to Remember: The Holy Spirit is the power and strength for every aspect of the Christian life.

Once we learn to walk in the Spirit, we can then choose to take the specific actions that will best unleash the incredible power of God and have the biggest impact toward the outcomes we all desire.

CHAPTER 18

THE "REAL HOW" AND THE "BIG FOUR"

Relying on God has to begin all over again
every day as if nothing had yet been done.[1]

C.S. LEWIS

Even with a deeper understanding and better perspective on the Holy Spirit and what it means to walk with him, there will always be a tension about how our efforts fit into what God has called us to do. As we were reminded in the last chapter, we all want our efforts to matter—and that's not a bad thing.

Thankfully, God has given us a great number of commands that, when followed, offer opportunity for personal growth and kingdom impact. There is a subset of those commands I call the "Big Four." They have to do with *forgiveness, gratitude, sexual purity,* and our *money.* In my experience, growth in these areas consistently yield the greatest outcomes, while protecting us from the most severe consequences of inaction or wrong choices. It's worth noting that these benefits and protections extend to everyone, regardless of the worldviews we hold, the cultures we live in, or even how we feel about Jesus. This confirms the wisdom behind the guidance. Even so, there is great resistance to following these commands.

So what's the problem? If the advantages are so obvious and apply to everyone, then why do so many people not follow this guidance? Primarily, it's because the culture of the world patently rejects these ideas, and any time we go against culture, we invite difficulty and ridicule. The easier path is to go with the flow. To be clear, following God's most countercultural commands is not easy; it's extremely difficult. It means we have to deal with our pride and our desire for control and independence.

As you've been reading and (hopefully) learning from this book, right now might be your best opportunity to learn how your efforts join with the Spirit for real transformation, allowing you to deeply experience the grace of God in an undeniable way. Are you ready? I hope so. Either way, this will be a hard chapter because of what we've experienced or been taught in the areas of forgiveness, gratitude, sexual purity, and generosity. Also, the enemy has been hard at work to prevent us from awareness, understanding, and a perspective on truth. Why? Because he knows that those who follow God's most difficult teaching, framed by a perspective and fellowship with the Holy Spirit, will be far less likely to believe his lies.

SEVENTY-SEVEN IS A BIG NUMBER

Sometimes I hear a person's story and immediately think to myself, *I would completely understand if there was never any forgiveness in that situation.* This was exactly the case when I learned about what Joan had been through before coming to our school.

Joan's mother had to make a decision no mother should ever have to make. After her husband left, she didn't have the means to take care of her children, so she decided to split them up amongst family (where possible) and foster homes. Unfortunately for Joan, she ended up in a very unsafe environment where she experienced unspeakable trauma. When she arrived at school, and for the first half of the school year, Joan was visibly broken. Her tall figure lumbered slowly around campus, always with her head down. She didn't have any friends and was not interested in building a relationship with her Family Mentors. I felt a deep sadness for her situation.

Her teachers and Mentors never gave up, however, and the consistent, loving, and safe environment started to have a noticeable effect. Slowly, Joan started smiling and engaging with her fellow students. She eventually joined the basketball team, and despite having no experience, she became the starting center and began to enjoy playing the game.

As she entered her second year, the degree of transformation was remarkable, if not miraculous. Joan had become a bit of a prankster and was displaying a wit and sense of humor I didn't think was possible, given her past trauma. Eventually, she confided in her Family Mentors and told them what we already knew: she had placed her faith in Christ.

This is not to say that things were rosy all the time. Joan still harbored deep resentment about being abandoned by her mother, and not surprisingly it manifested in various ways, and certainly limited her growth in her newfound faith. We tried to talk to her about the value of forgiveness, but in an honor/shame culture, it just didn't make a lot of sense to her. But we play a long game at our school and were patient in waiting for the Spirit to lead her to a place of forgiveness.

At the end of the school year Joan came forward and wanted to be baptized, along with a number of her fellow students who had become joyful Jesus followers. It was at this point that one of her Family Mentors, Auntie Jackie, had a bold, if not insane idea: she was going to try to find Joan's mom and invite her to come to the baptism.

This idea turned into a challenging task. Joan's mother was difficult to track down and was rumored to be at least two hours away in a place not easily accessible by public transport. Undeterred, Jackie diligently sought out her location, and eventually was able to identify the village where she was most likely living. Without knowing for sure, she made the trek to the location and was able to meet with Joan's mom. She was not a Christian but agreed to come to the baptism.

From the Amazima Blog: "The day Joan got baptized was the first time she had seen her mom in a long time. It was full of hesitant but joyful hugs, and cheerful shouts as Joan went down in the water to be buried with Christ and raised to walk in the newness of life!" The reconciliation was real and the debt was gone. Joan, with the help of the Holy Spirit, was able to genuinely forgive her mom. In the weeks that followed, her mother moved back to the area so Joan would have a home where she could stay over the breaks. It hasn't been easy but they've spent every term break together for the last three years, as well as the COVID lockdown. God has continued to heal them both and is writing a story of redemption worthy of the Gospels.

Our students struggle to forgive others for the same reasons we all do. When someone harms us, a debt is created in the relationship, making authentic reconciliation difficult. To actually forgive someone means canceling a debt that is owed to us. We are more likely to stubbornly hold on to the debt, and until it's paid, the relationship is not the same.

Although the choice for a Jesus follower is obvious, we will most often choose unforgiveness. This is in spite of the fact that we are all equally in need of forgiveness and commanded by God to forgive others.[2]

> Peter came to Jesus and asked, "Lord, how many times shall I forgive my brother or sister who sins against me? Up to seven times?" Jesus answered, "I tell you, not seven times, but seventy-seven times" (Matthew 18:21-22).

Jesus made sure there was no doubt about the critical importance of forgiving others. In the most unforgiving of cultures, he consistently forgave those who were considered the worst of sinners. In perhaps the most shocking act of forgiveness ever recorded, Jesus asked the Father to forgive the men who had just nailed him to a Roman cross: "Father, forgive them, for they do not know what they are doing" (Luke 23:34).

Let this sink in. Jesus was able to forgive the people who tortured and killed him—but somehow we still resist forgiving others, like it's the most unreasonable thing we've ever been asked to do. This unfortunate reality will not change until we choose to forgive through the power of the Holy Spirit.

The forgiveness of our sins is only available because of the finished work of Christ on the cross. Forgiven people, who have been reconciled to Christ, have been given the ministry of reconciliation and the power of the Holy Spirit to accomplish it.[3] I have repeatedly compared the limited good we are able to do ourselves against the great good that is possible when we join our efforts with those of the Holy Spirit. Perhaps forgiveness is where we find the biggest gap, because forgiveness is at the heart of God.

Sure, we can say we've forgiven others, and maybe we have to some extent. But the kind of forgiveness that fuels transformation in all areas of our faith is only available through the Holy Spirit. Our job is to think about who needs our full forgiveness, acknowledge our limitations, and ask the Spirit to do what only he can do. This is easier said than done. There is nothing natural or in our power to truly forgive.

True forgiveness is difficult. Expressing gratitude offers a more accessible opportunity and carries with it a greater potential impact on our rhythm with the Spirit.

DON'T JUST *BE* GRATEFUL

There are a lot of parenting philosophies out there, but there is at least one thing nearly all parents agree on: they want their kids to be grateful. My mom, probably like your mom, would often direct me to say thank you whenever someone had done something nice for me. It was especially awkward, however, when she would make me do it in front of the person. Is it weird that I'm fifty years old and it still happens?

Anyway, we have to tell our kids to be thankful because, like most other things we've discussed, it's not natural. We push for gratitude because regardless of our belief system, we all have a sense that it's somehow important. Being grateful is not an add-on. It's central to the Christian life and to our relationship with the Spirit. It might just be the most important perspective for us to mature into.

When we are grateful, we are also humble because they are two sides of the same coin. You can't be grateful without being humble and vice versa. Humility leads to a posture of grace that prevents us from pridefully thinking we are deserving of anything. A gracious attitude makes us available to the Holy Spirit, and protects us from the schemes of the enemy, who is actively trying to make us believe in our own strength and independence. Got it?

We can't just decide to become a more naturally grateful person, though. If you happen to be a grateful person, be grateful to God for your gratitude! Sure, we can do valuable things like counting our blessings, putting up sticky notes of items of thanks, and writing in a gratitude journal, but again, there are limits to the impact of such activities. They serve more to remind us than transform us.

If becoming a grateful or humble person is important, but we are limited in our own capabilities, is it as simple as saying, "I can't. You can. Please help"? Yes and no. Of course, acknowledging our limitations and asking for help is always beneficial, but in regard to gratitude, there is something else we can do to marry our efforts with those of the Holy Spirit. We learn about this from an important story:

> Now on his way to Jerusalem, Jesus traveled along the
> border between Samaria and Galilee. As he was going

into a village, ten men who had leprosy met him. They stood at a distance and called out in a loud voice, "Jesus, Master, have pity on us!" When he saw them, he said, "Go, show yourselves to the priests." And as they went, they were cleansed. One of them, when he saw he was healed, came back, praising God in a loud voice. He threw himself at Jesus' feet and thanked him—and he was a Samaritan. Jesus asked, "Were not all ten cleansed? Where are the other nine? Has no one returned to give praise to God except this foreigner?" Then he said to him, "Rise and go; your faith has made you well" (Luke 17:11-19).

If we pay close attention, we see that Jesus was not talking about *being* grateful, but rather highlighting the importance of *expressing* it. There is absolutely no doubt that all ten lepers in the story felt grateful. Having been healed from leprosy, they would soon be able to rejoin a society that, by law, had forbidden them from participating. If the story was just about being grateful, Jesus would have focused on all ten lepers, who at that moment would have been the most grateful people on the planet. Instead, Jesus shared about the one person who came back to express his gratitude.

This story is as amazing as it is important. Jesus took a brief departure from teaching about key doctrines and the kingdom of God to say this to us: when you're grateful, express it, and especially when you're grateful to God. Just feeling grateful is not good enough! How does this apply to our walk with the Spirit? We can choose to recognize our general lack of gratitude, and choose to ask the Spirit for help in becoming more grateful people. Then as we grow in gratitude, we can choose to express it.

I believe that gratitude is the oil for the powerful engine of the Holy Spirit because a grateful person is more sensitive to the work of the Spirit in their life, and more likely to be joyfully surrendered to his will. A humble and grateful person who is closely walking with the Spirit has the potential to embrace difficult but important teaching on another vital topic: sex and relationships.

RUN AWAY!

The world would have us believe that sex is just a physical act, and any potential consequences are minimal as long as things are consensual. In my opinion, based on working with high school and college students for so many years, this is the biggest and most devastating lie one can believe. When we believe this lie, we can fall for all the rest of the enemy's lies about sex—like the one that says sex outside of marriage is empowering for women, or that watching pornography is healthy and good.

Acting on the enemy's lies about sex leads to unavoidable brokenness. Danlyn and I have walked with dozens of students through all kinds of difficulties and have seen firsthand the reality of how people are specifically affected by casual sex and porn. Women are not at all empowered, but instead, experience deep depression and identity issues, which lead to more unhealthy choices and relationships. For our girls in Uganda who grow up in humble communities, the idea of enjoying sex is mostly a foreign concept. What they've been taught and experienced makes it extremely difficult for them to comprehend the truth.

In regard to pornography, the world says, "No problem," but in addition to being extremely addictive, neuroscience tells us that repeated exposure to pornography actually rewires the brain to change how we view identity, sexuality, relationships, and even how we process everything around us.[4] The inevitable damage done through sexual promiscuity doesn't care about your politics, generation, beliefs, or opinions. Worse, the consequences we experience do little to change our future decisions or behavior.

As you've probably noticed, I'm not a fan of legalism, so it shouldn't surprise you that I've never found much value in presenting any of God's rules by just saying, "You'd better not." With every group of students I've had the privilege of leading, we've had a camp or retreat where the topic was sexual purity. Before discussing the topic, I would always ask the students, "Why would I care if you have sex?" After a few dumb answers, mostly from teenage boys, someone would invariably say, "Because you care about us?" Of course, that is the right answer.

Having seen the damage that results from ignoring God's design for sex, I am strongly motivated to do whatever I can to encourage young people to choose the better path—which leads to great benefit and protects them from certain harm.

God cares about our purity in the same way, but much more deeply. Since God created sex with a purpose, he best understands the damage that results from moving outside of the protective boundaries of his design, and he works to keep us from harm. How do I know this? For one thing, God consistently gives clear warnings in Scripture. For another, there is no category of sin where the Holy Spirit is more active in convicting us.

The apostle Paul is in full agreement and used the strongest possible language to express his views:

- "Put to death, therefore, whatever belongs to your earthly nature: sexual immorality, impurity, lust, evil desires, and greed, which is idolatry" (Colossians 3:5).

- "Among you there must not be even a hint of sexual immorality, or of any kind of impurity, or of greed, because these are improper for God's holy people" (Ephesians 5:3).

- "The body, however, is not meant for sexual immorality but for the Lord, and the Lord for the body" (1 Corinthians 6:13).

- "For God did not call us to be impure, but to live a holy
  life. Therefore, anyone who rejects this instruction does
  not reject a human being but God, the very God who
  gives you his Holy Spirit" (1 Thessalonians 4:7-8).

Jesus, in his famous Sermon on the Mount, even equated lust
to adultery! To understand how radical and countercultural all this
teaching was, consider the first-century audience for Jesus and Paul.
In the Jewish community, women had become like property and
were generally in service to men. Men of high stature were permit-
ted to break Jewish law and commit adultery (which normally carried a penalty of death). For the Greco-Roman pagans in Palestine,
their sexual exploits would be too raunchy even for Netflix. My point
is, there has never been a time when God's teaching about sex and
purity was so countercultural. Though the culture of that day was
completely resistant, Jesus and his apostles consistently taught believers to treat their purity with the utmost care and respect.

We are perfectly capable of taking care of the things we believe
to be important. It's just a matter of what we consider sacred. When
I was in high school, I had a black Z28 Camaro with T-tops, a big
engine, and a killer sound system. It was my pride and joy. On Saturday nights I could usually be found cruising around East Cobb,
Georgia, and blaring Metallica for all to enjoy. You can be sure the Z
got a full treatment of care earlier in the day. I would wash every inch
of it, both inside and out, and spend a lot of extra time on the tires
and wheels. I went through a three-step wax process like an expert,
that resulted in near perfection.

Paul described our bodies as "members of Christ himself" and
"temples of the Holy Spirit" (1 Corinthians 6:15, 19). That is pretty
incredible language. If our bodies are infinitely more important than
our possessions (even more than my Z) then why don't we treat them
as sacred? In my view, either our motivation for obedience is wrong

or we have been too influenced by the culture. Also, we are likely failing to cooperate with the Holy Spirit.

If our reason for obedience to God's Word is one of avoiding consequences or legalistically following rules, and not because we trust that God wants the best outcomes for us, there will be no joy in our faithfulness. We will also be unlikely to ask the Spirit for help. Like everything else, there are limits to what we can accomplish in our own strength.

This problem shows up most prominently in the battle against pornography. In response to intense convictions from the Holy Spirit, Christians will take drastic steps to control their behavior. Depending on their level of willpower, these measures will work for extended periods of time. Ultimately, however, no one is strong enough to overcome or control sexual sin on their own; it requires the power of the Spirit. More specifically, it requires the supernatural fruit of self-control.

I have watched God redeem dozens and dozens of seemingly unredeemable situations stemming from sexual sin. Every time, it took the best efforts of human strength combined with the power of the Holy Spirit. While it's tempting to celebrate the consequences avoided, my greater joy comes from seeing the positive outcomes God has promised to those who trust him.

If fleeing sexual immorality is the best example of how our efforts can work together with the Holy Spirit to produce the best outcomes, a close second has to do with following what God says about money.

WHERE IS YOUR TREASURE?

Most of the time, when a pastor or priest begins a sermon about money, there is a collective sigh from the congregation and a temptation to tune out. Don't do that here. I will keep it short, and I promise not to be prescriptive about your finances. Of all the big-impact categories of commands, though, money is the one we struggle with the most. Way too often we are straight-up disobedient.

God is perfectly clear about how he feels about money and its potential impact on our lives. For professing Christians, ignorance is not a valid excuse. Neither is the influence of prosperity teaching. We know from Scripture that God is not against money itself. But he is against desiring, loving, hoarding, or even pursuing money.[5] The apostle Paul said it this way: "For the love of money is a root of all kinds of evil. Some people, eager for money, have wandered from the faith and pierced themselves with many griefs" (1 Timothy 6:10).

From this verse and others, we know why God wants us to avoid a money-centered lifestyle: it can lead to complete disaster.[6] We can debate what Paul meant by "ruin and destruction" but regardless, there's not much wiggle room here. Our attitude about money is critically important.

Jesus also had a lot to say about money. It may surprise you to learn that he spoke more about money than about other important topics like salvation, sin, grace, or love. From Jesus, we learn that money distracts us from the gospel[7] and that life isn't found in having lots of stuff.[8] In addition, he told us to not "store up treasures" for selfish reasons and to not value our wealth over our faith.[9] How do these principles from Jesus compare to what our culture teaches, or with how we actually manage our money? If you're not feeling any tension at this point, consider what Jesus had to say when teaching about money, eternal life, and the kingdom of God:

- "If you want to be perfect, go, sell your possessions and give to the poor, and you will have treasure in heaven. Then come, follow me" (Matthew 19:21).

- "Sell your possessions and give to the poor" (Luke 12:33).

No matter what you've been taught or what you know, this is a hard teaching from Jesus. It is even harder to process this statement: "Truly I tell you, it is hard for someone who is rich to enter the kingdom of heaven. Again I tell you, it is easier for a camel to go through the eye of a needle than for someone who is rich to enter the kingdom of God" (Matthew 19:23-24).

These verses are particularly tricky in Uganda because of the mix of legalism and prosperity teaching taught here. If local pastors were to take these words from Jesus as literally as they take certain Old Testament laws, being rich would completely disqualify someone from eternal life. Instead, most of the village churches teach that wealth is the ultimate goal and God is all for it.

I would instead say that any theology that teaches God wants us to be materially wealthy is completely wrong and indefensible. For the record, God does want us to be rich—it's just not at all about money.

> Command those who are rich in this present world not to be arrogant nor to put their hope in wealth, which is so uncertain, but to put their hope in God, who richly provides us with everything for our enjoyment. Command them to do good, to be rich in good deeds, and to be generous and willing to share (1 Timothy 6:17-18).

Let's go back to that "camel fitting through the eye of a needle" thing. If wealth itself is not a disqualifier (it's not), then why is it so difficult for materially rich people to enter the kingdom of heaven? The danger is more about what money does to our dependence on, or our need for, God. The more money we have, the easier it is for us to feel self-reliant, prideful, and entitled—all of which makes it more likely we will reject God's grace, and instead place our faith in our wealth. If you think your prosperity is a sign of blessing, well, enjoy your camel ride.

God wants us to be generous because it protects us from believing the enemy's lies about money and leads us to a place of availability and humility. At some point, even the wealthiest of us realize that money isn't the secret to a joyful life. I think the American Dream is a lie and always has been. In my experience, generosity is the key. But just like everything else we've discussed in this section, we must have the power of the Spirit in order to be generous for the right reasons.

It is certainly tempting to check the box with a 10 percent tithe or a big gift when we have extra funds in the bank account, but if we are generous for the wrong reasons, there is very little benefit of any kind. We can choose to be generous but must, at the same time, ask the Spirit for help to truly give for the benefit of others and for the glory of God. For me personally, learning to be generous has had a bigger impact on my faith and walk with the Spirit than anything else. True generosity is not natural and is definitely countercultural. For me, it was a confirmation of the power of the Holy Spirit and a catalyst for leaning into "I can't. You can. Please help" in every situation.

> **Something to Remember:** Choosing to forgive, to express gratitude, to flee from sexual immorality, and to be generous with the help and power of the Holy Spirit, together have the potential to grow your faith like nothing else.

To wrap things up, let's talk about outcomes. More specifically, the outcomes that God has promised to those who believe and choose a surrendered walk with the Spirit.

CHAPTER 19

LIGHT, HOPE, FREEDOM, AND JOY

Seek first his kingdom and his righteousness, and
all these things will be given to you as well.

MATTHEW 6:33

In these pages, I've done my level best to share the important things I've learned and been reminded of on my journey to an unexpected joy and an unshakable faith I never thought was possible this side of heaven. For the last twenty years or so, I believe that my life experiences serve as a testimony to the truth and wisdom of Scripture. From direct observations made in two different cultures, I've put forth a useful progression and framework for following Jesus and living the Christian life.

No matter what you might think about the specific ideas I've shared here, it would be hard to effectively argue against the idea that approaching life through the general frames and perspectives presented will result in a fruitful relationship with God, and a life that enjoys the fulfillment of his promises.

We can't experience the full benefits promised by God unless we recognize our limitations, surrender to the Holy Spirit, and rely on his strength. Our efforts are simply not enough on their own. We're not really depending on the Spirit unless we willfully embrace God's New Testament commands that, without exception, are intended for our good.

Becoming an obedient follower of Jesus, however, is not possible without the correct perspectives of God, his rules, who he made us to be in Christ, and ever-changing circumstances that are out of our control. We can't just change our perspectives like we can change our minds, but we can choose to become aware of what we truly believe, and then engage in the burdens God has impressed upon our hearts.

So, what's the payoff? What does a full life in Christ look like? How do God's promises tangibly show up as fulfilled in our lives? Those who walk in the Spirit have a noticeable confidence in God's grace (assurance), extraordinary fruit, irreducible hope, and genuine freedom from the trappings of this world. All of these characteristics are so countercultural and unnatural that we certainly recognize them when we see them in others or experience them for ourselves.

NIGHT TO LIGHT

When our students first arrive to campus, they come with an emotional wall of protection that is impenetrable—at least initially. Since most of our students are from hard places and difficult circumstances, they tend to be hesitant about trusting the staff or even their fellow students.

In our first-ever class at TAS, there was a student named Night (pronounced *nigh-tee*) who was maybe the most guarded student I'd ever come across. Honestly, I was genuinely scared of her. It didn't help that she was from the northern part of Uganda, known for its strong and fierce warriors. When Night met her roommates, she let them know that she was "off-limits" in every way, and to not mess with her belongings. She made it very clear that a failure to comply would result in serious consequences, including, but not limited to, bodily harm. As we would soon learn, Night was also the brightest student at the school (even to this day) and additionally, was very talented in many ways.

Over time, as she became more comfortable with our philosophy and got to know her Teachers and Family Mentors, Night began to soften. She became more accessible and was willing to engage in activities beyond the classroom, like Sewing Club and Debate. The most surprising of her endeavors was basketball.

Basketball as it's played in Uganda is definitely more of a contact sport than the American version. Maybe that was why Night was drawn to it. Because she is naturally athletic and fearless, the game was a good fit for her, and she soon became a fixture on the court. Eventually she qualified to be a member of the school team. For a while, there were scraps, scrums, and attitude problems, but by the end of the second school year, everything had apparently changed, even if we hadn't fully comprehended it yet.

Our girls' basketball team had traveled to a tournament held at one of the big schools in Kampala, the capital. By this time in the life of TAS, our students were largely unaffected by the abuse they would typically experience from the other students they interacted with in crowded environments. Everyone has their limits, though, so I was always nervous that something bad would happen when our kids were called "poor" or "orphans." Although our players and fans always did a great job of not responding, Uncle Kelly may have lost his temper a few times...but I digress.

In the second game of the tournament, Night was pushed so hard into the pole holding the backboard that several of her teeth were knocked right out of her mouth. At that moment, I almost rushed the court because I was sure Night was going to put somebody in the hospital. It didn't happen. Instead, there was nothing but grace from Night.

For reasons I won't get into, it took many days to get her treatment sorted out, and then for another couple of weeks her jaw was wired shut. Night endured a lot of pain and couldn't eat regular food. The worst part for her was that she missed a lot of school. Academics are extremely important to her and she was facing a lot of extra work to get caught up and stay on pace. Never once, however, did Night grumble or complain. In fact, her attitude didn't change at all even though her circumstances were incredibly trying.

At some point many weeks later, Night's Mentors finally processed all that had happened. Somehow, Night handled this terrible situation, from start to finish, with an incredible grace, joy, and maturity we'd never seen before in her. How had we missed her transformation? The Night we all knew would have exploded in anger and frustration when faced with this set of circumstances. The unfairness of it all might have driven her to quit school. One of her Family Mentors decided to ask her about it.

"How have you been able to handle all of this with such grace and peace? Nobody would have blamed you for being angry or acting out. What happened to that girl who was ready to fight anyone who wronged her?"

With the biggest, most beautiful smile you'll ever see, she replied, "Auntie, that was Night without Christ."

The moment was so profound that I received a call almost immediately after it happened. What was completely unnatural had become natural, because of the saving and transforming power of Jesus. In the coming months I paid close attention to Night, because admittedly, I was skeptical. My doubts, however, were absurdly unfounded. Depending on the day, you might find her leading worship, tutoring other students, participating in her D-group (discipleship group), or practicing a new dance with her friends. Even with all the new activity, Night remained the number-one academic student in the school.

Her transformation was so dramatic that at dinner one night I asked her about it. Without consciously knowing she was validating what Scripture teaches, she spoke of being accepted and belonging to a family. We all have a need for acceptance, but in Uganda, where broken families are so common, knowing it's God's will for us to be adopted "to sonship through Jesus"[1] has an empowering effect that is hard to describe.

Furthermore, Night talked about the impact of being assured of her salvation. Sure, she could point to the volume of verses that teach we're not capable of undoing the saving work of Christ on the cross,[2] but her assurance came from the presence of the Holy Spirit in her life. As the apostle John says, "This is how we know that we live in him and he in us: He has given us of his Spirit" (1 John 4:13). All of this adds up to a sense of freedom that allows her to experience the outcomes that only come from following Jesus, unencumbered by pride or shame.

After that conversation, I asked Night if I could, from that moment forward, call her "Light." Given her journey out of the darkness, it just made more sense to me. To this day, at least for me, her name is Light. When I asked her for permission to tell this story, she flashed a shy but beautiful smile that penetrated my heart and said, "If you think it will help people to know Jesus, then please share my story."

As was the case with most of our students, for Light the pandemic was more of an opportunity than a hindrance. Since all the students in the entire country were out of school for more than a year, Light used most of her time to teach elementary-age kids, making sure they didn't fall too far behind in their studies. Moreover, she was part of a group of girls who, on a weekly basis, traveled to different communities to share about the value of women and the inherent worth we have in Christ.

Light's life reflects her Savior. Even though she could just "cruise," being one of the smartest, most talented students at TAS, she has embraced her purpose to live a life worthy of the gospel, bearing fruit so others may come to know Jesus. Seeing this transformation unfold so dramatically also helped me to see more clearly another tangible and manifest example of God's promises, only this one had been with me my entire adult life.

SUPERNATURAL HOPE

My friend Greg Stubbs, who won the Top Gun trophy in the 1980s and was considered the best fighter pilot in the US military at that time, once said that Danlyn was the strongest person he'd ever known. I completely agree. To some, it might seem that the hand Danlyn has been dealt is patently unfair. In addition to the emotional burden from not being able to bear children and not having the physical strength to raise them, she's had to endure intense pain and debilitation for the last two decades.

When she was twenty-eight years old, we were living a storybook life (sort of). We had the money, the house, the cars, the boat, the friends, the travel, and were in top physical condition. When things are good it's easy to feel like you're invincible, but you can lose focus from what's important. That's exactly what was happening when we got the shocking news that Danlyn had a big problem, in the form of a grapefruit-sized, blood-filled mass that had grown on her liver, apparently over a period of fifteen years or so. Because the tumor was vascular, it would require a complicated and dangerous surgery to remove.

Danlyn was in the operating room for more than ten hours. The surgeon removed the liver from her body, performed a resection of the tumor, and then put what was left of the liver back where it's supposed to be. For good measure, they also removed her appendix and gallbladder. By every account, the surgery was a big success. The only reminder of the whole ordeal was to be a large "Mercedes symbol" scar. Unfortunately and tragically, however, the wound area got infected.

I was stupidly out of town on a business trip when I got a call telling me that Danlyn had been rushed to an emergency surgery. The infection had spread to her lungs, they were filling up with fluid, and there was an urgency to open her back up and deal with the infection. There was actually a moment when she stopped breathing.

I didn't know about this then, but when a sealed wound is reopened because of infection, it's not then sealed up again. You could imagine my shock when I made it to the ICU and saw a giant hole in my wife's belly. My first question to the doctor on call was, "When are you going to sew her back up?" He replied, "We're not closing it. The wound will have to heal on its own." What did that mean? Well, it meant that every day for about four months the wound area had to be cleaned and repacked with saline-filled gauze.

After the wound finally healed and closed, Danlyn then had to deal with a whole new set of challenges. Because of the infection, they removed a lot of her voluntary stomach muscles, which left her with a very weak core. Worse, over the next twelve months, her internal organs started pushing out, which required another surgery to install a large piece of mesh across her entire abdomen. At the time of the surgery, she had the dubious honor of having the largest piece of mesh ever surgically installed.

After the second surgery, Danlyn's new and perpetual reality would be characterized by migraines, back and neck issues from a lack of core strength, and wound pain from the titanium tacks used to attach the mesh. She also has endometriosis, which brings its own issues, including ovarian cysts. All this to say, she's had a rough go and nobody would've blamed her for questioning God or losing hope.

Despite my seminary training, ministry work, public speaking, success in business, and all the rest, God has probably used Danlyn more than me to inspire a generation of students. There is just something attractive and infectious about supernatural hope in an otherwise hopeless world. In Uganda, our female students call her "Miss Amazima" and hold her in the highest regard as a role model. When they give their testimonies, they often refer to her hope-driven contentment in the face of pain and difficult circumstances as the reason for their consideration of the gospel. They also can't believe she's put up with me for more than twenty-five years!

For Danlyn, hope is not a strategy or a coping mechanism. She is buoyed by the fact that because of Christ and what he's promised, her suffering matters greatly, and that's not just a platitude: it has been her exact experience. Further, I don't think you will find a person who is more excited about what God has promised for eternity. Danlyn is very much looking forward to being pain-free, with her new body, in heaven.

Scripture teaches that those who are not in Christ have no hope.[3] Conversely, followers of Jesus may have a certain hope.[4] The writer of Hebrews says that we should, "hold unswervingly to the hope we profess, for he who promised is faithful" (Hebrews 10:23). I believe that hope is the sure mark of a believer because hope is the promised outcome of a life lived with a kingdom perspective, characterized by a dependence on the power of the Holy Spirit.

JOY

In these brief stories about Light and Danlyn we see what happens— what the outcomes are—when we receive God's promises in faith. We don't have to struggle with our identity or our desire for acceptance because God has promised an adoption into his family and an identity in Christ. Our deepest fears and doubts are addressed in the promise of assurance in salvation. The deep longing every human being has for hope is found in the person of Jesus. All of these promises (and others) contribute to the most important outcome for a believer: *freedom*. The apostle Paul, writing to the believers in Galatia, reminded them, "It is for freedom that Christ has set us free. Stand firm, then, and do not let yourselves be burdened again by a yoke of slavery" (Galatians 5:1).

Followers of Jesus are meant to live in freedom. Freedom from the anxiety of performance, the stress of comparison, or the need for approval. Freedom from doubt, shame, and fear. Freedom to choose not to sin, and more importantly, freedom from the ultimate penalty of sin. Freedom to live with purpose. Freedom from trying to be justified by following the rules and being good. Freedom from the exhausting work of trying to live the Christian life in our own strength. Freedom to experience God's love and complete joy.

If you call yourself a follower of Jesus and this promised freedom doesn't fire you up, then perhaps you should ask yourself, "Why not?" In the first pages of this book, I said we would need to decide if Jesus and the life he has promised are enough, and better than what the world is offering. That is my big question to you now. What will you choose?

Your works or the finished work of the cross?

Your performance or his grace?

Your fruit or his fruit?

Your will or his will?

Your strength or his strength?

Your perspectives or his perspectives?

The wisdom of the world or the wisdom of Scripture?

Independence or dependence on him?

Something to Remember: To those who walk in the Spirit, God has promised a life full of his fruit, his hope, complete assurance, and total freedom from the snares of this world and the schemes of the enemy.

My prayer and challenge for you is that you'll joyfully choose Jesus in everything and experience, like I have, abundant and unexpected joy.

A MUGGS LIFE

In January of 2016 I was in Uganda for a short visit to shepherd a forty-foot container, full of medical supplies, through customs to be delivered to doctors, dentists, and clinics in the local Jinja area. At that point we'd already signed on to serve at Amazima, so naturally I was excited to visit the campus, which was under construction.

My driver was somehow able to follow the "interesting" directions, which was fortunate, since TAS was not yet on the literal map. We entered through the construction gate and were greeted by a man named Gary, who was overseeing the massive project to transform seventy acres of jungle into a secondary boarding school. The tour started with the administration building and what would eventually become the first classroom block. We then made our way down to the boys' houses that were newly started, with only a few courses of bricks out of the ground. Nearby, on the freshly graded area that would eventually become our football pitch, there was a dog watching us intently.

Intrigued, I made my way over to check on the dog. She was a street breed, very typical of what you see anywhere and everywhere in Uganda. I couldn't get very close without her retreating. Even so, she followed us for the next hour, at a distance. At the end of our time, I asked a few questions about the dog, since she seemed so comfortable on the campus. As it turned out, the dog was rescued from a slum and brought to the school for security, shortly after they'd broken ground. Unfortunately, the guards who were hired to look after things didn't want her around, and worse, the workers abused her whenever she tried to make friends.

Instead of turning her loose, Gary had her taken to Amazima's other property in a nearby village, about fifteen minutes away by car. There were other dogs at that property, and the thought was that she'd be happier with some company. That arrangement lasted about forty-eight hours. Against the longest odds, the dog found her way back to the secondary school property and never left. She had been living under a dump truck for almost six months when I met her. Casually and not so seriously, I told Gary to "keep her alive" and we'd see her again when we moved to Uganda later in the year.

As planned, we made it back to Jinja in the fall. After getting settled in the brick oven, we drove out to the campus to see the progress that had been made since my prior visit. Most of the buildings we needed for the first year of school were nearing completion. It was a spectacular scene. As we were about to leave, I noticed the dog I had met about seven months earlier hanging around the construction entrance. But this time she didn't look so good.

It was obvious she'd been surviving on her own strength, without much assistance. She was malnourished, completely unapproachable, and moving very slowly. The best word to describe her was "broken." Since we couldn't get near her, there was nothing we could do until we moved onto campus, which ended up being about three months later.

By the time our little house at the school was finally ready, the dog was in very bad shape. She'd lost the will to live and no longer cared if people came around her. A friend had introduced us to a quality vet so we made arrangements to have her evaluated. Dr. Ali called me to say the dog had a dead puppy inside of her that had also caused a nasty infection. His recommendation was to put her down instead of performing a surgery that could end in the same result. For reference, the cost for ending her life was $50 and about $150 for the surgical procedure. For reasons I still can't fully comprehend, we asked Ali to save her.

When we brought her home, she had a big bucket on her head since "cones" aren't available in Uganda. Oh, and because it was now apparent she would survive, we gave her a name: Muggle, or Muggs for short. For Potterheads, the name will make sense. For the rest of you, let's just say it's a name that honors her non-pure bloodline. Immediately, Muggle made herself at home. Within a minute or two of being in the house, she jumped up on the couch. It would be a harbinger of things to come. Muggle has never known a couch (or a chair) she didn't like.

In the coming months, we saw a complete transformation of Muggle. As she started to get to know the students and the staff who lived on her seventy-acre playground, she developed a confidence and joy that was hard to believe. She'd make her rounds, visiting the houses in the afternoon, and then head down to dinner with the students in the evening. Often she'd stay out all night patrolling with the guards on duty, and more than once identified and ran off some bad guys trying to break into the school grounds. Her favorite activity was "hunting" the various birds and wildlife who also called our campus home. Muggle lived like a dog who knew she was safe, loved, and free.

At the same time, she exhibited a level of trust, loyalty, and obedience not typical even for a rescue dog. For the entire time we lived in Uganda, Muggle never made a mess in the house, nor did she tear up or chew any of our belongings. She was fiercely protective of every student and staff member on campus. Whenever there were new faces around, we had to let Muggle know those people were okay. Amazingly, you only had to tell her once. With Danlyn and I, however, Muggle was more than just loyal: she was fully dependent on us, including for her extraordinary joy. The guards told us that every time we were gone for more than a day, Muggle would be noticeably less of herself.

By the start of 2021 we had grown to love just about everything about our life in Uganda. At that point, I would've said we were going to be in Jinja for a very long time. All things being equal, I could have lived the rest of my life there. Things rarely work out how we plan, though, right?

Danlyn's pain was increasing, and her overall health began to deteriorate at a concerning rate. The breadth of surgical options is limited in Uganda, so she would have to go back to the States for any kind of surgical solution to whatever was going on in her body. We had a choice: to leave our home and move back to the US, or to take a sabbatical for the surgery and then return to Uganda if and when Danlyn got better. Thankfully, the Spirit gave us the wisdom we needed to make the best decision. We laid plans to move back to Georgia.

If you would have asked anyone around Amazima how they thought I would handle walking away from Student Life and leaving the students, there would have been unanimous consensus that I would struggle to let go of leadership. It didn't happen. Oh, sure, there was sadness and grief, but how could there not be? Unexpectedly (or maybe not), what Danlyn and I more experienced in the last couple of months in Uganda was total peace and joy. But then we started to wrestle with what to do with Muggle.

It was a difficult decision. How could we take Muggle from the only home she'd ever known? How would she do without hundreds of people around, and dozens of acres to explore? What would happen when she would lose the freedom to roam? Could she survive the cold of winter? There were many other impossible questions, but ultimately, we decided to bring her back to the States with us. The three of us were in it together.

As I write these final pages, we've been back for a couple of months and I'm happy to report that the same unshakable faith and extraordinary joy we experienced in Uganda has not left us—nor do I think it ever will, because our perspectives have changed. With the right perspectives, we experience the benefits of following Jesus no matter what happens. Also, God has graciously given us a new assignment, to come alongside the organizations that sponsor students and provide post-secondary school support through mentoring, discipleship, job training, and placement. We launched a nonprofit in support of that effort called the 314 Community. You can check out our website at www.314community.org.

As it turns out, for Muggle, her joy and contentment weren't based on her environment or circumstances, but rather on *being with the ones who saved her and love her unconditionally.* In most ways, the circumstances of her life are less favorable than they were in Uganda. Gone are all her people and the treats awaiting her all over campus. She's traded the best climate in the world for seasons that change. Her walks are on a leash now and she's traded monkeys for squirrels. You get the point. As long as we're together, however, she's great.

For me, watching Muggle thrive in a completely different context reminds me of how simple life can be if we organize it around Jesus and trust his wisdom and guidance. It's not about our circumstances or our performance. If we have the right perspectives, framed by brokenness and grace, then we are free to engage the power of the Holy Spirit to accomplish our purpose and enjoy the promises of God. It's not about *where* we are or *what* we do, but more importantly about *whose* we are and *how* we choose to trust and follow.

NOTES

CHAPTER 1—UNCLE KELLY

1. Gregory Bateson, *Mind and Nature* (New York: Hampton Press, 2002), 14.
2. 1 Corinthians 3.
3. Gregory A. Smith, "About Three-in-Ten U.S. Adults Are Now Religiously Unaffiliated," *Pew Research Center*, December 14, 2021, https://www.pewforum.org/2021/12/14/about-three-in-ten-u-s-adults-are-now-religiously-unaffiliated.

CHAPTER 2—A NEW SET OF LENSES

1. Stephen R. Covey, *The 7 Habits of Highly Effective People: 30th Anniversary Edition* (New York: Simon & Schuster, 2020), 17.
2. Romans 3:20; 10:2-3; Ephesians 1:17; 4:13; Philippians 1:9; Colossians 1:9; 2:2; 3:10; 1 Timothy 2:4; 2 Timothy 2:25; 3:7.

CHAPTER 3—A JOURNEY BEGINS

1. Francis Chan, *Crazy Love* (Colorado Springs, CO: David C. Cook, 2013), 122.
2. Dambisa Moyo, "Why Foreign Aid Is Hurting Africa," *The Wall Street Journal*, March 21, 2009, https://www.wsj.com/articles/SB123758895999200083.

CHAPTER 4—UNDERSTANDING UGANDA

1. Online, this quote is attributed to Idi Amin, but its original source is unknown.
2. Romans 7:4; 11:6; Galatians 2:21; 3:18, 23-24; 5:4.

CHAPTER 5—FALSE GODS AND FALSE GOSPELS

1. Galatians 1:6; Romans 9–11.
2. Psalm 135:6; Matthew 5:45.
3. John 14:6; Acts 4:12; Galatians 2:16; 3:10-11; Romans 9:16.

CHAPTER 6–SUFFERING AND HOPELESSNESS

1. Philip Yancey, *Grace Notes* (Grand Rapids: Zondervan, 2009), 111.

CHAPTER 7–EQUALLY CREATED, EQUALLY VALUED

1. "Statistics," *NSVRC*, https://www.nsvrc.org/statistics.

2. A.W. Geiger and Leslie Davis, "A growing number of American teenagers—particularly girls—are facing depression," *Pew Research Center*, July 12, 2019, https://pewrsr.ch/2xCxEmP; Stephanie Doupnik, "I treat teens who attempted suicide. Here's what they told me," *Vox*, updated November 6, 2019, https://www.vox.com/the-highlight/2019/10/30/20936636/suicide-mental-health-suicidal-thoughts-teens.

3. Genesis 1:26-28.

4. Luke 13:10-17.

5. Matthew 9:20-22.

6. Luke 7:36-50.

7. Genesis 1:26-28; Judges 2:16, 18; 4:4-5; 2 Kings 22:14–23:25; Esther 9:29-32; Joel 2:28-29; Micah 6:4; Matthew 12:49-50; Mark 3:34-35; Luke 8:21; 10:38-42; 11:27-28.

CHAPTER 8–WHO WE ARE (ON OUR OWN)

1. Genesis 25:28-34.

2. Robert A. Pyne, *Humanity and Sin* (Nashville, TN: Thomas Nelson, 1999).

3. Romans 1:21-32.

4. Romans 3:23.

5. Romans 6:17-20.

6. Romans 3:12.

7. Romans 7:14-25.

CHAPTER 9–WHEN HELPING DOESN'T HELP

1. The Ugandan currency.

CHAPTER 10–GOD'S GRACE

1. Romans 10:13.

2. Luke 15:11-32.

CHAPTER 11–GOD, US, AND IDENTITY

1. A.W. Tozer, *The Knowledge of the Holy* (New York: HarperCollins, 1978), 1.

2. C.S. Lewis, *The Weight of Glory* (New York: Macmillan, 1966), 10.

3. David Kinnaman and Gabe Lyons, *UnChristian: What a New Generation Really Thinks About Christianity...and Why It Matters* (Ada, MI: Baker Books, 2012), 99.

4. John 13:35.

5. Dr. Stephen Flick, "The Christian Founding of Harvard," Christian Heritage Fellowship, September 8, 2022, https://christianheritagefellowship.com/the-christian-founding-of-harvard/.

6. John 10:30, 17:21; Philippians 2:5-6; Colossians 2:9-10.

7. Debra Heine, "DNC Panel Features 'Mermaid Queen-King' Who Calls for the Abolition of ICE, Police, and Prisons," *The Tennessee Star*, August 21, 2020, https://tennesseestar.com/2020/08/21/dnc-panel-features-mermaid-queen-king-who-calls-for-the-abolition-of-ice-police-and-prisons/.

8. 2 Corinthians 5:17.

9. John 16:13-14.

10. John 8:36; Romans 6:6, 18, 22; 8:1; Galatians 5:1, 24.

11. John 15:16; Ephesians 1:11; 1 Peter 2:9.

12. Psalm 107:8-9; Isaiah 54:10; John 13:34; Acts 10:43; Ephesians 1:5-8; 1 John 1:9; 2:2, 12; 3:1.

13. Romans 8:15; Galatians 4:5; Ephesians 1:5.

14. John 1:12; Acts 10:34; Galatians 3:28; 1 Corinthians 12:27; 1 Peter 2:9.

15. 1 John 4:16.

CHAPTER 12–GRACE AND CIRCUMSTANCES

1. 2 Corinthians 11:23-28.

2. James 1:2.

3. 1 Peter 4:13, 16.

4. Acts 7:60.

5. Maria Abenes, "Teens in America: How the COVID-19 Pandemic Is Shaping the Next Generation," *Psychiatric Times*, November 12, 2021, https://www.psychiatrictimes.com/view/teens-in-america-how-the-covid-19-pandemic-is-shaping-the-next-generation.

6. 1 Peter 1:7.

CHAPTER 13–PERSPECTIVE ON GOD'S RULES

1. A.W. Tozer, *The Pursuit of God: The Human Thirst for the Divine*, updated edition (Chicago, IL: Moody Publishers, 2015), 103.

2. Lee Rainie, Scott Keeter, and Andrew Perrin, "Trust and Distrust in America," *Pew Research Center*, July 22, 2019, https://www.pewresearch.org/politics/2019/07/22/trust-and-distrust-in-america/; Megan Brenan, "Americans' Trust in Government Remains Low," *Gallup*, September 30, 2021, https://news.gallup.com/poll/355124/americans-trust-government-remains-low.aspx; Felix Salmon, "Media trust hits new low," *Axios*, January 21, 2021, https://www.axios.com/media-trust-crisis-2bf0ec1c-00c0-4901-9069-e26b21c283a9.html.

3. Genesis 12:1-3; 26:4.

4. Galatians 3:1-9.

CHAPTER 14–JOYFUL OBEDIENCE

1. James 1:22.

2. Romans 2:17-24.

3. John 15:1-17.

4. John 15:5.

5. Genesis 3:6.

6. Acts 7:39, 51.

CHAPTER 15—WWJ(HU)D?

1. J.K. Rowling, *Harry Potter and the Deathly Hallows* (New York: Arthur A. Levine Books, 2007), 722.

2. Matthew 7:1-3.

3. Deuteronomy 6:5; Leviticus 19:18.

4. Luke 6:27-31.

5. 1 Corinthians 13:1-3.

6. 1 Peter 3:15.

CHAPTER 16—THE "REAL HOW" IS A "WHO"

1. Dallas Willard, *The Great Omission: Reclaiming Jesus's Essential Teachings on Discipleship* (San Francisco, CA: HarperOne, 2014), 34.

2. Ephesians 2:10.

3. Philippians 2:12-13.

4. Matthew 19:26; Romans 1:16-17; Titus 3:5-7.

5. Acts 11:18; 2 Timothy 2:25.

6. John Calvin, *Institutes* 3.3.1.

7. John 14:26; 16:13.

8. 2 Corinthians 3:18.

9. Matthew 10:20; Mark 13:11; Luke 12:12; Acts 13:9-11; Hebrews 3:7; 10:15.

10. Romans 12:2.

CHAPTER 17—WALKING WITH THE "REAL HOW"

1. 3 John 1:4.

2. Watchman Nee, *The Normal Christian Life* (Wheaton, IL: Tyndale, 1977), 161.

3. 1 Corinthians 1:20; 3:19.

4. Proverbs 3:7.

5. 1 Corinthians 1:19.

6. 1 Corinthians 1:27.

7. 1 Kings 4:29; John 14:26; 1 Corinthians 2:12-13; 1 Corinthians 12:8.

8. Mark 4:18-19.

9. Romans 8:5-6.

10. John Calvin, *Commentaries on the Last Four Books of Moses, Arranged in the Form of a Harmony*, vol. 1 (Edinburgh: Calvin Translation Society, 1852), 389.

CHAPTER 18–THE "REAL HOW" AND THE "BIG FOUR"

1. Wayne Martindale and Jerry Root, *The Quotable Lewis* (Wheaton, IL: Tyndale, 1989), 156.
2. Ephesians 4:32.
3. 2 Corinthians 5:18.
4. William M. Struthers, *Wired for Intimacy: How Pornography Hijacks the Male Brain* (Downers Grove, IL: InterVarsity, 2009).
5. Psalm 62:10; Proverbs 23:4-5; 11:28; Hebrews 13:5.
6. 1 Timothy 6:6-10.
7. Luke 8:14.
8. Luke 12:15.
9. Matthew 6:19, 24.

CHAPTER 19–LIGHT, HOPE, FREEDOM, AND JOY

1. Ephesians 1:5.
2. Romans 6:8; 8:13-14, 30, 38-39; 10:11; Ephesians 2:8-9; Hebrews 6:11; 10:22.
3. 1 Thessalonians 4:13.
4. Titus 3:6-7; 1 Peter 1:3.

To learn more about Harvest House books and
to read sample chapters, visit our website:

www.HarvestHousePublishers.com

HARVEST HOUSE PUBLISHERS
EUGENE, OREGON